P9-DZZ-910

Food & Society

Principles and Paradoxes
Second Edition

Amy E. Guptill, Denise A. Copelton, and Betsy Lucal

polity

Copyright © Amy E. Guptill, Denise A. Copelton, Betsy Lucal 2017

The right of Amy E. Guptill, Denise A. Copelton, and Betsy Lucal to be identified as Author of this Work has been asserted in accordance with the UK Copyright, Designs and Patents Act 1988.

First published in 2013 by Polity Press
This edition first published in 2017 by Polity Press

Polity Press
65 Bridge Street
Cambridge CB2 1UR, UK

Polity Press
350 Main Street
Malden, MA 02148, USA

All rights reserved. Except for the quotation of short passages for the purpose of criticism and review, no part of this publication may be reproduced, stored in a retrieval system, or transmitted, in any form or by any means, electronic, mechanical, photocopying, recording or otherwise, without the prior permission of the publisher.

ISBN-13: 978-1-5095-0183-0
ISBN-13: 978-1-5095-0184-7(pb)

A catalogue record for this book is available from the British Library.

Library of Congress Cataloging-in-Publication Data

Names: Guptill, Amy E., author. | Copelton, Denise A. | Lucal, Betsy.
Title: Food & society : principles and paradoxes / Amy E. Guptill, Denise A.
  Copelton, Betsy Lucal.
Other titles: Food and society
Description: Cambridge ; Malden, MA : Polity Press, 2016. | Includes
  bibliographical references and index.
Identifiers: LCCN 2016015422| ISBN 9781509501830 (hardback : alk. paper) |
  ISBN 9781509501847 (pbk. : alk. paper)
Subjects: LCSH: Food--Social aspects. | Food habits--Social aspects.
Classification: LCC GT2855 .G86 2016 | DDC 394.1/2--dc23 LC record available at
https://lccn.loc.gov/2016015422

Typeset in 10.5 on 12pt Plantin by
Servis Filmsetting Ltd, Stockport, Cheshire

The publisher has used its best endeavours to ensure that the URLs for external websites referred to in this book are correct and active at the time of going to press. However, the publisher has no responsibility for the websites and can make no guarantee that a site will remain live or that the content is or will remain appropriate.

Every effort has been made to trace all copyright holders, but if any have been inadvertently overlooked the publisher will be pleased to include any necessary credits in any subsequent reprint or edition.

For further information on Polity, visit our website: www.politybooks.com

Contents

Acknowledgments

We heartily thank Polity editors Jonathan Skerrett and Emma Longstaff, as well as several anonymous reviewers, for their vital guidance and kind enthusiasm. We are also indebted to many friends, colleagues, mentors, and students who have provided invaluable resources, feedback, and encouragement. They include Joyce Altobelli, Amy Bonn, Amanda Earl, Brian Fletcher, Amy Fuhr, Thomas Happell, Jennifer Haytock, Jennifer LiPira, Paul Loomis, Alison Moss, Jaymeson Moss, Xavier Moss, James Rose, Joan Spade, Marybeth Stalp, Jason R. Titus, Beth Tracton-Bishop, and Rick Welsh. Our thanks to them all.

Amy Guptill
The College at Brockport, State University of New York

Denise Copelton
The College at Brockport, State University of New York

Betsy Lucal
Indiana University South Bend

1
Principles and Paradoxes in the Study of Food

Case study

Each year, all over the United States and around the world, competitors and spectators gather to witness and celebrate the ability of some to quickly consume enormous quantities of a single food. The most famous of these competitions is a hot-dog eating contest that takes place on Coney Island, New York, each July 4 (US Independence Day). In 2015, the winner of this contest, Matt Stonie, consumed 62 hot dogs – with buns (which competitors soak in water to enhance speed of consumption) – in ten minutes. That's more than six hot dogs a minute, or one hot dog every 10 seconds! In 2009, Joey Chestnut set event, US, and world hot-dog consumption records by eating 68 hot dogs in the allotted time. In case you're wondering, separate men's and women's events have been held since 2011. In 2012, Sonya Thomas wolfed down 45 hot dogs; the 2015 winner, Miki Sudo, ate 38.

Welcome to the world of "competitive eating," the latest version of the classic pie-eating contest from county fairs. Eating contests have a long history in the United States, dating to at least the 1700s (Vardi 2010). They have a growing fan base in the United States and Japan (Halloran 2004). You can view these events not just on the Food Network, but also on ESPN. You can root for Takeru Kobayashi, a skinny Japanese guy; successful newcomer, Sonya "the Black Widow" Thomas; and "Cookie" Jarvis, whose large stature better represents the stereotype of "big" eaters, as they eat as many jalapeño peppers, pancakes, baked beans, or tamales as possible in the allotted time. Commentators marvel at the Black Widow's ability to outeat her male competitors and at Kobayashi's capacity to consume more than his heftier rivals. The International

Federation of Competitive Eating (www.ifoce.com) supervises and regulates these events, stressing, above all, that competitions must be safe. Interestingly, the website section on safety does not address the possible risks of this sport for its participants who, among other aspects of their training, imbibe huge quantities of liquids in the days before a competition to stretch their stomachs. As in other sports, these competitors take these risks and provide viewers with an engaging spectacle of a well-developed skill.

Contrast today's competitive eating with the "racial eating contests" (Vardi 2010) staged by whites for white audiences at the turn of the twentieth century. Such events pitted African Americans against each other, requiring them to consume, in most cases, "watermelon, pies, crackers or rice" (Vardi 2010: 376). These contests were presented as "light entertainment" at "club meetings, civil organization forums, and professional conferences" (Vardi 2010: 376). While eating contests were a popular form of entertainment and amusement for audiences across races, these racial eating contests were different, as we can see from white media coverage. According to Itai Vardi, accounts in the white press characterized the consumption by black contestants as animal-like and/or "likened [them] to mighty gustatory machines" (Vardi 2010: 381). Given that this time period was one of nutritional scarcity for many African Americans (Harris 2011; Warnes 2004; Witt 1999), participation in such contests may have been tempting, despite the potential to reinforce horrible racist stereotypes about blacks as less than fully human.

While these racial eating contests and today's competitive eating are similar in form, their social and cultural contexts make them sharply distinct, which raises fundamental questions about how to understand and explain food practices. As Warren Belasco (2002: 13) explains, "what we think about food may have little to do with the actual material properties of the food itself." Patterns of food production, preparation, and consumption are not universal, natural, or inevitable (Germov and Williams 2004). These patterns are created and continually recreated by individuals' actions and interactions. At the same time, individuals navigate among existing patterns in the decisions they make, and some have more freedom and influence than others. When we study food, as with any dimension of society, we confront fundamental questions: Where do these patterns come from? How can we discern their meaning? And how do individuals conform to and/or subvert these patterns?

Introduction: invitation to the feast

Welcome to the study of food! You are joining a growing community of students, scholars, and activists who are exploring perennial questions about the human experience through what Anthony Winson (1993) calls "the intimate commodity." Unlike other things we buy, food is taken into our bodies multiple times a day. It is a meaningful and sustained arena of action and interaction, one that connects us to others on deeply significant terms. While scholars throughout the humanities and social sciences have been finding important insights through the study of food for at least a century, food studies as an interconnected field emerged more recently. These connections are still forming, as people with backgrounds as varied as urban planning, literature, sociology, bioethics, cultural studies, feminist history, and global geography discover and create points of connection in food. Food also connects thinkers and writers within colleges and universities to those in other arenas. Food writers often function as public scholars, bridging academic ideas and diverse popular engagements with food. The field is hugely diverse and, obviously, no single text can satisfyingly capture it all.

This text is entitled *Food & Society*, rather than, say, *Food & Culture*, which is to say that this book puts insights from disciplines like anthropology, sociology, geography, political economy, and, to a lesser extent, history in the foreground. Anthropologists, with their focus on the role of food in the construction and maintenance of social systems (Ferguson and Zukin 1995), have long been at the forefront of scholarly discussions of food. Claude Lévi-Strauss (1983), for example, demonstrated that social convention, rather than biology, determined what was edible by members of a given society. He also examined how certain foods were designated as suitable either for men or for women, or should only be consumed on holidays or never by children. In introducing the field, we weave together insights like these with more structural ones, ones that focus, for example, on the institutional context of food entertainment (chapter 3) or the persistence of hunger amid food surpluses (chapter 8).

This introductory chapter first discusses foodways and the food system as two key concepts for understanding this field of study. We then discuss three principles that help explain the patterns we present in subsequent chapters. Next, we outline the notion of paradox: how apparent contradictions in food-related patterns raise key questions about their underlying dynamics. As you will see, these paradoxes stem from the fundamental questions raised in this chapter's opening case study. The introduction ends with a synopsis of each chapter's animating paradox and key insights.

Foodways

Foodways* are the patterns that establish "what we eat, as well as how and why and under what circumstances we eat" (Edge 2007: 8). The concept of foodways focuses our attention on food preparation and consumption, as well as cultural dimensions of food and eating.

A key element of foodways is what we eat. There is an enormous range of substances that are edible by humans (or that can be made edible through techniques of preparation to make them safe and tasty to eat). As Marvin Harris (1985: 13) wryly notes, "We can eat and digest everything from rancid mammary gland secretions to fungi to rocks (or cheese, mushrooms and salt if you prefer euphemisms)." Yet any one of us consumes only a tiny portion of that range. Part of this fact has to do with personal "taste"; but even individual taste is not a simple matter of determining whether a substance produces a positive or negative sensation in the mouth and on the tongue. On the other hand, humans will go to great lengths to turn inedible items into palatable ones. For example, the wild cassava eaten in tropical regions of the world is poisonous until it is pounded and soaked for days. Similarly, most olives are inedibly bitter until they undergo a lengthy curing process.

Realizing that even the most basic understandings of food are socially defined raises interesting questions about why we eat the foods we do and how we view them. Consider, for example, the centrality of meat in many US foodways. Marvin Harris (1985: 27) points out that many cultures have a "special esteem for animal flesh," and that it is common to use "meat to reinforce the social ties that bind campmates and kinfolk together." More prosaically, restaurants in the southeastern United States often offer meals known as "meat and threes." Eaters pick a meat – such as fried chicken, chicken-fried steak, or meatloaf – and three vegetable sides – such as coleslaw, greens, pickled beets, mashed potatoes with gravy, cheese grits, applesauce, or macaroni and cheese. Only in this context is macaroni and cheese a "vegetable." Many of these restaurants accommodate vegetarians by offering a "farmer's plate" composed of

---

* Items in bold appear in the glossary.

chosen "vegetable" sides. It is not a coincidence that the restaurants call these meals "meat and threes" rather than "vegetables and ones." For many Americans, eating meat and a couple of "starches" (usually some kind of potato, less commonly rice or pasta) and vegetables is what makes a "meal," or, more specifically, a "balanced meal." In many other cultures, cuisines are composed around a staple starch – such as potatoes, rice, or maize – and flavored with meats, vegetables, herbs, and spices, a category anthropologists summarize as "relish" (Mintz 1985). While the relish is nutritionally crucial, it is the starchy food that makes the meal. The focus on meat may seem natural to people who participate in American and similar foodways, but it reflects a particular cultural history shaped, in part, by the abundant natural resources made available through the conquest of North America (Cronon 1992).

While the concept of foodways helps draw our attention to the social and cultural context of food-related practices, it is so broad that defining a pattern as part of a foodway does not go very far in explaining why that pattern has emerged and persisted. Different academic traditions emphasize different factors in explaining foodways, and the burgeoning field is constantly producing new insights. Thus, while 'foodways' is a useful touchstone concept, it is not the only way to frame our understanding of food. We must also consider the food system, which focuses our attention on other aspects of humans' relationships with food.

The food system

While the concept of foodways focuses on what we eat and why, we must also use another lens to examine the relationships among food, individuals, and society. The concept of a **food system** – the set of vast, interlinked institutions and processes that transform sunlight, water, and soil into meaning-laden foods – highlights the production, processing, and distribution of food and necessarily turns our attention to the materiality of the food we eat. A system is made up of a set of interdependent parts that create a unified whole. For a system to operate properly, all of its parts must be in place and working (Hesterman 2011). The arrangement of parts influences how the system works; and changes to one part of the system create changes (sometimes unpredictable ones) in other parts of it.

The major purpose of a food system is "to provide nutrition to keep us all alive" (Hesterman 2011: 4). How well it does so depends on each of the parts of the system and their relationship to each other. Stress or strain in one part of the system will be felt in other parts of the system. A breakdown in some aspect of the system will influence the ability of the system as a whole to operate. Of course, we need to keep in mind that, while humans are fundamental to all parts of the system, some things – like weather – are beyond human control.

Historically, food systems were quite small and localized. For a long time, humans produced and processed much of their own food, depending only on their family or clan for what they needed. As technologies advanced and populations grew, food systems become more complex and humans became more interdependent. Some people produced food or items that could be processed into food; other people processed it; still others distributed it. Eventually, most people in industrialized nations ended up far removed from these social processes and now participate in the food system largely as consumers.

Indeed, such changes have been crucial to the development of humans as a species. Oran Hesterman (2011: 9), writing about the United States, puts it this way: "A food system that allows less than 2 percent of our population to feed the rest of us . . . is exactly the system you want to free the other 98 percent to develop other sectors of our economy, such as manufacturing, health care, social services, the arts and sciences, and education."

But this arrangement also means that, for most people, the workings of much of the food system are invisible and they may not understand just how complex that system is. As we will show in chapter 6, the industrialization of the food system, which allows for the efficient feeding of vast numbers of people, also has serious costs with respect to the environment, human health, and people's traditional ways of living. In other words, there are high costs associated with the cheap food this system is able to produce. Similarly, advances in technology have created a global food system that allows wealthy people to enjoy virtually any food any time – while also creating patterns of food scarcity that make it almost impossible for others to acquire adequate food, despite its actual abundance (see chapters 7 and 8).

To get a sense of the array of processes that must come together for a food system to work, consider the following. Let's start with food production. Many foods are grown from plants. Seeds are planted, often with the help of machines; inputs like water and fertilizers are added; plant growth is monitored and facilitated. The success of this aspect of the process relies on a great deal of knowledge and technology, as well as some amount of luck. When the crop is ready to be harvested, people and machines come together to make that happen. But, once the crop has been picked, unless it is a fruit or vegetable that can be eaten as it is, it must be processed. And even if it can be eaten as is, it still must be distributed and sold for consumption.

Processing is the next step. While some crops are processed only minimally, others "become ingredients for a myriad of processed products" (Hesterman 2011: 5). In *The Omnivore's Dilemma*, food writer Michael Pollan (2006) details how the processing of No. 2 field corn results in an incredible range of corn-based food products. Each year in the United States, billions of bushels of this corn are taken to wet mills, where it is turned into "the building blocks from which companies like General Mills, McDonald's and Coca-Cola assemble our processed foods" (Pollan 2006: 86). The most valuable product that's created from the processing of corn is high-fructose corn syrup, which finds its way into hundreds of processed foods, some of which you wouldn't expect to contain sweetener. The remaining fractions of the corn kernel are turned into non-food items, other sweeteners, corn starch, and so on. As Pollan (2006: 91) notes, today, "you would be hard-pressed to find a . . . processed food that isn't made from corn or soybeans," another versatile food crop.

Once they have been processed into something edible by humans, these food products are still a long way from the individuals who will consume them. They now must be distributed. In the United States, that means traveling an average of 1,500 miles (2,400km) from where the food was produced to where it will be consumed (Hesterman 2011: 7). Since most food is not purchased directly from producers or processers, after being distributed to grocery stores, restaurants or other outlets, it must be purchased by individual consumers before it's actually eaten.

And while you might assume that consumption is the end of the line for a food product, there is one more part of the food system to account for: How will we deal with the waste produced? Not just the human waste that results, but, "All those parts of our meal that we do not eat – including packaging, wastewater and chemicals from processing, and food that is prepared but not eaten – end up either in a landfill or compost heap to be recycled back into soil" (Hesterman 2011: 7).

As you can see, the production, processing, and distribution of food comprises a complex and wide-ranging set of processes, not all of them under human control. Too much or too little rain can interfere with production. A strike by workers can shut down processing. A blizzard or hurricane can interrupt distribution, as can a trucking company going bankrupt. The food system is, indeed, a complicated and sometimes fragile entity. As two perspectives on the same phenomena, foodways and food systems provide a more complete picture of the relationships between food and society.

Here's an example that illustrates the relationship between foodways and the food system. Jewish people who keep kosher do not consider edible material to be food unless it is prepared according to a particular set of practices. Kashrut, the practice of keeping kosher, means, among other things, not mixing meat and dairy in meals; not consuming pork, shellfish, and some birds; and eating only kosher meat. Meat is kosher only if the slaughter of animals to be consumed by observant Jews is overseen and certified by a rabbi to ensure that the act is done in accordance with the rules. Utensils, pots and pans, and other tools used to prepare meats cannot be used to prepare dairy foods unless they have been kashered through prescribed processes of heating, scouring or scalding, infusing or soaking. These rules are subject to debate and interpretation, and they also differ depending on whether one is orthodox or conservative. For example, according to strict orthodox rules, non-stick pans coated with Teflon cannot be kashered; conservatives say they can (Stern 2004).

In order to keep kosher, Jewish people need to be part of a food system that can produce, process, and distribute food according to the relevant religious principles. In order to observe these foodways, Jews need access to food products that receive special treatment and handling as they move through the food system. Enjoying a meal out requires finding a restaurant that has adhered to these religious restrictions all the way to the point of consumption.

Having discussed foodways and the food system as complementary perspectives in the study of food, next we profile three explanatory principles that we revisit in subsequent chapters. They capture some of the essential insights of the field and help us integrate an astonishing variety of ideas and findings.

Three principles

Three basic principles underlying the interdisciplinary study of food and society help frame our understanding. First, food is both richly symbolic and undeniably material. Consider the common notion of **comfort foods**, dishes and products consumed specifically for an emotional boost. We tend to think comfort food choices simply reflect idiosyncratic, individual tastes. However, Locher and colleagues (2005: 274) conducted a study with college students and found that "both the social and physiological dimensions of food" help explain food choices. Socially, students' chosen comfort foods shared three traits: (1) they invoked a feeling of familiarity and of being cared for; (2) students ate them when they needed an emotional boost; and, (3) even though these foods evoked feelings of being cared for, they tended to eat these foods when they were alone.

Eating these foods made them feel connected to a group – their family – that was physically absent but made psychologically present. In explaining their choices, students also highlighted the physical attributes of their comfort foods: how soups or ice creams are soft, spooned, and filling, or how crunchy foods enable a stress-relieving physical activity (Locher et al. 2005: 287). Some respondents also emphasized that their comfort foods must be convenient, which reminds us of another important material reality: how many kinds of "junk" foods are widely available and cheap.

The case of comfort foods also highlights a second key principle of food studies: that people's experiences with food are both individual and social. For example, differences in eating patterns help distinguish social groups from each other, becoming a form of **cultural capital** (Bourdieu 1984), the relatively rare and highly valued knowledge, skills, attitudes, and tastes that help define an elite status. As we describe in more detail in chapter 2, knowing and using upper-class table manners – knowing which fork to use for what foods, for example – marks a person as having a particular class status in society. Before the twentieth century, fine dining was largely limited to the elite (McMillan 2012); but, when eating out boomed along with the ranks of the middle class in the 1950s, many had to learn the "bodily management and emotional control" inherent in Victorian-era table manners (Kasson 1991: 182). As another example, gender shapes the choice of comfort foods: men tend to prefer hot meals, while women prefer snack foods (Wansink 2007; Wansink, Cheney, and Chan 2003). Researchers explain that men more often eat meals prepared by others, and associate these hot dishes with being cared for. Women, conversely, often do the work of preparing meals, and find ready-to-eat foods a mark of indulgence. As these two examples illustrate, the practices we participate in (or avoid) reveal much about our social location and multiple identities.

The third principle that organizes our approach to understanding food has to do with inequality. Because they stand at the intersection of social forces, foodways and food systems both reflect and shape **social inequality**, persistent patterns in which some people enjoy more material and cultural privileges than others. As we explain in all of the following chapters, foodways are used both to maintain and to contest inequalities of power and privilege with respect to gender, social class, race and ethnicity, sexuality, and age. As we note in several chapters, even something as prosaic as school lunches reveals profound underlying dimensions of inequality. One vivid example is obento, the Japanese practice of constructing elaborate, visually appealing boxed lunches that young children eat at school. Mothers are expected to prepare them with meticulous care, and students are expected to eat them quickly and in their entirety. In a classic analysis, anthropologist Anne Allison (1991: 195) explains that this almost compulsory practice "situates the producer as a woman and mother, and the consumer, as a child of a mother and a student of a school . . . Both mother and child are being watched, judged, and constructed." Power is at work in the obento practice, maintaining women's unequal burden in child-rearing and families' subordination to the state. While school lunches in the United States are not as elaborate or scrutinized, chapter 2 explains that US food practices are still highly gendered, and chapters 4, 6, and 8 explore the dynamics of inequality in the food system that help explain what ends up on cafeteria trays or in brown bags.

These three principles provide a conceptual framework that organizes our exploration of this wide-ranging and dynamic field. There is no unitary or dominant "theory of food"; but there are some integrating concepts and ideas that help connect different perspectives. The different traditions we draw on in this text emphasize some underlying features over others, but these three principles help us make clear connections among these disparate insights. The chapters parse out topics within food studies that sometimes cohere with and sometimes cross disciplinary traditions. We could have grouped findings from the field in many different ways; we chose these particular topics because they each center on a key compelling question revealed by a paradox, that is, an apparent contradiction. The following section elaborates the notion of paradox in relation to the fundamental questions raised by the opening comparative case study of competitive eating. These questions underlie the specific paradoxes that animate each chapter.

Paradoxes: the individual and society

Oft quoted is Karl Marx's famous aphorism from *The Eighteenth Brumaire of Louis Bonaparte* (2001 [1852]: 7): "Men make their own history, but they do not make it just as they please; they do not make it under circumstances chosen by themselves, but under circumstances directly encountered, given and transmitted from the past." Looking beyond the sexist writing conventions of the time, we see that Marx puts his finger on one of the central questions that impels all of social inquiry: to what extent are individuals free to create the conditions of their own lives amid the myriad social and cultural forces they must navigate? Ascertaining the relative influence of the individual and society – of the personal/psychological and the social – has long posed a challenge for sociologists and other students of social life. As we explained above in our discussion of the three basic principles organizing our book, this relationship is important to the study of food and society as well.

In earlier decades, social science was dominated by a structuralist perspective; that is, one that focuses on enduring social patterns and how they shape human behavior. This perspective highlights how food production, processing, preparation, and consumption are organized through institutions, organizations, and groups. For example, sociologists of agriculture employ structural insights to track and explain the "disappearing middle" in the agricultural sectors of the United States and other wealthy countries (Lyson, Stevenson, and Welsh 2008). The largest industrialized farms are growing in number, as are the smaller "boutique" farms in peri-urban regions while mid-size or "family-scale" farms are shrinking. This trend can be explained structurally in terms of how the largest farms often benefit the most both from agricultural subsidies and relationships with large food manufacturers, and from the growing demand for alternative, non-industrial foods among relatively well-off urban consumers. In other words, this is an issue that focuses our attention on the food system and how it operates.

In more recent decades, a social constructionist perspective arose, in part out of frustration with **structuralism**'s tendency to make existing structures seem inevitable and immutable and, consequently, to frame individuals as passive. **Social constructionism** emphasizes individual agency, reminding us that, as people make choices and behave in particular ways, they help to shape the social world in which they live. When patterns persist, it is because they are continually reproduced by human action. In emphasizing individual agency, the constructionist perspective on food tends to focus on the meanings we attach to our engagement with foodways and how they relate to practices and relationships. As the opening case study vividly illustrates, even practices that seem to have the same form can have vastly different underlying meanings. Similarly, the analysis of comfort foods (Locher et al. 2005) shows that individuals actively construct these practices according to their treasured social relationships. Agency does not mean freedom from social influence; rather, it means navigating and shaping social and cultural landscapes both individually and collectively.

While there have been many scholarly and activist debates that have fallen along structuralist-constructionist lines, most food scholars appreciate how the dialogue between these two perspectives reveals more than each could reveal on its own. We present them here, not as opposed alternatives, but as complementary lenses. Empirical research shows that foodways are neither frozen nor fluid, and together food scholars have produced more insight by employing different emphases. For example, consider the differing approaches to the question of why we eat what we do. Connors and colleagues (2001) focus on individuals and find that people have "personal food value systems," a set of processes they use to make choices about foods they eat. Taste, health, cost, time, and social relationships were the five main values around which these systems revolved, but safety, quality, waste, ethics, symbolism, and variety also played a role. Other scholars emphasize the broader forces that shape, for example, our taste in bread (grainy or white?) and which foods we are most likely to find on the supermarket shelf (see chapter 5).

Clearly, delving into any particular pattern quickly shows both the individual and society as important. For example, consider analyses of vegetarianism in the United States. As more individuals have adopted vegetarian diets, more restaurants have begun to offer vegetarian-friendly options on their menus, which in turn shapes the choices patrons can make about what to eat (Maurer 2002). Researchers also note that some vegetarians participate in vegetarian organizations or otherwise identify themselves as activists within a social movement, while others see avoiding meat as simply a personal choice (Maurer 2002). Mainstream food writing often promotes regular meatless meals as boons to health for meat-eaters (see chapter 4), and so vegetarianism is not as much of a departure from dietary conventions as it once was. This mainstreaming of vegetarianism may be seen as a boon or a detriment to the movement. Clearly, then, vegetarians make vegetarian foodways, but not out of whole cloth. And vegetarian foodways are influenced by the food system itself, which affects the variety of vegetarian foods that is available at a given time and in a given place.

Each of the chapters opens with a case study that illustrates its animating paradox, and each of these paradoxes relates, in some way, to the fundamental question about how individual agency works within these shifting social structural realities. Thus, the paradoxes should not be seen as problems to be solved but rather as points of ongoing, productive dialogue. Celebrating a paradox as a point of departure is wholly in keeping with the adventurous spirit of food studies, a field that bridges the material and the symbolic, the intimate and the global, the sacred and the profane, the eternal and the ephemeral.

Plan of the book

In the rest of this book, we examine many dimensions of foodways, using the key explanatory principles to maintain some common orienting threads. Each chapter also offers suggestions for further reading and exploration.

In chapter 2, "Food and Identity: Fitting In and Standing Out," we examine how food is central to both individual and group identity. Foodways mark membership in some groups and signal outsider status in others. They unite the people who consume the same foods in similar ways, while serving as a means for others to show that they are "different" and, depending on the context, better. We show how food is implicated in the social construction of identity, including national and regional, racial-ethnic, class, and gender identities. These patterns, which change over time, reproduce cultural beliefs about appropriate behavior for people based on group affiliation.

Chapter 3, "Food as Spectacle: The Hard Work of Leisure," shows these patterns in another context, the production of food-based leisure experiences that require an enormous amount of work – most of it invisible to those who consume it, literally or figuratively. The paradox examined in this chapter is the hard work done by some people to provide spectacular leisure experiences for others. The amount of work by restaurant employees that goes into the production of a fine-dining experience for customers is remarkable. Food entertainment media are another realm in which food functions as a spectacle. Our focus is on "food porn," a kind of media that allows viewers to experience the pleasures associated with food in a vicarious manner. They get to watch or read about others doing the work needed to prepare a complex recipe and then enjoy the results on the screen or page.

Chapter 4 explores "Nutrition and Health: Good to Eat, Hard to Stomach," taking up the paradox that pairs US government

nutrition guidelines and food marketing with the food choices made
by consumers. Despite fairly widespread agreement over the past few
decades among academic nutrition professionals about what constitutes a "healthy diet," consumers often report confusion about what
is and is not healthy and experience difficulty following a "healthy
diet." This is because information about "healthy" eating is both
abundant and contradictory. We explore how lobbying and marketing by the food industry and the dual and conflicting mandate of the
USDA to protect US agriculture and simultaneously offer nutritional
advice to the American public produces confusing nutrition messages. We end by discussing another health issue linked with diet –
the so-called "obesity epidemic." We consider the consequences of
the dominant view linking diet with weight and health, as well as the
moral undertones such a linkage tends to obscure.

Chapter 5, entitled "Branding and Marketing: Governing the
Sovereign Consumer," examines these interactive processes by going
beyond the "enchanting myth of consumer sovereignty" (Korczynski
and Ott 2004: 575) to explore the complex interplay of corporate
influence and consumer choice when foodways are embedded in a
broader consumer culture. We explain that brands are symbols; they
are the legal property of corporations, but also part of the broader
cultural lexicon where consumers imbue them with other meanings.
We also address the self-service supermarket as a **social institution** that embodies the paradox of consumer sovereignty within a
rigorously monitored and controlled environment. The significance
of these questions is clear when it comes to the impact of consumer
culture on children, so the chapter considers those questions as well.

The vast production system that supplies supermarkets and other
mass outlets is the subject of chapter 6, "Industrialization: The High
Costs of Cheap Food." It begins with the issue of antibiotic resistance, one of the social and environmental costs that industrial food
production exacts. It then describes the cultural and material process
of industrialization with reference to the case of fluid milk. The latter
part of the chapter explains why some critics of industrial food characterize its "cheap" food as distressingly costly.

Chapter 7, "Global Food: From Everywhere and Nowhere,"
builds on the industrialization narrative to explain global food connections while highlighting the role of corporations in managing
transnational supply chains. Privileged eaters in the current global
food system consume foods from around the world whose origins are
surprisingly murky. The chapter explains this paradox by examining
the food connections between the global North and the global South

through three broad eras: the modern colonial period, the development decades, and globalization. Throughout, we ask how the costs and benefits of the system are distributed and why.

Chapter 8, "Food Access: Surplus and Scarcity," examines inequality of food access through a critical lens. It begins by noting the conjoined problems of food surplus and food scarcity in national and global food systems and then reviews how social problems are defined and understood. The important semantic differences between "hunger" and "food insecurity" reveal a contested terrain, questioning the meaning of food deprivation and the means by which we address it. We last explore criticisms of anti-hunger efforts and why some allege that they do more harm than good.

The final chapter, "Food and Social Change: The Value of Values," narrates the burgeoning food movement and the diverse ways in which individuals and organizations are seeking positive social change through food, both face to face and across geographic and social differences. In surveying these efforts, we explore a key question that many of these efforts confront: Can market forces be directed toward enduring, significant change? Or do the inexorable laws of supply and demand put insurmountable limits on how much alternative markets can ameliorate social inequality? In other words, can we build a more just food system on the scaffold of market relations? We close this volume with the concept of food democracy because, as Karl Marx and Friedrich Engels (1969 [1845]: para. 11) famously put it, "the philosophers have only interpreted the world in various ways; the point is to change it."

We hope that reading this book is just one moment in a lifelong engagement with the rich insights from food studies. In studying food, you are joining this vibrant intellectual community, bringing your own unique experiences and insights like a bottle of wine to a dinner party. None of the research presented here is the final word on its topic; you will have something to add. As a reader, you are not a member of an audience but rather a guest at a table. Bon appétit!

Further reading

Edge, John T. (ed.). 2007. *Foodways*. Chapel Hill, NC: University of North Carolina Press. A volume in *The New Encyclopedia of Southern Culture* (ed. C. R. Wilson), this book describes southern US foodways from African-American food and barbecue to Tabasco sauce and wine.

Le Billon, Karen. 2012. *French Kids Eat Everything*. New York: HarperCollins/ Morrow. Writing as a parent and academic, Le Billon argues that differences between US and French foodways can help explain the significant difference between obesity rates in the two countries.

McMillan, Tracie. 2012. *The American Way of Eating: Undercover at Walmart, Applebee's, Farm Fields and the Dinner Table*. New York: Scribner. McMillan, a journalist, provides insights into the relationship between foodways and the food system in the United States. Her focus is on the difficulties of eating well in that context.

Pollan, Michael. 2008. *In Defense of Food: An Eater's Manifesto*. New York: Penguin. While encouraging individuals to exercise agency in their choices about what to eat, Pollan's follow-up to *The Omnivore's Dilemma* also examines a number of structural constraints on those choices, such as how they are shaped by food science and the industrialization of eating.

Sack, Daniel. 2000. *Whitebread Protestants: Food and Religion in American Culture*. New York: Palgrave. Focusing on US Protestants, Sack shows, for example, in a chapter on "Liturgical Food," how the holy meal of bread and wine has been defined differently across time and place.

Further exploration

1 IN CLASS: Describe the best meal you have ever eaten. What made it the best meal ever? What did you eat? With whom did you eat it? Was it a special occasion? Are the foods you ate likely to be foods with which your classmates are familiar? Why or why not?

2 FOR DISCUSSION: Watch a film that features a ritual meal of some kind (e.g., *When Do We Eat?*, *Soul Food*, *What's Cooking?*, *Babette's Feast*, *The Wedding Banquet*). Discuss what is eaten, how and when it is eaten, who shares the meal, and where it is eaten. Based on what you see, how strict are the rules for what foods are to be consumed, how they are to be prepared, who participates in the meal and how the meal is structured?

3 ONLINE: Visit the International Federation of Competitive Eating website (www.ifoce.com) and look at the eater profiles and list of records posted there. What patterns do you see in the profiles? What records are most surprising?

2
Food and Identity:
Fitting In and Standing Out

Case study

In October 2006, newspaper headlines announcing "US Bans Vegemite" enraged Australians at home and abroad (Healey 2006). One Australian in New York exclaimed, "In Australia the slogan is that Vegemite puts a rose in every cheek; but today America has slapped the cheek of every Australian" (Nichols 2006: para. 6). Just the thought of the United States banning this quintessential Australian food seemed a rejection of everything "Aussie."

Vegemite is a brown vitamin-rich paste made from brewer's yeast popular in Australia where it is spread on toast like peanut butter or jam. It was created by the Fred Walker Cheese Company in 1922 as the Australian counterpart to the popular British spread Marmite. As a former British colony, Australia initially "held on tightly to all things British" but, by the 1920s, Australian entrepreneurs were introducing Aussie-made products as competitors to popular British items like Marmite (Richardson 2003: 60). Vegemite's popularity grew slowly until World War II when Vegemite was indelibly linked with nationalist sentiment. It was included in Australian soldiers' rations, a fact the company advertised heavily, in part to explain why Vegemite was in short civilian supply. This created a solid link between Australian national identity and Vegemite ("The Vegemite Story").

The 2006 Vegemite controversy stemmed from false media reports that customs officials were not permitting travelers to enter the United States with Vegemite, paired with the US Food and Drug Administration's (FDA) restrictions on folic acid supplementation. Folic acid is the synthetic form of folate, a water-soluble B vitamin hailed for its role in preventing birth defects. Because excessive amounts of folic acid may mask vitamin B12 deficiencies, the FDA restricts folic acid supplementation to enriched breads, cereals, flours, and other grain products. Brewer's yeast is rich in naturally occurring folate, so these FDA restrictions do not apply. Although the FDA denied an import ban, and media reports later clarified that imports for personal use were legal, the anger it provoked indicates how closely Vegemite is linked with Australian national identity (Bosch 2006; "US Government Denies" 2006).

Two years later, Australians were again outraged when, in an effort to promote local food vendors, the Beijing Organizing Committee for the 2008 Olympics prohibited teams from shipping imported food into the Olympic Park for athletes' consumption. While the ban applied to all national teams, the Australian team was particularly incensed because it severely limited athletes' access to Vegemite. Louise Burke, the Australian Olympic team nutritionist, explained that the foods they planned to ship, including Vegemite, were "not readily available in China" and that such foods were "crucial" because they provide "familiar foods in the heat of competition," making "athletes feel at home" (English 2008: paras 9–10). The Australian team considered Vegemite necessary for ensuring optimal performance and winning medals. Happily, disaster was averted when, upon their arrival in Beijing, Australian athletes found Vegemite in their official welcome bags ("Australian Athletes" 2008).

Rozin and Siegal (2003: 63) call Vegemite "the best predictor of national identity of any food in the world." Their survey of undergraduates at a large Australian university found that students who were at least third-generation Australians were more likely than non-Australian students to report liking Vegemite. Students closely associated Vegemite with "Australia," second only to its strong association with "toast." The link between Vegemite and Australian national identity persists, despite the fact that the Vegemite brand is now wholly owned by the US company Kraft Foods.

The popular website YouTube.com is filled with video clips of non-Australians trying Vegemite for the first time. Typically, these depict the novice preparing toast and spreading it with butter and a thin layer of Vegemite in the Australian tradition. However, unlike Australians, the novice usually grimaces, spitting out the first bite. On one hand, these videos demonstrate the novice's adventurous spirit and willingness to cross cultural thresholds by sampling food associated with a cultural "other." However, the predictable negative reaction signifies that incorporation of foodways often occurs on the culinary terms set by the novice. In short, eating Vegemite marks Australians *as Australians*, while not eating it or reacting negatively to it marks one *as not Australian*.

As the case of Australians and Vegemite illustrates, foodways are a central feature of both group and individual identity. They mark membership in particular nations, geographic regions, racial-ethnic groups, social classes, and genders. Maintaining culinary distinctions sustains group identity and fosters a sense of personal belonging. This chapter explores the paradox of how food signifies both exclusion (difference) and inclusion (acceptance) through the association of food and national, regional, racial-ethnic, social class, and gender identities.

Introduction: food and identity

Individuals creatively define who they are and craft a social identity, both in terms of idiosyncratic and personal characteristics and relative to the various social groups to which they belong (Howard 2000). What foods we eat, how and when we prepare, serve, and consume them, are all types of **identity work** – activity through which we define for ourselves and others who we are socially and culturally (Caplan 1997; Howard 2000; Lupton 1996). Consumption choices, such as clothing, transportation, and housing, powerfully indicate the type of person we are and how we want others to see us. Whether we wear designer or second-hand clothing, drive a Mercedes or ride a bicycle, or live in a luxury town-home or public housing complex, each of these class-based status symbols offers clues to the various social statuses or positions we occupy in society. A **symbol** is something that stands for something else. As such, symbols carry shared meanings within particular cultures. **Status symbols**, then, are objects that signify one's position (or social status) in society. While we have some choice in what clothes we wear, modes of transport we use, and places we live in, these "choices" are also clearly structured by the larger opportunity structure in which we are located. Poor persons will be hard-pressed to realize the "choice" to drive a Mercedes, for example, just as their "choice" to eat fresh fruits and vegetables out of season may be constrained (see chapter 8). The relationship between food and identity is thus a good example of the complex interplay of individual and society noted in chapter 1.

By offering hints about our key statuses, food also functions as a status symbol, shaping both how we see ourselves and how others view us. We engage in identity work by learning to like and dislike particular dishes and choosing to consume certain foods but not others. Because food is literally consumed through the social act of eating, it plays a significant role in the social construction of identity.

The popular saying "You are what you eat" is not just a nutritional adage. If you eat Vegemite every day, you are probably Australian; if you nosh on grits and collard greens, chances are high that you are from the southern United States; if you eat steak and lobster regularly, you are most likely middle or upper class; and, if you normally consume salad and other "lighter fare," you are probably a woman.

Examining the "how" of foodways highlights how the symbolic meanings of foods are often established and maintained through **rituals**, social activities performed primarily for their symbolic significance, rather than for practical ends. The Christian ritual of taking communion, for example, entails consuming a small piece of bread or wafer with wine or grape juice. While Roman Catholics believe that these foods are transformed literally into the body and blood of Christ (through a process called transubstantiation), other Christian traditions believe these are simply symbolic representations of the same. In either case, the ritual is a powerful symbolic act within the Christian faith. The actual amounts of bread and wine consumed are too small to be nutritionally significant, but that is not the point. Christians consume these foods in a highly patterned manner not for any practical end; rather, they do so to sustain and renew faith. By participating in rituals, individuals publicly affirm the shared values of the group and incorporate new members into the collectivity.

Emile Durkheim (1965) explored how religious rituals contribute to **social solidarity**, the feelings of "we-ness" within groups. The highly scripted and repetitive activities of rituals give participants strong feelings of connection to other past and present members, who presumably also engage, or did in the past, in the same patterned acts. Rituals are key to maintaining group identity and values, but they are also powerful agents of social transformation. For example, coming-of-age and wedding rituals symbolically convert outsiders into insiders by transforming children into adults and single persons into spouses. Thus, many food rituals, from everyday practices to special occasions, create and sustain distinctive social identities while simultaneously offering opportunities for social change.

This chapter examines the paradoxical ways in which foodways both socially unite and divide individuals. We detail how the US Thanksgiving ritual creates and sustains a core national identity and explore the role of food in the maintenance of distinctive regional differences. Racial and ethnic identities are also reinforced by distinctive foodways and serve as both a point of ethnic pride and, at times, a source of fierce nutritional contention. Foodways also reflect and reinforce social class differences, with the upper and working classes within affluent societies demonstrating clear distinctions in food presentation and consumption. Gender differences are also reinforced and sometimes traversed through foodways. We conclude the chapter with an exploration of culinary tourism that demonstrates how participating in the foodways of others can signify acceptance of cultural difference while simultaneously reinforcing it. The relationship between food and identity thus demonstrates how food is both individual and social, material and symbolic, and shows how foodways function as key mechanisms of social inequality, reflecting and reinforcing national, regional, racial, class, and gender hierarchies.

Food and national and regional identity

Nations, and the different geographic regions within them, construct **cuisines** – distinct sets of ingredients, flavor principles, and cooking techniques – and these cuisines foster unique national and regional identities. Consider the differences between Szechuan- and Cantonese-style Chinese dishes. Szechuan style hails from western China and is known for its use of the hot Szechuan chili pepper in dishes like Kung Pao chicken and Szechuan chicken. Cantonese style hails from southern China and is known for dim sum (dumplings or rolls filled with a variety of meats, vegetables, or shrimp) and the cooking techniques of steaming and stir-frying. While both are considered part of a single national cuisine, they reflect the varied regional climates, crops, cultures, and tastes within the vast nation.

Similarly, Italy has regional variations differentiating northern cuisine, with its greater reliance on rice and corn dishes such as risotto and polenta, from southern cuisine, with its heavy reliance on olive oil, pasta, and tomato sauces. To many non-Italians, Italian food simply consists of pizza and pasta; but any self-respecting Venetian would disagree, being more likely to identify polenta, the corn-based dish for which the Italian region of Veneto is known, as an iconic dish. Clearly, regional variation exists within national cuisines, adding a critical element to our understanding of food and identity.

National and regional cuisines stem from distinctive local agricultures, as well as ethnic, religious, and other social differences associated with the people of a given area, representing structural and cultural dimensions, respectively. Structural differences, in particular, have more to do with how economic and political systems, as well as geography and climate, shape foodways. These structural issues demonstrate that the link between food and identity is not simply a matter of individual preference or choice; rather, identities are shaped by social structural features beyond the control of any one individual.

Consider the donut. Although considered a Canadian food icon, the donut has different regional connotations, linked to urban and rural, as well as class, differences. Before the 1970s, popular media outlets constructed donuts as American fare, and for good reason: donuts were an American import. Penfold (2008) traces the transformation of donuts from an American food to a distinctively Canadian and, more specifically, Ontario-based food. As late as the 1970s, restaurant magazines promoted donuts as a means for Canadian restaurateurs to attract American tourists (Penfold 2008: 172). But, in the context of disintegrating Canadian "cultural anchors" in the 1980s and 1990s, the donut emerged as a powerful symbolic representation of Canadian life (Penfold 2008: 178). In particular, a sense of shared national values came under attack as Canadian provinces, particularly francophone Quebec, increasingly voiced disagreement on constitutional matters. Second, the postindustrial economy increasingly divided consumers into the haves and the have-nots. This class fragmentation was reflected in the emergence of upscale coffee shops catering to the middle and upper classes and donut shops catering to the working class. Within this context, the unpretentious donut, affordable to rich and poor alike, served as a **social unifier** in an increasingly divided Canada.

Donut shops became the Canadian equivalent of the English pub, a place all social classes could afford to patronize and where they could mix comfortably to discuss important matters of the day and forge community ties. Such spaces are often termed **third places** to distinguish them from home and work – the first and second places (Oldenburg 1989). The symbol of the donut as a social unifier was supported in popular culture via "donut lore." Citing statistics, such as the most donut shops per capita, rural towns and suburbs erected welcome signs proclaiming to be the donut capital of Canada, claims that were reinforced verbally by residents. According to Penfold (2008: 176–7), donut lore "stands in opposition to a cultural centre – most often Toronto with its 'world-class' pretensions" and "plays on a sense of ironic pride in marginal status, simultaneously poking fun at the unsophisticated hinterlands and the pretentious metropolis." While Toronto and other Canadian urban centers might boast world-class eateries and entertainment, rural and suburban Canada had the democratic donut, a point of pride for those living in the shadows of so-called urban sophistication. The donut wasn't fancy; but it was affordable and tasted good. The donut was thus clearly linked to systems of social inequality through class distinctions and rural and urban differences.

Despite their strong national symbolism, Penfold (2008: 176) argues that donuts are more accurately a regional food. Even though they were found throughout Canada by the 1980s, donut shops are still most concentrated in the central province of Ontario, and few towns outside Ontario claim to be a donut capital. In the western province of British Columbia, other pastries are preferred to donuts, and upscale coffee houses outnumber working-class donut shops.

Because many industrialized countries include different cultural, racial-ethnic, social class, and religious groups, national rituals of solidarity are especially important for generating feelings of social cohesion and symbolically incorporating new members. National holidays are a case in point, and many involve food rituals. Take the US Thanksgiving holiday, celebrated annually on the last Thursday in November. Examining the history of Thanksgiving as both myth and historical reality demonstrates how food rituals construct and maintain national identity, creating distinctive in- and out-groups.

What images come to mind when you think of the US Thanksgiving holiday? While Pilgrims, Native Americans, the Macy's Thanksgiving Day Parade, and American football likely figure prominently, turkey with all the trimmings – stuffing, mashed potatoes, gravy, cranberry sauce, and pumpkin pie – spring to mind for many. The ample meal is based on the US Thanksgiving story, as retold annually in elementary school pageants. According to tradition, the winter of 1621 was devastating for the Pilgrims of Plymouth Colony. Were it not for the Native Americans, who shared their food, hunting methods and knowledge of local foods and growing techniques, the Pilgrims would have perished. After a successful fall harvest, the Pilgrims celebrated with their Native American friends by sharing a feast and giving thanks to God. This story, however, is more myth than reality, as historians, social scientists, and food scholars explain. More accurately, the Thanksgiving tradition was invented to promote American national solidarity following the Civil War.

According to Siskind (2002: 42), participating in the Thanksgiving ritual "transforms a collection of immigrants into Americans by connecting them to a cultural history stretching back to the 'founding' of the country." As we have noted, this founding story, in which Pilgrims and Native Americans supposedly shared their bountiful harvest in a lavish feast, is largely invented; that is, the tradition is based on a culturally constructed and idealized version of the first Thanksgiving. Though based on a fictionalized past, **invented tradition**s like these serve at least three important purposes. First, they symbolize social cohesion and create a strong collective identity. Second, invented traditions establish new social institutions and legitimize existing ones. Finally, invented traditions socialize individuals into the shared norms and values of the group practicing them (Hobsbawm 1983: 9). Thanksgiving is an important invented tradition grounding the present in an invented past, symbolizing national unity, and reaffirming a distinct national identity based on the institution of the family (Siskind 2002).

Where did our modern notion of the original Thanksgiving come from? Historically, days of thanksgiving were spiritual occasions proclaimed by religious leaders, in which feasting played only a minor role. Days of fasting were called in times of hardship, famine, or drought, while days of thanksgiving were observed to express gratitude for a successful harvest, victorious battle (often over Native Americans), or other signs of divine favor. Thanksgivings were primarily days of worship, not days of nation-building. Historians argue that the story of the first Thanksgiving is best understood as a community-based fall harvest festival (Loewen 2008; Pleck 1999; Siskind 2002).

How, then, did Thanksgiving evolve to represent nationalism and to valorize the family? Throughout the eighteenth and early part of the nineteenth century, Thanksgivings were largely limited to New England. Beginning in 1846, Sarah Josepha Hale, the editor of *Godey's* magazine, hoping to unite the nation and avert civil war, encouraged her readers to celebrate Thanksgiving and beseeched state leaders to proclaim it a legal holiday (Pleck 1999). During the US Civil War between northern and southern states, President Abraham Lincoln declared several days of thanksgiving to celebrate northern victories. In 1863, Lincoln declared Thanksgiving a national holiday to be observed on the last Thursday in November (Pleck 1999). The goal was to unify the divided nation through a core ritual celebration centered on the family.

Southern states, with wounds still fresh from the loss of the Civil War, were not eager to accept a national day of unity based on a northern tradition, especially since many northern ministers used Thanksgiving sermons to preach abolition (Siskind 2002). Only after the postwar Reconstruction period, when Southern states became free to implement segregationist policies protecting the power of white elites, was Thanksgiving celebrated throughout the American south (Siskind 2002). In the same era, Thanksgiving was infused with images of Pilgrims, Native Americans, and the mythical story at Plymouth (Pleck 1999; Siskind 2002). School pageants taught children the importance of Thanksgiving as part of the national origin; and grade schoolteachers encouraged immigrant students and their families to celebrate it. According to Siskind (2002: 52), "With the addition of the Pilgrims and the first Thanksgiving, the holiday became a full-fledged ritual re-enactment of an origin myth of the nation."

Amid this mid-nineteenth-century coalescence, Thanksgiving was solidified as a domestic occasion linked to images of a rural home-coming (Pleck 1999; Siskind 2002). Rapid industrialization follow-ing the Civil War facilitated rural-to-urban migration, spreading extended kin. Consequently, Thanksgiving was increasingly expe-rienced as a rural homecoming, as family members traveled from urban centers back to rural hometowns to celebrate. The popular Thanksgiving song "Over the River and Through the Woods" reflects this emergent meaning.

The dual significance of Thanksgiving as a national day of unity and a domestic occasion is captured humorously in the 2000 US film *What's Cooking?* which depicts the celebrations of four families in Los Angeles, California, with divergent social locations. While all four celebrate with the traditional stuffed turkey, each also prepares unique dishes representative of their cultural heritage. The Mexican-American family serves homemade tamales and tortillas, while the upper-class African-American family includes shitake mushroom stuffing, fresh asparagus and fruit compote. The working-class Vietnamese family, in deference to the divergent tastes of both the first and third generations, prepares a single turkey with traditional Vietnamese spices on one breast and traditional Thanksgiving spices on the other, accompanied by both spring rolls and canned sweet potatoes. By participating in the ritual while incorporating traditional ethnic dishes, they simultaneously affirm their national affiliation and the unique cultural heritage of their family. The element of home-coming is captured in the film, as family members travel from across the country to celebrate together, thus renewing family ties through a national holiday. In this way, new immigrant groups are symbolically incorporated into the nation, while the family is reaffirmed as the foundation of a strong society.

The US Thanksgiving ritual is just one of many invented traditions that promote national solidarity. All countries, and particularly mul-ticultural ones, need rituals to create a sense of national community.

Benedict Anderson (1991: 6) calls nations **imagined communities**
since "members of even the smallest nation will never know most of
their fellow-members, meet them, or even hear of them, yet in the
minds of each lives the image of their communion." Lacking reciprocal social ties with all citizens, the ties linking a nation's people
are largely imagined. Anderson's concept helps to explain why
Thanksgiving and the Thanksgiving meal is such an important ritual,
despite the historical distortions on which it is based. All nations
engage in the ritual reaffirmation of shared identity and values; the
features of the modern US Thanksgiving reflect the country's particular historical and cultural conditions.

While widely practiced and inclusive in spirit, the Thanksgiving
ritual also reflects persistent inequalities. Just as Southern states
initially resented a national holiday based on a northern ideal, contemporary Native Americans challenge the social construction of
Thanksgiving as a day of national unity. The myth of Pilgrims and
Native Americans celebrating collectively obscures the violence
Native Americans faced at the hands of white colonists. Pilgrims
brought diseases, against which Native peoples had no immunity,
bloody wars, and other social and legal policies, such as a belief in
private ownership of land, that were anathema to Native peoples'
ways of life. For Native Americans, Thanksgiving may not signify
national unity and social cohesion; rather, it signifies continued political oppression, with some Native Americans treating Thanksgiving
as a "National Day of Mourning" (Baker 2009; Mihesuah 1996).
Native perspectives on Thanksgiving demonstrate how this ritual
both unites and divides, and remind us that the meanings of ritual
meals are often contested.

Food and racial-ethnic identity

The United States is typically depicted as a cultural melting pot.
Given the unique combinations of native peoples and immigrant
groups and their distinctive food traditions, the culinary landscape
is diverse (Gabaccia 1998). Many cultural groups maintain and
reinvigorate distinctive foodways to retain and express their unique
heritage, while simultaneously adapting new culinary elements to
create a hybrid cuisine. The Gullah, for example, descendants of
slaves from the coastal islands of South Carolina and Georgia, have
been especially successful in preserving foodways centered on rice,
rice cultivation, and food self-reliance through gardening and forag-

ing over generations of changing social contexts (Beoku-Betts 1995). In other cases, ethnic foods have become largely untethered from their cultural origins. The prevalence and variation of hybrid cuisines illustrate the diverse origins of many foodways.

"Soul food" is a rich example of a dynamic, hybrid cuisine (Opie 2008). It is "distinctively African American but was influenced by Europeans, who introduced corn to African foodways and then provided cornmeal, meat, fish, and other ingredients as rations to the first enslaved Africans in southern North America" (Opie 2008: 134). Enslaved and poor African Americans fashioned a culinary repertoire reliant on less valuable cuts and types of meat, such as pig ears and feet, chitterlings, ham bones, and chicken, and used strong flavorings to spice up and extend meals to feed large families over several days. Based on diverse African ancestries and the deprivations imposed by slavery and Reconstruction, these culinary skills served poor African Americans well in times of scarcity.

In the early decades of the twentieth century, African Americans from the southern United States began moving to northern cities in large numbers in what is called the Great Migration. Seeking industrial work and escape from poverty, tenant farming, sharecropping, and blatant discrimination in the South, poor African-American southerners brought to the North the culinary repertoire on which prior generations had relied (Poe 2002).

During and after the Great Migration, southern African-American foodways offered psychological comfort to migrants in northern cities, functioning as a comfort food that reminded them of home (Poe 2002). African-American foodways also offered new arrivals business opportunities in the form of neighborhood groceries and restaurants, appealing prospects to new migrants because of their low start-up costs, the relatively few skills required for entry, and migrants' established familiarity with cooking techniques (Poe 2002). However, upper-class African Americans in northern cities often rejected the foodways of poorer migrants, preferring instead to eat like their white upper-class counterparts in an attempt to assimilate to the dominant white culture (Poe 2002). Working-class African-American foodways were more difficult to maintain during the economic hardship and food scarcity caused by the Great Depression in the 1930s. Food assistance programs, including the distribution of surplus commodities, soup kitchens, and breadlines (see chapter 8), offered an array of non-ethnic products to many poor African-American families. Wealthy white families also sometimes shared extra food with their African-American cooks and domestic servants, who brought leftovers home to their hungry families (Opie 2008). The once-thriving black-owned restaurants and grocers faced difficulty during these lean times and, because of the refusal of many white-owned banks to extend credit to black business owners, many small grocers and restaurants closed (Poe 2002).

Beginning in the 1950s and continuing into the 1970s, African-American social movements valorized African-American culinary traditions, renaming the cuisine "soul food" (Opie 2008; Poe 2002). The Black Power and Black Nationalist movements, for example, called for the creation of a distinctive Afrocentric consciousness and culture to contest the devaluation of African-American culture in white America. These movements sought to develop and promote a new, positive black cultural identity that would unite African Americans. Along with music and literature, African-American foodways were a key part of this Afrocentric culture (Opie 2008). According to Opie (2008), African-American authors began publishing cookbooks and defining soul food as an important part of a unique African-American heritage. The Black Power movement, in particular, championed soul food as a distinctively African-American creation and urged blacks to take pride in this unique culinary legacy. African-American celebrities, including James Brown and Muhammad Ali, invested in African-inspired chain restaurants as the popularity of soul food soared (Opie 2008).

Nevertheless, like upper-class black northerners during the Great Migration, some African Americans continued to criticize soul food. Soul food held "complex meanings in the 1960s, serving as a source of ethnic and family pride to some and as a reminder of slavery and nutritional miseducation to others" (Opie 2008: 181). Despite endorsing Black Nationalism and welcoming the creation of a unique Afrocentric culture, the black separatist movement known as the Nation of Islam (NOI) popularized by figures such as Elijah Muhammad and Malcolm X, rejected soul food on both religious and cultural grounds. As a religious movement preaching a unique brand of Islam, the NOI rejected pork, a soul food staple, believing pigs to be unclean and prohibited under Islam. Additionally, the NOI rejected soul food on the grounds that its strong reliance on animal products and frying made it unhealthy and, as such, part of a white conspiracy to undermine the physical and political vitality of African Americans. Elijah Muhammad, the head of the NOI throughout the 1950s and 1960s, preached that white elites "promoted the consumption of unhealthy processed food and spicy and greasy food in order to weaken and eventually wear out black[s]" (Opie 2008: 159).

Additionally, some question the distinctiveness of soul food as an African-American culinary tradition, claiming that soul food represents regional southern foodways more generally. White southerners regularly publish cookbooks on "southern" cuisine that prominently feature many of the same dishes commonly associated with soul food, like sweet potato pie, chitterlings, greens, fried fish, and pulled pork. Nevertheless, soul food has maintained its pivotal position as an emblem of black cultural identity. Soul restaurants remain popular, and soul-themed canned goods and convenience foods, including Sylvia's brand, now appear in conventional supermarkets.

The rise of soul food in the 1960s and 1970s was one part of a culinary revolution in the United States marked by the rising popularity of ethnic foods, health foods, and other alternative cuisines (Belasco 1987, 2007). The ethnic food boom emerged from the **ethnic revival** of the 1970s, when Americans sought to reclaim their ethnic heritage as a response to the **hegemonic process**, the way dominant cultural forms incorporate and thereby erase cultural distinctions. Reclaiming a lost ethnic heritage creates a **neo-ethnicity**. In seeking neo-ethnicity, members of the grassroots ethnic revival embraced traditional cultural forms, including ethnic foodways. An ethnic food boom resulted, and food corporations saw ethnic foods' growing popularity as a profitable business opportunity. In a process termed **corporatization**, food corporations in restaurant, retail, and manufacturing began producing ethnic foods and promoting them to a growing and affluent market comprised of core ethnics (those with actual ties to the ethnic culture from which the product hails) as well as counterculturalists, gourmets, and **culinary tourists** – those who view ethnic food as an enjoyable respite from normal and mundane foodways. Moreover, because ethnic food was linked to high-quality ingredients and supposedly authentic and time-consuming cooking techniques, manufacturers could present packaged ethnic food as a specialty product with a correspondingly higher price.

To some, the corporatization of ethnic food represents a rise of cultural pluralism; to others, it marks the homogenization of cultural difference that weakens both the symbolic and economic links between a particular racial-ethnic group and its foodways (Belasco 1987). While core ethnics typically did the arduous work of starting and growing successful ethnic restaurants and groceries, mainstream corporations acquired these businesses to expand their profits by moving from mass marketing to **micro-marketing**: promoting specific products to narrowly defined consumer groups based on age, gender, ethnicity, and other social statuses (also discussed in chapter

5). Through micro-marketing, corporations could market ethnic goods to middle- and upper-class families who could afford their higher costs, as well as second- and third-generation immigrants who lacked the time and technical knowledge to cook ethnic food from scratch (Belasco 1987).

As an ethnic cuisine is corporatized, its association with the original ethnic group weakens. In fact, the popularity of a food item beyond group borders – outside the nation or region from which it originated, or beyond the ethnic groups with which it was initially linked – usually signals a decline in the association of that food with a distinctive social identity. Mexican food is a good example. Taco Bell has become so ubiquitous that it is no longer firmly associated with a distinctive ethnic group. Each year, millions of people around the globe "run for the border" (Taco Bell's advertising slogan from the 1980s) without ever actually crossing any borders, real or symbolic. Even Burger King and McDonald's offer a multitude of sandwiches in the form of the non-ethnic sounding "wrap," which is actually a flour tortilla (Lind and Barham 2004). Clearly, while foodways may help form and maintain racial-ethnic distinctions, they are constantly changing via their mainstreaming and adaptation by ethnic others.

Food and social class identity

As we noted in the example of upper-class African Americans' rejection of soul food as a working-class cuisine during the Great Migration, social class distinctions are frequently made visible in, and reinforced by, foodways. Importantly, lower-class groups tend to have poorer diets than higher-status groups (Andrieu, Darmon, and Drewnowski 2006; Bernstein et al. 2010; Cade et al. 1999). Because healthier foods cost more than less nutritious foods, cost produces a social class gradient in diet and nutrition. An analysis of 27 different research studies from around the globe calculated an average daily price difference of US$1.50 per person between the healthiest and least healthy diets (Rao et al. 2013). Another recent study of food expenditures in Washington State found that higher-cost diets were also significantly higher in all seven nutrients examined (vitamins A, C, and E, fiber, calcium, magnesium, and potassium) and in overall nutrient density (Monsivais, Aggarwal, and Drewnowski 2010). Chapter 8 examines in greater detail the problems of poverty and food insecurity, as well as societal responses to these. Here, we focus more on the symbolic meanings of food and foodways for designating persons as social class insiders and outsiders.

As we have discussed throughout this chapter, what we eat is determined as much by food's symbolic meanings as by its material or nutritional qualities. Therefore, the way social class influences foodways extends well beyond access to a nutritious and abundant diet. Bourdieu (1984) coined the term we introduced in chapter 1, cultural capital, to describe how tastes, usually thought of as idiosyncratic personal preferences, together with manners and social skills, mark membership in particular social classes. Bourdieu (1984) noted three differences between upper-class and working-class foodways. First, upper-class foodways require one to defer gratification, while working-class ones embrace immediate satisfaction. Second, upper-class foodways valorize difficult and time-consuming dishes, whereas working-class ones celebrate simple and quick ones. Third, upper-class culture prioritizes form, while working-class culture emphasizes substance and function. Many people in affluent countries participate in both upper-class and working-class foodways at times; but Bourdieu (1984) notes that social class strongly influences which ones a person finds accessible and enjoyable. As the economy separates individuals into distinctive social class positions, these positions shape people's access to cultural capital.

The class distinctions identified by Bourdieu (1984) are aptly illustrated in many fictionalized films featuring social class makeovers of the rags to riches variety. For instance, in the 2001 film *The Princess Diaries*, 15-year-old Mia Thermopolis is visited by her estranged paternal grandmother who she learns is the queen of Genovia, making Mia a princess and heir to the throne. The Queen and her entourage undertake to instruct the socially awkward middle-class teen in all the forms of cultural capital befitting a royal, including classic dance, literature, and of course, table manners. To teach Mia proper table posture, the queen straps Mia to the chair-back to prevent her from slouching. Later, at a state dinner, Mia is served sorbet between courses, a common practice in fine dining, believed to cleanse the palate – to neutralize or clean the flavors in the mouth left over from the previous course so that the diner can fully savor the flavors in the next course. Mia scoops a large portion into her mouth and then becomes noticeably uncomfortable as the cold sorbet freezes her mouth. This and other dining blunders demonstrate clearly that Mia has much to learn about fine-dining etiquette if she is to live comfortably among the royals, for whom form and etiquette are paramount.

As another example, in 1990's *Pretty Woman*, Vivian, a prostitute played by Julia Roberts, is hired by Edward, a rich businessman, to be his companion for a week. In their first morning together, Vivian awakes to find Edward eating his room-service breakfast in their hotel penthouse. Instead of taking the time to sit on a chair and assemble her breakfast on a plate as Edward had done, Vivian cheerfully perches on the edge of the table to eat a croissant with her hands and talks with her mouth full. In short, Vivian takes the opportunity to enjoy immediate gratification through a one-item breakfast, while Edward finds it necessary to hold to the form of slowly consuming a more elaborate meal.

Later in the film, Vivian makes a major effort to acquire enough cultural capital to pass as upper class. Employing working-class solidarity, she asks the hotel manager for help in selecting a dress and learning the appropriate table etiquette for high-end dining. Like Mia in *The Princess Diaries*, we clearly see the limits of her quick training. Vivian gets flustered when, instead of the salad she had expected, the dinner begins with an elaborate and rare dish, escargot (snails), a food she is unfamiliar with and thus unable to eat properly. As she struggles to discern which utensil to use amid the expansive array at her place setting, the unpretentious self-made businessman they are dining with helps ease her discomfort by claiming that he, too, often forgets which one to use. In doing so, he implicitly pokes fun at the upper-class obsession with form over function in fine dining and allies himself with working-class culture. Nevertheless, though he and Vivian constitute fully half of their table, they both still hew to the upper-class norms that suffuse the fine-dining institution. It is not just that working-class and upper-class foodways are different; they are also unequal.

Food and gender identity

Some of the most evocative areas of food studies examine the multiple ways food is gendered. First, within a culture, particular foods or dishes are constructed as masculine or feminine. Second, men and women also have different relationships with food, with women reporting greater concern with food and weight. Third, while men have increased their share of household labor, women still perform the bulk of housework, including **feeding work**, which entails planning and provisioning meals as well as preparing and serving them (Charles and Kerr 1988; DeVault 1991). Men and children are often the beneficiaries of women's feeding work, and, even though men increasingly participate in it, they often do so in ways that maintain, rather than disrupt, gender distinctions (Deutsch 2005; DeVault 1991).

In every culture, some foods are considered masculine and others feminine (Counihan and Kaplan 1998). Meat, so central to US foodways (see chapter 1) is strongly associated with masculinity. According to Sobal (2005: 137), food studies research demonstrates conclusively that "Animal flesh is a consummate male food, and a man eating meat is an exemplar of maleness." In most cultures, hunting is traditionally assigned to men and hunting and meat-eating symbolically represent men's domination over nature and incorporation of the vanquished animal's strength (Adams 1990). In western cultures, salads, vegetables, and "light" foods are linked to femininity, mirroring women's concern with weight and body size (Adams 1990; Amiraian and Sobol 2009). Reflective of the association of masculinity with meat and femininity with vegetables, women are much more likely than men to be vegetarians (Maurer 2002).

Men and women are rewarded for conforming to gendered foodways and sanctioned for deviating from them. In particular, people's perceptions of others' attractiveness, as well as their femininity and masculinity, are affected by what and how much one eats. In one experiment, college student participants rated a video of a woman eating a small salad as significantly more appealing than a video of the same woman eating a sandwich (Basow and Kobrynowicz 1993). In another study, subjects rated women eating large meals as significantly less attractive than those consuming smaller ones. However, ratings of men were not affected by meal size, suggesting a sexual double standard. Subjects also rated persons consuming large meals as significantly less feminine and more masculine than those consuming smaller meals, regardless of gender (Bock and Kanarek 1995).

These ratings relate to internalized food rules. In her examination of food rules among college students, Counihan (1992: 58) found that women worry more than men about calories, and calories override women's concerns about vitamins, minerals, fats, carbohydrates, and protein. She concludes that "The sexes are enjoined to eat differently – men to eat heartily and abundantly, women daintily and sparingly" (Counihan 1992: 61). Given the link between attractiveness and eating, it is not surprising that women are more concerned with calories and are more likely to diet than men. Nor is it surprising that women eat less when they are with men than when dining with other women, a difference especially marked in heterosexual dating encounters (Counihan 1992; Young et al. 2009). Women tend to favor easy-to-eat and neat foods as appropriate for a date, a difference researchers attribute to women wanting to avoid food spilling on and staining clothing or sticking to their teeth (Amiraian and Sobol 2009: 230). Men, on the other hand, do not adjust their eating behaviors when dining with women (Young et al. 2009), underscoring the stronger link between women's food consumption and physical attractiveness. Nevertheless, some research indicates that men are more likely than women to restrict their food choices to those considered gender appropriate (Gal and Wilkie 2010). Gender nonconformity is more threatening for men because it represents the loss of a valued and powerful social status. Because femininity is not as highly valued as masculinity, women's gender nonconformity is less disruptive of gendered power dynamics.

Power dynamics are also relevant to men's and women's different relationship to feeding work, which is still more often performed by women in multiple countries. For example, Dutch women spend an average of 9.1 hours a week cooking, whereas Dutch men spend an average of only 3.7 hours (van der Lippe, Tijdens, and de Ruijter 2004). In Australia, among adults aged 26–36 years, 65% of women had sole responsibility for meal preparation compared to 29% of men, while 23% of women and 27% of men reported that they shared the task (Smith et al. 2010). A recent time-use survey in the United Kingdom found that 85% of women versus 60% of men reported any time cooking, and 60% of women versus 33% of men reported 30 or more continuous minutes of cooking. British women spent a median of 50 minutes, whereas British men spent a median of only 10 minutes cooking (Adams and White 2015). In the United States, women did 9.3 times as much cooking as men in 1965, but by 1998 this ratio had dropped to 2.2 (Harnack et al. 1998). Clearly, men are doing more than in the past, but US women still perform more than twice as much feeding work as men. Among the specific tasks that comprise feeding work, US men are most likely to shop and least likely to plan meals, with meal preparation falling in between. Men's participation in meal planning and preparation is higher among younger men, those with wives working full time, or those from smaller and/or poorer households (Harnack et al. 1998).

Women's feeding work is often taken for granted and goes unnoticed, unless it is not done, despite the fact that it entails considerable mental planning, including monitoring family members' taste preferences, and requires physical labor in the form of shopping, cooking, and cleaning (Charles and Kerr 1988; DeVault 1991). Research with diverse Canadian families outlines the rationales family members offer for why women perform more feeding work than men. Respondents claim that women have more flexible schedules and free time in which to complete feeding work, know more about nutrition, have more cooking skills, and want to avoid upsetting family members, especially husbands. Although rarely stated explicitly, all of these explanations include an assumption that feeding work is women's work (Beagan et al. 2008). Because men are often considered exempt from the responsibility for feeding work, they frequently garner special praise when they perform it (DeVault 1991).

As more women with children have entered the paid labor force in the last few decades, the pressures of the unequal burden of feeding work have increased. Women now spend fewer hours on housework, while men spend about the same; thus, even though men are doing a larger proportion of the total housework, their burden hasn't actually increased (South and Spitze 1994). Of all domestic tasks, men are most likely to cook, and the pressures have resulted in shifting some of the work of cooking to restaurants, takeout meals, and supermarket "meal solutions." This shift in labor is called **domestic outsourcing** (van der Lippe, Tijdens, and de Ruijter 2004). Single women are significantly less likely than single men to dine at restaurants or eat takeout, while married women are the least likely to do so (Kroshus 2008; Smith et al. 2010; van der Lippe, Tijdens, and de Ruijter 2004).

Given these gendered divisions, how is feeding work accomplished among same-sex couples? Few studies examine gay men's and lesbian women's contributions to feeding work within cohabiting relationships. Instead, most focus on household labor more generally, where partners' contributions to feeding work are combined with other domestic chores (Coltrane 2000; Kurdek 2007). Gay and lesbian cohabiting couples are eager to present their relationships as fully egalitarian, which stems, in part, from being in a society that still considers their families to be illegitimate. Interestingly, Carrington's (1999) research on gay and lesbian couples found that feeding work was not equally divided. Moreover, less involved men claimed to perform more feeding work than was actually the case as revealed by direct observation. Carrington (1999) argues that less involved male partners are seeking to heighten the masculine image of their more involved male partners. Conversely, the more involved female partners tended to underplay their work as a means of protecting the feminine status of their less involved partners.

Given the persistence of gendered foodways, it is unsurprising that gender also pervades the culture of dieting. Dieting is usually seen as a feminine concern. Things shifted, however, with the Atkins diet, one of the first diet programs centered on restricting carbohydrate intake to achieve weight loss, promoting high-protein and fat-laden foods like red meat, bacon, and butter over traditional dieting fare like salads and vegetables. Amy Bentley (2004: 35) argues that, by promoting red meat and other foods linked to masculinity, Atkins "allowed men to come out of the closet with regard to dieting." Men could safely declare they were on a diet and pursue a weight-loss regimen without threatening their masculinity. Other weight-loss products have attempted to capitalize on the gender-bending success of the Atkins diet. Nutrisystem, for example, a popular weight-loss program based on ready-made meals, now features separate diet plans for men and women on its website (www.nutrisystem.com). The company hired Dan Marino, former US football star and Hall of Fame quarterback for the Miami Dolphins, as their spokesman to encourage men to "man up and slim down."

Just as men can diet in decidedly masculine ways, they can also reinforce gender boundaries through cooking. The next chapter notes the preponderance of men in high-status chef positions, but men's cooking can maintain boundaries in domestic spheres as well. Jonathan Deutsch (2005) analyzes food preparation among male firefighters, who cook and eat together while on duty. Deutsch finds that firefighters bring a masculine identity to the performance of traditionally feminine work. For example, they prize the rotating job of cook because it gives one control over the menu and delegation of duties such as chopping onion or setting the table, making it a powerful masculine role. Second, their behavior is peppered with sexualized banter, such as referring to chicken breasts as "chicken tits" and positioning foods to approximate body parts, as well as the exuberant use of profanity. This kind of banter, which is the most pointed and frequent when the men are performing the most feminine tasks such as serving meals, insulates men from the implicit threat to their masculinity that cooking poses (Deutsch 2005). Paradoxically, then, these firefighters are recreating gender boundaries through the very process of crossing them. The following section describes culinary tourism as a similar way of reinforcing lines of distinction while simultaneously engaging in food practices associated with others.

Culinary tourism

In her pathbreaking work, Mary Douglas explored how the social act of sharing a meal both maintains and disrupts significant group boundaries (Douglas 1972; Douglas and Nicod 1974). According to Douglas (1972), while drinks might be consumed with co-workers, snacks with acquaintances, and hors d'oeuvres with friends, meals are shared with family and others we wish to welcome into the family. For example, for many new couples, bringing a romantic partner to a family dinner for the first time is a pivotal social event because it is a sign of social acceptance and inclusion within the family unit. But, at the same time that meals allow us to be inclusive of others, they also function to exclude certain individuals and groups from significant social relationships by clearly delineating a boundary between "us" and "them." For instance, in the popular film *Bridget Jones's Diary*, Bridget, the single protagonist, has dinner with a group of married friends. Though included in the meal as a member of this friendship clique, Bridget is the only single person at the event, making the number of people at the table an odd number, which literally and symbolically makes her the odd person out. Dinner conversation, which centers on Bridget's single status, reinforces this point. This fictional example shows how sharing a meal can be both inclusive and exclusionary at the same time.

Cuisines define those who share given foodways as *cultural insiders*, while simultaneously marking as *cultural outsiders* those who do not. Crossing culinary boundaries by participating in the foodways of cultural others can signify inclusiveness and openness to diverse experiences. Yet we often cross culinary thresholds in ways that maintain, rather than disrupt, the "us" and "them" distinction. Consuming "ethnic food" can illustrate open-mindedness and adventure, but it does so in ways that typically maintain the "us" and "them" dichotomy.

Consider typical reactions of North American viewers to the popular television show *Bizarre Foods with Andrew Zimmern*. The host travels the world sampling such foods as grilled cow udder and *chunchules* (braided intestines) in Chile, and ants and poisonous cane toads in the Australian Outback. Most North American viewers would be hesitant to try these "strange" foods, and viewer reactions, ranging from disgust to cautious curiosity, illustrate how powerful cultural forces and social distinctions are in shaping one's appetite. Even Anthony Bourdain, the adventurous eater and host of the Travel Channel's *No Reservations*, has particularly strong negative reactions when he visits the Namibian Bushmen in southwestern Africa (Aga and Soholt 2007). Squeamish, but wanting to be a good guest, Bourdain attempts to hide his distaste when he eats cooked ostrich egg baked in sand and ash, warthog head cooked in hot embers, and warthog anus roasted directly on a fiery log. He proclaims the dirt- and ash-laden meal "the worst, most difficult, even horrifying meal of my life," presumably because it departs so forcefully from his understandings of what is good and safe to eat. To his Bushmen hosts, these same foods and cooking techniques hardly qualify as bizarre. We see, then, that when culinary tourists consume foods of ethnic "others," they still experience them on their own terms. In that sense, Zimmern's and Bourdain's eating adventures represent the crossing of boundaries, but in ways that maintain the "us" and "them" distinction.

Like Zimmern and Bourdain, affluent consumers increasingly participate in **culinary tourism**, an encounter with an unfamiliar culinary culture that reinforces the tourist's identity as an adventuresome and sophisticated person. A satisfying tourist experience hinges on the elusive notion of **authenticity**; tourists want to experience tastes and other sensations that are true to the cuisine they are sampling (Johnston and Baumann 2015). However, ethnic restaurants must adapt cuisines and foodways to make them both legible and palatable to the customers they serve, and the regional variations within say, Thailand, are compressed on the menu of a Thai restaurant in Toronto. No restaurant can give patrons the true experience of eating as if one were a member of the represented culture.

Authenticity is not an objective quality that adheres to a dish; rather, authenticity is a social accomplishment produced by the interaction of diners' expectations and restaurateurs' design of the dining experience (Germann Molz 2004; Grazian 2003; Lu and Fine 1995). Interestingly, diners only identify things as authentic when they are considered foreign. For example, it is unlikely that a North American has ever remarked, "What an authentic peanut butter sandwich!" Rather, a dish feels "authentic" when it meets a certain essential standard in the mind of the diner. For example, the popular Thai noodle dish, pad Thai, despite its wide regional variations within Thailand, has to look, smell, and taste a certain way for North American and European diners to consider it authentic. Restaurateurs, in turn, have to make diners feel comfortable without making them feel completely "at home." The decor, food, menu, and music of ethnic restaurants are carefully arranged to give diners the impression that they have been transported to another country but are also adapted to American palates and assumptions (Germann Molz 2004). Authenticity, then, does not reside in the restaurant nor in the mind of the diner; instead, it resides in the moment of interaction and is best understood as a social accomplishment (Lu and Fine 1995).

Conclusion: The complex relationship between foodways and identity

As this chapter shows, identity is not merely about the free choices that individuals make; rather, identities are strongly patterned by our structural position in society. Food rituals, key elements of foodways, reinforce both belonging and difference through fostering identification with in-groups; they challenge difference through crossing culinary thresholds via culinary tourism and corporate mainstreaming. Moreover, the meanings of particular foods and food rituals can be highly contested, as the examples of Canadian donuts, Thanksgiving, and soul food demonstrate. As a result, foodways are constantly in flux, as people attempt to alter the meaning and content of food rituals, vary their participation in them, and redraw culinary boundaries. Thus, foodways are both individual and social. They mark insiders and outsiders and, paradoxically, both preserve identity and promote social change.

The findings and insights from this chapter also show that our relationship with food is structured by our social location within complex systems of social inequality. Our geographic region and nation, race and ethnicity, social class, and gender structure our relationships to food; and these relationships, in turn, can alter or reinforce patterns of social inequality. The next chapter builds on this exploration of food and social inequality by examining in greater detail the distinctions between food as leisure or entertainment for the privileged, accomplished through the hard work of others.

Further reading

Baker, James W. 2009. *Thanksgiving: The Biography of an American Holiday.* Durham, NH: University of New Hampshire Press. Baker provides a richly detailed historical account of the iconic American Thanksgiving ritual celebration, including a particularly interesting chapter on Native American perspectives and protests.

Gabaccia, Donna R. 1998. *We Are What We Eat: Ethnic Food and the Making of Americans.* Cambridge, MA: Harvard University Press. Gabaccia offers a detailed history of ethnic food and ethnic identity in the United States. The introductory chapter includes a short, highly readable account of the transformation of the bagel – first from an Eastern European baked good into a Jewish food icon, and, eventually, into a mainstream American food.

Glassner, Barry. 2006. *The Gospel of Food: Everything You Think You Know*

About Food is Wrong. New York: Ecco. Glassner, a noted sociologist, explores food and foodways in this book aimed at a popular audience. Of particular relevance for issues of food and identity are the chapters dealing with both "classy" (chapter 4) and fast-food restaurants (chapter 6), and social hierarchies that esteem fresh above processed foods (chapter 3). Also of interest is his detailed discussion of "food adventurers" in search of authentic dining experiences.

Inness, Sherrie. 2005. *Secret Ingredients: Race, Gender, and Class at the Dinner Table*. New York: Palgrave Macmillan. Inness explores the links between gender, race, and class and cooking through an examination of American cookbooks over time. She examines how gender and racial stereotypes were constructed and reinforced, as well as challenged, through cookbooks. Of special interest is her argument that cookbooks contained the seeds of social rebellion against particular food stereotypes.

Shortridge, Barbara and Shortridge, James (eds). 1998. *The Taste of American Place: A Reader on Regional and Ethnic Foods*. New York: Rowman & Littlefield. An oldie, but goodie, this edited volume explores the many varied links between geographic regions, ethnic groups, and foodways. It includes introductory chapters on regional and ethnic foods, as well as select chapters on the association between particular ethnic groups and specific foods (e.g., Jews and Chinese food, Cajuns and crawfish), and the performance of ethnic identity via food (e.g., among Italian Americans).

Further exploration

1 IN CLASS: Bring an ethnic canned or packaged food to class with you. Briefly describe the item, including its labeling. As a class, determine which items seem the most authentic and which the least authentic. What characteristics led you to rate those items as most authentic? What characteristics led you to rate items as the least authentic? How do these characteristics relate to the social construction of authenticity discussed in the chapter?

2 FOR DISCUSSION: Describe a regional food in your area. How do locals regard it? How do outsiders regard it? Is it well known outside your region? If so, has this changed the way locals and outsiders regard it? What are the specific structural and cultural factors that link this food with your particular region?

3 ONLINE: Locate the words to the Thanksgiving song, "Over the River and Through the Woods" (there are a number of versions available). Discuss and analyze how the lyrics reflect and reinforce popular images of Thanksgiving explored in the chapter.

4 ONLINE: Visit the Radcliffe Institute for Advanced Study at Harvard University's website for their 2007 conference on "Women, Men, and Food: Putting Gender on the Table" (http://athome.harvard.edu/food/). Watch the clip of Ruth Reichl's presentation on "Identity and Food."

Click "Watch" and follow the link for "Writing Food, Writing Lives: You Are What You Cook." Then select Reichl's presentation from the video menu. How does her talk reflect larger issues of food and identity discussed in the chapter?

3

Food as Spectacle: The Hard Work of Leisure

Case study

In 2014, the word "foodies" was included on Lake Superior State University's annual "List of Words Banished from the Queen's English for Mis-Use, Over-Use and General Uselessness." Comments about the word noted that, since it means "people who love food," it's a pointless term that applies to everyone and that we don't refer to people who love beer as "beeries" or those who love sleep as "sleepies" ("LSSU Continues its New Year Tradition" 2015).

In 2015, Canadian sociologists Josée Johnston and Shyon Baumann published the second edition of their groundbreaking empirical study of foodies, who *aren't* just "people who love food." Foodies characterized themselves as "well-informed, discovery-minded, discerning consumers (and most often food producers as well) who lead food-focused lives and present themselves to others as uncommonly passionate about food" (Johnston and Baumann 2015: 60). US foodies balanced democracy and distinction in their quest to be seen as experts on food without being dismissed as snobs. Furthermore, they defined food as worthy of their consumption based on two criteria: authenticity and exoticism. Authenticity has a number of dimensions, including geographic specificity, "simplicity," personal connection, history and tradition, and ethnic connection (Johnston and Baumann 2015: 65). As art historian Alison Pearlman (2013: 142) explains, "Exemplary foodies eat everything – or, at least, what they think counts – without reservation." And these days, that's true whether it comes from a food truck, an out-of-the-way ethnic restaurant, or a Michelin three-star, fine-dining mecca.

Here, we see one way that eating as a hobby and leisure experience is both individual and social. For foodies, being a foodie is part of their identity. An identity that at once distinguishes them from non-foodies and connects them to a community of foodies. At the same time, individuals dining out at chain restaurants with their friends and families may not identify as foodies, but they want to have a particular kind of experience when they eat at a restaurant. People expect to derive pleasure from eating out (Warde and Martens 2000). They want to have an experience that is both familiar – and perhaps even offers a menu of "comfort food" – and pleasurable because they are paying for an experience, not just a meal. The hunger they seek to satisfy is both material and symbolic. They need to nourish their bodies and would like to do so with tasty food (or perhaps simply food they don't have to prepare themselves). But they also expect to be waited on and "taken care of" appropriately in the process. And, in the United States, where tipping is expected, they will show their esteem, or lack thereof, for the service by the amount they leave their server.

Foodie or not, few people ever think about all of the behind-the-scenes – and not-so-hidden – labor that goes into their leisure experience. They go to a restaurant to be impressed and entertained, not to wonder whether the bus boy is being exploited because he is an undocumented worker, whether the fish cook will be able to send his three children to college or if the captain really loves the salmon as much as he claims. But that's the paradox we explore in this chapter: the grueling work that goes into creating spectacular leisure experiences for others.

And what about the food media spectacle that fuels foodies' hunger for knowledge about all things related to food? That's the focus of the second part of the chapter.

Introduction

The act of "eating out" hasn't always been associated with having a good time with friends, celebrating an accomplishment, or getting together with family. Historically, people ate out only when they were traveling, eating at the same inn where they rented a room for the night. And, beginning in the fifteenth century, the establishments called "restaurants" were much narrower in their service, offering only restorative substances, especially broths, for consumption (Spang 2000). In England, near the end of the eighteenth century, eating out for pleasure began in private gentlemen's clubs (Warde and Martens 2000).

Hotels first served meals via room service (since it wouldn't have been proper for a lady to dine in public) and only opened their dining rooms to non-residents in the late nineteenth century. So-called modern restaurants – public establishments that specialized in serving meals for a price – were almost exclusive to Paris until well after the middle of the nineteenth century (Spang 2000).

In their early days, the "whole purpose" of a restaurant "was to eclipse the kitchen, to pull a curtain of illusion across the real conditions of production, to aesthetize and tidy" (Spang 2000: 236). As historian Rebecca L. Spang (2000: 234–5) explains in *The Invention of the Restaurant: Paris and Modern Gastronomic Culture*, "From the kitchen, often located in the basement, steam was said to bellow as from the mouths of Hell; there, filth-spattered cooks sweltered in the life-threatening heat of pitched battle" while they, along with "dozens of unseen workers transformed the dirty, hairy, slimy, or feathered products of the market" into something that looked good enough to eat. Customers never saw the ingredients or witnessed the cooking of the food. As Spang (2000: 236) tells it, "they waited [in the dining room], drinking wine and swallowing oysters, until the waiter . . . appeared with a paradisiacal bounty of flavors, smells, textures and sights."

In other words, as Erving Goffman (1959) would have put it, restaurants separated the back stage of the kitchen and other food preparation areas from the front stage of the dining room. This distinction remains today in language used by restaurant workers. The "back of the house" refers to the kitchen and other backstage areas, while the "front of the house" encompasses the dining room and waiting areas such as the bar.

This wall – literally – of separation between a restaurant's kitchen and dining room remained intact for decades, particularly in fine-dining establishments. Until the 1980s in the United States, for example, "exposed kitchens were largely confined to inexpensive, commonplace eateries" (Pearlman 2013: 70). Open cooking served a variety of ends, including advertising the food, making the most of a cramped space or, most commonly, gaining public trust. As Pearlman (2013:71) notes, "Exposed kitchens reassured customers of honesty and hygiene in the historically lowbrow sector of the restaurant business."

Yet the early 1980s marked the beginning of a trend toward exhibition kitchens and the related phenomenon of chef's tables in fine restaurants. It began in California in 1982, when chefs Alice Waters and Wolfgang Puck made "wood-burning ovens, grills and ranges a component of gourmet-dining-room décor" (Pearlman 2013: 73). As individual chefs gained fame for their personal styles of cooking and the number of self-identified gourmands and foodies grew, there was a demand for access to knowledge about the processes by which food was prepared.

However, exhibition kitchens didn't show restaurant patrons everything (Pearlman 2013). And there was no clamoring for demonstrations of mundane kitchen tasks like preparing *mise en place* to serve two hundred people ordering from a menu of twenty-five different options of appetizer, soup or salad, entrée and dessert or washing hundreds of dishes each night. In other words, there was little interest in the less glamorous aspects of cooking for a crowd of demanding customers, increasing numbers of whom fancy themselves experts on food and expect to be treated in particular ways as a result. There was little interest in the hard work behind the spectacular leisure experience that restaurant patrons sought.

In their study of eating out in England, sociologists Alan Warde and Lydia Martens (2000: 23) write that, "The emergence of specialised places to eat out, particularly where there was a choice of food rather than a limited menu, was essentially a commercial innovation of the twentieth century." Reflecting immigration patterns, England saw the rapid expansion of restaurants serving ethnic food – specifically, Chinese, Indian, and Middle Eastern – between the mid-1950s and mid-1970s (Warde and Martens 2000).

In the United States, "elite American food culture was dominated by French *haute cuisine* [i.e., high-brow food] at the turn of the twentieth century" (Johnston and Baumann 2015: 7). This focus on the superiority of French cuisine and restaurants persisted well into the century, with most of the best American restaurants being "modeled after the French restaurant Le Pavillon (Manhattan [New York], 1941–72), considered the pinnacle of fine dining in the country from the 1940s through the mid-1960s" (Pearlman 2013: 3). By the 1970s, however, new American cuisine, also known as California cuisine, was in ascendance at restaurants like Chez Panisse (opened in 1971), and gourmet culture in the United States was off and running.

Chefs went from being viewed as blue-collar laborers to skilled professionals, even artists and rock stars. Food media expanded in form and scope, beginning in the 1960s when Craig Claiborne introduced the concept of the restaurant review in the *New York Times* (Harris and Giuffre 2015). Nina and Tim Zagat democratized the reviewing process in 1979 when they started publishing their diner-survey-based books of reviews (Johnston and Baumann 2015).

And, of course, the internet opened that field even wider by allowing anyone with computer access to write and post a review of a restaurant. Afraid that bad reviews will ruin their reputation, restaurateurs now comb websites looking for negative reactions to their businesses.

But it wasn't just reviews that went online. As cell phones added diverse capabilities and it became commonplace for people to have an internet-ready digital camera with them when eating out, it became popular to take and post pictures of restaurant dishes on social media sites. Foodies want to show off their good taste by sharing photos of the food they were consuming. Some chefs are determined to restrict this practice, fearing that other chefs might steal their creations this way. Clearly, eating out has progressed far beyond restorative broths prepared under mysterious conditions hidden from their consumers.

Dinner at a fine-dining restaurant is "an event, an occasion to be experienced" (Shelton 1990: 514). But, as Allen Shelton (1990: 513) explains, the consumer is "at the end of a long line of invisible laborers, culminating with the waiter taking the order." This chapter focuses on the segment of the line within the restaurant itself. Michael J. Broadway and Donald D. Stull (2010: 60–1) document "the human suffering hidden in our food." Sarah D. Wald (2011) notes, for example, the invisible labor done on farms and in food-processing and -preparation facilities by undocumented workers, who are over-represented in food-systems occupations. In this chapter, our story begins after the stewards in charge of ordering and maintaining supplies have done their work (Brenner 2003). All of this work is carefully structured to ensure a positive experience for the diner.

Shelton (1990: 507) defines a restaurant as "a theater for eating, looking and thinking" that offers patrons assistance in "fashioning a self." As discussed in chapter 2, dining at such restaurants is a way to accumulate and show off one's cultural capital, or more specifically, one's **culinary capital** (LeBesco and Naccarato 2008: 224): it signals good taste, refinement, and a particular class identity that makes one worthy of inclusion. As Warde, Martens, and Olsen (1999: 122–3) contend, a "broad repertoire of culinary experience (for purposes of communication, comparison, companionship)" is a tool for intra-class (within one's social class) communication and a way to claim this form of cultural capital (see chapters 1 and 2). As David Kamp (2006: xiii) explains in *The United States of Arugula*, prosperity and culinary advances in the United States have led to "the creation of an expanded leisure class that treats food as a cultural pastime, something you can follow the way you follow sports or the movies." While LeBesco and Naccarato (2008: 223) view the phenomenon of culinary capital as "help[ing] to sustain class hierarchies by promoting the illusion of class mobility," it is clear that there is a burgeoning use of food to signal taste, if not actual social class standing. As Roseberry (1996: 763) explains, there is a "widening spectrum of foods – including wines, beers, waters, breads, cheeses, sauces and the like – through which one can cultivate and display 'taste' and 'discrimination.'" Even heirloom tomatoes have come to symbolize the "cultural nobility" of their consumers (Jordan 2007).

In the first part of this chapter, we examine the invisible labor that makes this leisurely dining experience possible. We explore the modern restaurant as a unique social space of consumption where diners consume an identity-affirming leisure experience produced by (mostly) low-paid workers who bring a distinct set of meanings to the interactions in that setting. Whether the spectacle on display is the diner, the locale, the food or the staff, we detail the paradoxical way in which enormous amounts of largely invisible work are performed to produce it. As Warde and Martens (2000: 5) explain, it is not just the food that a restaurant provides that is important; restaurants also provide a performance in which "the atmosphere, appeal to sensual perception and the character of the service" are equally important.

In the second half of the chapter, we shift to another realm of food as spectacle: the explosive rise of food entertainment media in such diverse forms as newspaper food sections, increasingly varied and narrowly focused culinary magazines, and cooking shows on public television and, in America, on the Food Network. On most nights, more people are watching the Food Network than are watching any single cable news channel (Pollan 2009). We explore how food media have become a vehicle for serving up another kind of leisure experience: a spectacle consumed off the page or screen that is, for most, about looking rather than about doing. While celebrity chef Giada de Laurentiis is a culinary-school-trained food expert, is everyone who watches her television show focused on the food? Or are they distracted a bit by her beauty? The spectacle and fantasy inherent in food media have led some to term it "food porn" – food pornography, a characterization we explore in this chapter.

Fine dining and invisible labor

While invisible labor is critical to producing any dining experience, its scope and depth are remarkable in fine dining. This labor is invisible to the patrons but not to the people who do it. Leslie Brenner (2003:

141), a journalist who spent a year documenting life at Daniel, the namesake restaurant of well-known chef Daniel Boulud in New York City, points out, "it is far from uncommon for hours of work to go into a single element out of dozens on a plate." The tiny, artfully arranged salad that accompanies an entrée may include glazed pecans made in-house, plus a chef's signature vinaigrette made from vinegar she distills herself. As Michael Ruhlman (2006: 115) recounts, the vast majority of professional cooking is "dominated by the crushing monotony of daily prep." The ability of restaurants to put out high-quality meals relatively quickly is a product of that preparation, known as *mise en place*. *Mise en place* refers to having as many elements of dishes prepared and organized before service as possible. It is "the organizational foundation of the professional kitchen" (Brenner 2003: 9) without which cook and restaurant would be lost. The array of tasks is enormous, the range of required skills impressive, the difficulty of the work often overlooked. Such skills, insiders assure us, are built on repetition, "mind-numbing, day after day, repetition" (Ruhlman 2006: 27), as individuals learn not only to prepare the food for service but to look at the number of "reservations, the number of portions available, [and] the semi-predictable habits of the clientele" to know how much of each item to prepare (Boulud 2003: 82). Waste of time or ingredients is anathema in the professional kitchen; the restaurant can afford neither. Among the tasks to be completed are "simmering stocks, making sauces, cutting garnishes, peeling, slicing, dicing vegetables, [and] portioning out meats, poultry and fish" (Brenner 2003: 9). Imagine doing this work in the space described by journalist Francis Lam (2006: 263) that "packs nine cooks into a 9- by 27-foot kitchen, playing pinball with hot stockpots." This work begins several hours before the restaurant opens to customers and leads to long, physically demanding days for the cooks and chefs.

Many of us envision chefs, outfitted in their crisp whites, working briskly but artfully, in a gleaming kitchen. In reality, the work is physically taxing and somewhat dangerous. Journalist Michael Ruhlman (2006: 161) puts it this way: "This is physical work and you have to be in good shape – it gets hard." The hands and skin of cooks are often in harm's way, with cuts and burns being a common hazard. There are other occupational hazards, too: "Slip, trip and fall incidents are the leading sources of occupational injuries in restaurants" (Chang et al. 2011).

The work does not get easier when service begins. Food orders, course by course, are called in by the expeditor, who works to keep the pace of food production moving and to maintain an orderly progression. All of the food for a table needs to be ready at about the same time, but dishes take differing amounts of time to prepare. Cooks are usually juggling food for multiple tables, and must keep track of what items are at which stage of doneness, what items take longer or shorter lengths of time to cook, and which sauces and garnishes go with each item. There is an enormous amount of information to master and multiple and ever-changing demands to juggle. Consistency in the food prepared is important, as "dishes must taste and look exactly the same" for as long as they remain part of the menu (Leschziner 2007). Each station in the kitchen is responsible for producing different elements of the meal and for coordinating its work with the people at other stations. For example, the saucier doesn't just make sauces but also cooks the meats to order, while the pastry station bakes rolls and bread but also makes desserts.

In writing about restaurant work, there is much discussion of getting "into the weeds," the term used for falling behind in one's work and not being able to keep up with the orchestrated pace of ordering and production. A cook who gets into the weeds during dinner rush may not get out until ordering stops. Others may lend a hand to help this person catch up, but they usually have their own work to do and cannot afford much time away from their own station. Desired by all instead is "the dance," which happens when the kitchen staff is working well together (Ruhlman 2006: 27).

Once cooked and plated, the food goes to the expeditor, often the executive chef or sous-chef (second in command). Laura Faye Taxel describes this aspect of the expeditor's role:

> Every plate comes to him for inspection before servers bring it out to the dining room. Each gets a split second of his full and undivided attention. He cleans the edges, rearranges pinches of micro-greens, moves a tiny cup of sauce an eighth of an inch to the left. Anything that doesn't measure up to his exacting standards is sent back. (Taxel 2008: 197)

The expeditor gets orders out of the kitchen efficiently but is also focused on the diner's visual and gustatory experience of the food.

Other restaurant work varies in its visibility to diners. In the kitchen, or the "back of the house," for example, dishwashers handle massive numbers of containers used in food preparation – including "huge stockpots, bus pans, sauté pans" (Brenner 2003: 95) – as well as all of the plates, silverware, glassware, and so on used to serve it. It is low-prestige work, but utterly crucial to the restaurant as a whole. Work in the dining room, or the "front of the house," may be witnessed but not necessarily seen. For example, Brenner (2003) describes how the reservationists at Daniel walk a fine line between accommodating and controlling guests. They need to ensure a sufficient number of customers but also that they arrive on a suitable schedule. As customers arrive, the host or hostess is in charge of seating them but has little or no control over how fast they are served or when they finish their meals and vacate the table. The more reservations, the more times tables must be "turned" and the more chance that later reservations will have to be delayed. As Brenner (2003: 65) explains, "The assigning of tables is an art in itself." Kuh describes how the process goes awry:

> Around the hostess desk, there is a crush of people. The seating plan for the evening has gotten off to a bad start. Early reservations showed up late, parties that the manager had put down as no-shows (and given their tables away) showed. Voices are being raised ever so slightly.
>
> There's the sense that the carefully monitored fifteen-minute slots that make up the reservation book are starting to pop like rivets in a doomed sub. [But t]he manager and the hostess are calm. It's just another busy night in a successful restaurant. (Kuh 2001: 212)

Much of the mental and emotional energy that goes into the work of hosting is, by demand, invisible to the customers, even though hosts and customers almost always interact face to face.

Let's move to the table, which Erickson (2004: 86) calls "the spotlight of the restaurant drama; it's the reason that everyone has arrived for the show." There is much activity to organize here. Fine-dining restaurants often use teams of two waiters to serve a table, a front waiter (also known as a captain) and a back waiter. A maître d' oversees the dining room, making the customer "feel well taken care of" (Brenner 2003: 61). A server, interviewed by Alison Owings (2002: 158) for her book *Hey, Waitress!*, characterized the role of the front waiter as "the greet-the-customers, take-their-orders, and see-how-everything-is-going" job. It is also the captain who "takes most of the heat" when customers are unhappy (Owings 2002: 158). To the back server falls "the get-the-food-together and serve-it job" (Owings 2002: 158). Damrosch (2007: 34) characterizes this job as "practically invisible to the guest" and sees it as "mindless and fairly thankless," but it involves numerous tasks. The back server "pours the water, serves the bread, marks the table (meaning that he or she sets the silverware for any number of courses), helps clear each course, fetches glassware, removes empty glasses, and pretty much runs the station" (Damrosch 2007: 34).

In some restaurants, servers are joined by runners; they pick up food in the kitchen and take it to the tables. A head runner serves as a dining-room-side expeditor, "keep[ing] track of which tables are eating which courses, which plates have gone out, and which should go out next" (Brenner 2003: 13). These workers help service run smoothly, getting food to the table while it is still hot and making sure that the entire table is served at the same time. In some restaurants, a course is put on hold if a guest leaves the table to use the restroom or make a phone call. Such an approach further complicates the demands of service for both back- and front-of-house staff.

Like other restaurant jobs, serving tables is physically and mentally demanding work. It also requires **emotional labor** and **emotion management** (Hochschild 1983; Leidner 1993) that other restaurant workers need not do because they do not have direct contact with customers. Emotional labor "requires one to induce or suppress feelings in order to sustain the outward countenance that produces the proper state of mind in others," which is emotion management (Hochschild 1983: 7). Chef Boulud (2003: 110) observes that, "The client–restaurant relationship is one of the few opportunities the customer has to be in a position of superiority. Bad day at the office? Got blamed for something you didn't do? Belittled for a shortcoming? You can always take it out on the waiter." Mistakes made by the kitchen staff are likely to be taken out on the server, too, despite the fact that they are not her/his fault. In his classic study of restaurant kitchens, Gary Alan Fine (1996) addresses "culinary disputes" between cooks and customers that must be mediated by servers. The chef believes s/he has cooked the food as it should be eaten; a customer believes that her/his preferences must be accommodated. The server's wage depends on pleasing customers to maximize tips; the chef believes her/his culinary expertise must be respected. Dublanica (2008) uses the notion of "waiter armor" to describe servers' tactics for dealing with these intractable demands. As Ehrenreich (2001: 35) wryly notes, "Customers are in fact the major obstacle to the smooth transformation of information [i.e., orders] into food and food into money."

A major part of emotional labor is learning to anticipate guests' needs and put them at ease; servers must "be present when needed or wanted, but also ... disappear when not needed or wanted" (Damrosch 2007: 23). Emotional labor is also cognitive: "the social interaction in a good deal of service work presents its own cognitive demands: observing and interpreting behavior and expression, inferring mood and motive, taking on the perspective of others, responding appropriately to social cues, and knowing when you're understood" (Rose 2004: 203).

A server's tips, the majority of their income in the United States, depends, in part, on successful emotional labor. As Dublanica (2008: 108) points out, "Waiters have one of the few jobs where their compensation depends on the whims of their customers." Rose (2004: 23) puts it this way: server–customer interaction "involves a good deal of economically motivated emotion management and interpersonal manipulation, all centered around the tip, which, itself is laden with symbolism and feeling." Just as customers size up their entire dining experience – not just the work literally done by their server – in deciding how much to tip, servers make their own assessments. Paules (1991) notes that servers often see tips as reflecting the quality of the customer rather than of his or her work. This ascription of quality may be made in advance. In their article, tellingly titled, "Because They Tip for Shit!," Rusche and Brewster (2008) examine "tableside racism," showing how assumptions about the poor tips predicted to be left by black customers relate to discriminatory behaviors by servers. Furthermore, Brewster and another colleague (Brewster and Lynn 2014: 545) demonstrate that "both black and white restaurant customers discriminate against black servers by tipping them less than their white co-workers."

The tidy clothes and formal posture of servers in fine-dining restaurants belie the physical demands of the job. Erickson (2004: 80) notes that good servers must be "quick on [their] feet and able to maneuver the small spaces and crowded passages of the restaurant." Serving is hard on a person's legs and feet, fingers, and spine (Rose 2004). Dublanica (2008: 49) details one hazard associated with serving food: "I balance the hot platters on my hands and arms and set out across the restaurant to deliver the entrees to my table. Halfway to my destination I realize I misjudged the temperature of the plates. I can feel the platter balanced on my forearm radiating intense heat through the sleeve of my shirt." After an eight-hour dinner shift, Damrosch (2007: 104) describes servers as "exhausted, irritable and wide awake." In a busy restaurant, there will have been little or no time for a break to drink a glass of water or visit the restroom.

Another realm of physical work takes place before service starts and after it ends. They sweep, scrub, refill, and restock to prepare for the next period of service. They may wipe down menus with window cleaner or vinegar (Brenner 2003); fingerprints may need to be polished off the clasps of the menus as well (Damrosch 2007). The front-of-the-house staff irons tablecloths, decrumbs chairs, and polishes glassware and water pitchers. This "side work" can comprise up to a third of a server's job (Ehrenreich 2001).

Overall, then, Frank Bruni (2006: 319, 325), a former restaurant critic for the *New York Times*, is not necessarily exaggerating when he describes waiting tables in a busy restaurant as "a back-straining, brain-addling, sanity-rattling siege," in which servers are "trying to be fluent in the menu, calm in the face of chaos, patient in the presence of rudeness, available when diners want that, invisible when they don't." The result of all this invisible labor – if it is indeed successfully hidden from restaurant patrons – is an experience of dining as leisure, of eating as a confirmation of one's self-concept of high status and good taste. It allows diners to experience food, drink, and – importantly – themselves as spectacle rather than as a product of repetitive, backbreaking labor and strict emotional regulation. The highly structured nature of this work is what makes feeding an ever-changing crowd of customers possible; but the fact that the labor involved becomes visible only occasionally allows the diner to view the experience as leisurely. Inequality of status is necessary to the institution.

In addition to the work they perform, front-of-house and back-of-house workers also differ in other characteristics that contribute to the social inequality central to restaurants and restaurant work. "Work in the restaurant industry is characterized by low-paying, low-skilled jobs, which offer variable and often unpredictable work hours marked by high turnover rates" (Sachs et al. 2013). Women and ethnic minorities are overrepresented among these low-wage workers; and research shows that this inequality is spatialized within restaurants (Sachs et al. 2013). For example, front-of-the-house staff are most often white or light-skinned women (as hosts and servers), in part because of the feminization of service and the emotional work it entails (Sachs et al. 2013). Back-of-the-house positions, except for chefs, are increasingly filled by immigrant (perhaps undocumented) and racial-minority men. Most chefs and head cooks are white men, and, although Latinos play a vital role in kitchens throughout the United States, they are most often located in lower-status positions such as cooks, food-prep workers, and dishwashers. The gendered division of labor in professional kitchens reflects a stereotype linking women with domestic, but not professional, cooking (Harris and Giuffre 2015). In *Taking the Heat: Women Chefs and Gender Inequality in the Professional Kitchen*, sociologists Deborah A. Harris and Patti Giuffre (2015) show how these chefs navigate the gendered landscape in their struggles to establish themselves as professionally competent and to take on leadership roles when promoted to higher-status positions.

Interestingly, this gendered and racialized division of labor usually remains unseen by foodies and non-foodies alike, as the back-of-the-house is largely invisible to all. But what about the prolific food entertainment media, which often promise viewers access to the "behind-the-scenes" dimensions of the food world? Do they really offer insights into this hidden reality?

Food entertainment media

In some ways, food media takes readers and viewers into the back of the house where gourmet cooking takes place. This is not to say such depictions are accurate, entertaining as they might be. As Andrew Chan (2003: 47) notes, contemporary shows "create a gap that separates the viewer from the reality of actual cookery." In fact, Kathleen Collins (2009: 223) explains that, "Television cooking shows, and the media in general, are largely responsible for glamorizing what will always be, in actuality, toiling, sweaty labor." She also concedes, however, that such media coverage – and the public's seemingly insatiable appetite for programming related to food and eating – "has brought deserved attention to a previously uncelebrated class of laborers and artisans" (Collins 2009: 223). As such, the media has made visible some of the hidden work that goes into producing our eating experiences but often in ways that are more fantasy than reality.

Viewers are, ostensibly, encouraged to perform this work themselves, as a form of leisure, but research reveals that few do. Time spent cooking is on the decline, even though food is a growing media realm. As Collins (2009: 136) notes, "the most persistent paradox of all, which still puzzles us to the present day [is this]: people love to watch cooking, but it does not mean they love to cook or that they even do it at all." Instead, their leisure experience involves consuming the labor of others. In other words, the media are appealing to something other than, or at least in addition to, individuals' interest in learning new cooking techniques or finding new recipes to try at home. For example, describing a cookbook written by Thomas Keller, chef at The French Laundry (commonly regarded as one of the best restaurants in the United States), Phoebe Damrosch (2007: 14) writes: "This is not restaurant cooking for the home chef; this is a secret pleasure for the jealous voyeur." Thus, while it intersects with a do-it-yourself aesthetic, much of food media is simply another form of food as spectacle.

Not surprisingly, food entertainment media rely on their own hidden labor to create the visual spectacle on the page or on the screen. Consider the invisible labor involved in putting a show together on the Food Network (Segan 2010). The network employs two people whose job it is to cover up the brand-name labels on products used on the air. Fifteen to twenty people do behind-the-scenes work for a basic cooking show on the network. Culinary producers are responsible for all details of an episode, planning everything from "swap outs," the examples of a recipe at different stages of completion that are shown on air, to what ingredients need to be in the cupboards and refrigerator. Many Food Network hosts wear a small earphone during taping. They are given instructions such as where to put their hands so as not to cover up a key ingredient. At the same time, they are cooking and watching for instructions from the studio director about which camera to face. Even shows that present as casual conversations between friends are presenting viewers with a carefully constructed experience.

There has been a veritable explosion of food entertainment media in the last two decades, with newspapers and magazines giving more coverage to food (Brown 2004). Two US TV networks are devoted to food and cooking, though they are by no means the only place to view content about food and eating. In addition to books about food and eating, numerous websites provide millions of recipes, videos demonstrating techniques and preparation, and other information about food and eating. And books themselves continue to proliferate, ranging from ever-more specialized cookbooks to memoirs by food-industry workers to entire books on a single type of food (like donuts or hamburgers) or method of food preparation (such as grilling or braising).

Our focus in this chapter is on magazines and television shows about food and eating. These media shape people's decision making about food and eating and more broadly a society's foodways: what people eat and the meanings they attach to a wide variety of foodstuffs and preparation and consumption activities. As Michael Ruhlman (2006: 237) notes, "Television is arguably the most powerful force shaping the culinary landscape today. More people are reached through television – entertained, educated, changed in some little or large food-related way – than through any other medium by far." Television can offer sensory elements (Collins 2009), especially visual and auditory elements, which other types of media cannot. While viewers must rely on the show's host to get a sense of the smell and taste of food, they can hear bacon sizzling in a pan and see the array of colors of heirloom tomatoes in a salad. It is surely no coincidence that hosts commonly describe the tastes that different elements bring to a dish and tell viewers that "It's already starting to smell good in here" when they, say, add onions to a skillet to begin a recipe. Cheri Ketchum (2005: 222), analyzing the appeal of Food Network programming, contends that it promises viewers "the pleasure of either fantasy or actual sensual delights."

Before the TV Food Network (now the Food Network) was launched in 1993, most cooking shows were on public television. The first star chef on public television was Julia Child who, with her co-authors, brought the perceived sophistication of French cooking to the United States with the book *Mastering the Art of French Cooking* (1961). Her show, *The French Chef*, began in 1963 on PBS's Boston affiliate, WGBH. Child was by no means the first person to cook on television (see Collins 2009), but she captured the public's attention with her accessibility and likeability. She was also in the right place at the right time, riding the wave of increased interest in food and cooking as status symbols and conveyers of good taste. She "introduced viewers to new ingredients and products" (Collins 2009: 82), as well as techniques, thus broadening people's palates, increasing demand for these items and, presumably, increasing people's expectations for their consumption and dining practices. She helped garner more respect for the profession of cooking, something from which later television chefs surely benefited (Collins 2009).

The Food Network, unlike PBS, is "an unabashedly commercial, entertainment- and profit-driven enterprise" (Kamp 2006: 345). At its inception, it was touted as "the kitchen equivalent to CNN, broadcasting food twenty-four hours a day" (Buford 2006: 45). From its shows, viewers learn less about how to cook than about how to consume; they learn how to taste and talk about food (Pollan 2009). Bold and brash restaurant chef Emeril Lagasse was its first star. Collins (2009: 5) explains that, "As the role of food changed from mere necessity to a means of self-expression and a conspicuous lifestyle accessory, the nature of cooking shows has shifted from didactic to entertaining." Her description of the "new style of cooking show" (Collins 2009: 169) reflects this change. For example, *Emeril Live* (chef Lagasse's hugely popular but now canceled show) included a live audience, a studio band and a chef who emerged from backstage to cheering crowds of adoring fans. While Julia's fans wanted to learn to cook like the French, Emeril's viewers want to observe an energetic spectacle of food preparation and be entertained by it. Hansen (2008: 58) argues that these new cooking shows "have eliminated cooking as labor" by "presenting [it] as 'easy' and 'fun,'" despite the fact that "cooking as a professional chef is the antithesis of easy and fun." Hansen (2008: 58) further notes that programs also "disavow the relationship between time and labor" by showing cooking in real time only when it's against the clock.

The Food Network has made chefs into celebrities and influenced consumers' expectations about food, everything from what their local grocery store stocks to what their experience will be like if they dine at a featured restaurant. New York City restaurateur Danny Meyer explains that, "Americans have come to follow restaurants, chefs and their activities 'like a spectator sport'" (Kamp 2006: 322). As Ruhlman (2006: 9) notes, "like baseball stars, [chefs] have their own cards and are famous for specialties within the industry." They "have been welcomed into the repertory company of American celebrity" (Pollan 2009). The result? "[C]ooking-struck, chef-adoring, restaurant-crazy consumers" (Ruhlman 2006: 11).

The rise of the celebrity chef is part and parcel of today's food media. Beyond television, chefs also have become performers in their own right, barely associated with their restaurants at all and capable of commanding huge appearance fees (US$35,000–US$50,000 per live show) (McLaughlin 2009). These chefs already have multiple shows on the Food Network that feature them, as well as websites, books, food products, and other ways for fans to connect with them. Yet there are always new ways to capitalize on their popularity. Not satisfied with watching their shows or buying their cookbooks, legions of fans appear willing to pay the price to catch a glimpse of their favorite chef in person. In fall 2009, chef Guy Fieri (winner of *The Next Food Network Star* in 2006) went on tour, with shows scheduled in twenty-one cities around the United States (McLaughlin 2009). Audience members paid up to US$250 a ticket to watch him cook, listen to his banter, and, perhaps, eat some of his food – an experience included only with the most expensive tickets. Chefs at this level must decide whether to focus on continuing to develop their food-related skills or shift their focus to marketing themselves as a product or brand (Ehrmann, Meiseberg, and Ritz 2009).

Clearly, the appeal here is about something other than, or in addition to, the food. Collins (2009: 182) notes that fans of chefs are interested in "the whole person," and the Food Network has obliged with *Chefography*, hour-long shows that recount chefs' and hosts' biographies. Not all Food Network stars are trained chefs; Rachael Ray is not a trained culinary professional but she is the subject of a *Chefography* episode, likely because she is among the most popular hosts on the network. What is it that makes food programming on television, as well as food-oriented magazines, so appealing to consumers – even, or perhaps especially, those who don't cook? What is the allure of this spectacular enterprise built on so much behind-the-scenes labor? Why is this particular leisure experience so attractive to so many people? How can we make sense of this social phenomenon?

Food porn

Because the voyeuristic elements of food entertainment media seem to be based on fantasy rather than reality, the phenomenon has been dubbed food pornography or **food porn** for short. Others (including Kamp 2006) use the term "gastro-pornography," perhaps used first by journalist Alexander Cockburn in 1977. Cookbook author and journalist Molly O'Neill (2003: 39) offers this definition: "prose and recipes so removed from real life that they cannot be used except as vicarious experience." Bill Buford (2006) concurs, noting that it is not an erotic experience but an unreal one that makes something food porn. It is a term that "generally evokes the unattainable" (McBride 2010: 38). Johnston and Baumann (2015: 62) explain that gastroporn "focuses on sensual close-ups of food and aspirational eating involving fantastical creations that, like many stereotypical porn scenarios, are probably never realized in the audience's homes." Clearly, food has a sensual appeal that many other topics of media coverage lack. Furthermore, food is a positive element in most people's everyday lives, creating pleasurable sensations and associations. Cockburn wrote about the "curious parallels between manuals on sexual techniques and manuals on the preparation of food" (quoted in McBride 2010: 38). And, like sex, food "is part of everyone's life in some way, shape, or form" (Collins 2009: 190). While comical on the surface, the concept of food porn has revealed important social dimensions of food media.

Food porn is an important concept for understanding the new emphases in cooking shows. "Though the recipes might often be the same then as now, presentation trumps content. Add to that the sexy hosts and kitchens, close-ups of food, fingers, lips, Emeril's 'oh yeah babe,' groans of pleasure from the hosts and the aroused audience, and it's tough to argue against the analogy" (Collins 2009: 189). Chan (2003: 48) explains the appeal of such food entertainment media this way: "Each show offers a virtual form of fast food or a 'quickie' instead of a real meal or mutually satisfying experience. This . . . leav[es] viewers unsatisfied or still hungry, [so] they'll keep coming back for more." Hansen (2008: 50) claims that, "Celebrity chefs . . . create an appetite that can never be satisfied." Or, as Michael Pollan (2009: n.p.) puts it: The target audience of the Food Network has shifted from people who like to cook to those who like to eat, those to whom "hyperexuberant, even fetishized images of cooking" appeal.

Emeril Lagasse was, perhaps, the first celebrity chef "to discover that cooking before a bleachers crowd, primed to respond raucously to theatrical additions of garlic or chili flakes or bacon ('Let's take it up a notch'), can make for inexplicably compelling television" (Buford 2006: 43). Discussing shows like *Two Fat Ladies* (featuring recipes oozing with butter and other fats), *Nigella Bites* (featuring a sensual host, Nigella Lawson, who "exud[es] passion and emotion as she handles food") and *Emeril Live* (with "king of the culinary come-on," Emeril Lagasse), Chan (2003: 50–1) explains that, when watching these shows, "the viewer is teased, tantalized, and titillated by the unfolding spectacle." Chef Chris Cosentino describes food porn as "the ability of food to elicit a positive and euphoric reaction, as well as to make others covet what you are eating" (quoted in McBride 2010: 41–2). The images are deliberately structured to shape viewers' experiences.

Some observers take the analogy further, focusing on the literal comparisons between depictions of food in entertainment media and pornographic films and photographs. Frederick Kaufman (2009: 5) asserts that, "the relationship of the recipe to the typical American cook has transformed into something akin to the relationship between sexual intercourse and the voyeur." Perhaps the best illustration of this phenomenon was when, near the beginning of her Food Network career, Rachael Ray appeared in a series of photos in the men's magazine FHM. Here is a description of one of these photos: "the most popular . . . proved to be one of 'Ray-Ray' (as her fans call her) in frilly underwear, licking chocolate syrup from the tip of a pendulous wooden spoon" (Kaufman 2009: 19).

Chan takes the analogy a step further, analyzing the "money shots" of culinary shows. In pornography, the money shot is male ejaculation; in cooking shows, it is "the achievement and presentation of the finished dish" or of the chef or an audience member tasting the food (Chan 2003: 52). Kaufman (2009: 18) describes watching the "climax" of an episode of *Food 911* in which hunky chef Tyler Florence helps home cooks rescue a favorite dish: "the editor kept looping their wet mouths and rapt faces as they pushed forkful after forkful of *arroz con pollo* past their lips, chewed, and swallowed – and pushed and chewed and swallowed again and again." Kaufman (2009: 12) explains that, "the closer the shot, the more detail revealed, the more fetishized the food." Journalist Bill Buford writes about "beauties," particular kinds of camera shots that highlight ingredients. Here is his description of a camera operator setting up a "beauty" of pecans:

> The pecans, surrounded by five spotlights, were resting on a bent piece of Plexiglas, for a hundred-per-cent reflection (pecans both in a bowl and somehow below it, like mountains on a placid lake), while [the camera man] inched closer and closer . . . He then manipulated a knob so that some nuts were in focus, while the ones behind, backlit, receded into an arty blur. (Buford 2006: 43)

Buford (2006: 46) maintains that shows on the Food Network "are full of exacting, intimate, amplified, and exaggerated beauties." His description of the preparation for this photo clearly highlights the amount of labor that goes into creating such visual experiences for consumers.

Television is not the only outlet of food entertainment media. Books and magazines about food, cooking, and eating abound. Cookbooks and food magazines like *Gourmet* (now defunct) and *Bon Appétit* are full of lush photographs and gaudy descriptions of food in exotic locales. Here is Molly O'Neill (2003: 39) on her experience at a book signing for one of her cookbooks, writing about her fans: "They saw me as the high priestess of a world that exists almost exclusively in the imagination, the ambitions, and the nostalgic underpinnings of American culture." Also: "People tell me they read my cookbooks 'like novels,' to enter an alternate universe where cooking is slow and leisurely and imbued with a comforting glamour" (O'Neill 2003: 45). Somewhat akin to the culinary tourism experience described in the previous chapter, this kind of food entertainment offers consumers the thrill of entering a new social space with little of the discomfort of traditional travel. The boundaries between fantasy and reality are recreated, even as they are pleasurably blurred.

Clearly, some people have discovered cooking as a concrete leisure activity, so whether such pleasurable viewing/reading is voyeuristic for everyone is up for debate (McBride 2010). It is clear from these descriptions that food entertainment media do indeed provide consumers with a leisure experience, a spectacle to be watched or read. And, just as they often have little idea how much work went into the production of the meal they consume at a fine-dining restaurant, they have little sense of how much work goes into creating the images they consume from food entertainment media or how challenging it would be to recreate the dishes they admire.

Conclusion: spectacle or reality?

The phenomena of food as spectacle are complex; they arise from many distinct trends and features within contemporary social life and, in turn, have an influence on other realms. As we discuss in chapter 2, American culture and foodways are shaped by a populist ideal, the notion that anyone with sufficient motivation and hard work can achieve lofty heights. Americans often celebrate upward social mobility as a marker of freedom and, as a corollary, minimize the existence or importance of persistent inequality. The difficult, invisible labor that enables fine dining or other mediated forms of food entertainment belies these populist assumptions and the fact that labor must remain invisible for the institution to succeed. Thinking about the struggles in other people's lives does not, after all, create much of a leisure experience. This discussion also shows some ways in which food is not just a material substance that satisfies physical hunger but also serves to symbolize our social status and identity. Whether a celebrity chef who commands five-digit appearance fees, an aspiring foodie who wants to be an expert on fine cheeses, or a family member looking for a good place to celebrate a birthday, all seek more than a full stomach.

The next chapter moves to a different arena in which definitions of and messages about "good" food relate to, but do not determine, what people actually eat. Our exploration of nutrition and health examines the dietary advice produced by the US government, the multiple stakeholders who shape it, and the complex ways this advice is perceived by regular eaters. This discussion provides a stark illustration of the ways in which food choices are both individual and social. Chapter 4 also analyzes the so-called "obesity epidemic" and the highly moralized discourse that surrounds it. Within a very different topic, the next chapter continues our exploration of how individuals perceive, navigate, influence, and sometimes contest the structured aspects of foodways and the food systems that shape our lives and identities.

Further reading

Collins, Kathleen. 2009. *Watching What We Eat: The Evolution of Television Cooking Shows*. New York: Continuum. This historical overview of how cooking shows have developed and changed over time provides great insights into the genre and its increasing popularity.

Fine, Gary A. 1996. *Kitchens: The Culture of Restaurant Work*. Berkeley: University of California. Gary Alan Fine was one of the first sociologists to analyze restaurant work. The chapter on "Cook's Time: Temporal Demands and the Experience of Work" is particularly interesting in the context of the discussion here.

Harris, Deborah A. and Giuffre, Patti. 2015. *Taking the Heat: Women Chefs and Gender Inequality in the Professional Kitchen*. New Brunswick, NJ: Rutgers University Press. Harris and Giuffre take readers into the social worlds of women chefs, trying to establish themselves in a career viewed by most as the province of men – despite the association of women with home cooking.

McBride, Anne E. 2010. "Food Porn." *Gastronomica* 10(1) (Winter): 38–46. McBride reports on a discussion about food porn held with chefs and academics.

Warde, Alan, and Martens, Lydia. 2000. *Eating Out: Social Differentiation, Consumption and Pleasure*. Cambridge, UK: Cambridge University Press. Warde and Martens examine eating out in the United Kingdom from both a constructionist and a structuralist perspective.

Further exploration

1 FOR DISCUSSION: Describe your last experience dining in a restaurant. What did you eat? Where did you eat it? Whom did you eat it with? How would you describe the meal from beginning to end? How fancy was it? How did it feel to engage with this spectacle of eating?

2 IN CLASS: Watch an episode of *America's Test Kitchen* (PBS) and an episode of a program featuring a celebrity chef. Compare them: How are the sets, host and food similar and different? What other elements do the two shows share? How else are they different?

3 ONLINE: Look at the website for a restaurant (maybe a famous one, such as The French Laundry, Le Bernadin or Naha), examining its menu and other elements that give you a feel for what it would be like to dine there. What kinds of information does the website provide? Are the foods described on the menu familiar to you? How much and what kind of detail is provided in their descriptions? Would you say that the restaurant's website functions as a kind of "food porn"? Explain why or why not.

4

Nutrition and Health: Good to Eat, Hard to Stomach

Case study

The Kellogg Company, the largest cereal manufacturer in the world, promotes its Special K cereal brand with the "Special K Challenge," a diet plan promising to deliver a weight loss of up to six pounds in two weeks. The plan entails eating a bowl of Special K cereal with skim milk for breakfast and again for lunch or dinner. Alternatively, one could replace the second bowl with a Special K Protein Meal Bar or a Special K Protein Shake, two **line extensions** of the Special K brand. Richard Mattes (2002) examined the impact of replacing two daily meals with cereal for two weeks. He compares the use of a single cereal, Special K, with a variety of cereals and with a non-diet control group receiving no instructions on what to eat. Subjects in all three groups lost weight, but those in the Special K group lost more than those in both the variety cereal and the control groups. The Special K group lost 4.4 pounds, compared to 3.3 pounds in the variety cereal group. Also, 88 percent of those in the Special K group and 81.5 percent in the variety cereal group lost fat. Is a difference of 1.1 pounds enough to justify choosing Special K instead of another cereal? Moreover, is a two-week dietary change likely to lead to long-term weight loss? While these questions should alert readers to problems in the study design, additional ones are raised by the note at the end of Mattes's (2002: 577) report that the study "was supported by the Kellogg Company."

The Dole Food Company, the world's largest producer and marketer of fresh fruits and vegetables, advertises the Dole Banana Diet for weight loss and general health. The diet consists of eating two Dole bananas for breakfast, a nutritious lunch and dinner, and a snack of fresh fruits or vegetables. They report that bananas provide fiber and vitamin C, which may aid in weight loss, and cite research demonstrating that eating breakfast helps increase metabolism. Dole's literature also notes that "bananas contain resistant starch, which ferments in [the] large intestine, creating by-products (butyrates) that block conversion of some carbohydrates into fuel" (Dole Food Company 2009: n.p.). However, the study Dole cites for this claim does not actually examine the role of bananas per se. Instead, it compares four test breakfasts, each with different total amounts of resistant starch derived from a variety of foods. All four test breakfasts include banana muffins, and, actually, the test breakfast containing the *least* amount of banana muffin is the only breakfast found to have a statistically significant effect on carbohydrate metabolism (Higgins et al. 2004). Do Dole's claims about the role of bananas follow logically from this research?

The Special K Challenge and the Dole Banana Diet are two examples in a long line of **meal replacement diets** aimed at weight loss. Most dietitians would probably agree that Special K cereal and Dole bananas are better choices for overall health and weight loss than a breakfast routine of donuts or fast food, and dieters lost weight on both regimens. However, research shows that meal replacement diets generally work in the short term by limiting calories, not because of any special property of the replacement food (Nestle 2006). Once a dieter returns to his or her normal eating patterns, pounds shed are typically regained.

Food restriction diets, in contrast, limit the number of foods consumed but permit unlimited quantities. These diets facilitate weight loss because, as people inevitably tire of eating the same foods, they eat less of them (Wansink 2007). The Atkins diet, which limits carbohydrates like potatoes and white rice, and maximizes high-protein foods like beef and cheese, does facilitate weight loss. However, as food manufacturers jumped on the low-carb bandwagon in the late 1990s and early 2000s, producing and marketing more products as "low-carb," the variety of permissible foods increased, thus decreasing dietary boredom. With the expansion of low-carb products, Atkins followers ate more instead of less, decreasing the diet's effectiveness (Wansink 2007). This may also help explain why the Special K-only diet produced slightly more weight loss than the variety cereal diet.

Fad diets such as the Special K Challenge, the Dole Banana Diet, and the Atkins diet abound, as do diet drugs and weight-loss supplements. Despite tremendous growth in the diet industry, increasing proportions of the populations of industrialized countries are overweight or obese. Why do many people find diet and nutrition plans that are promoted as good to eat (i.e., healthy) so hard to stomach? And are these diets actually sound plans for healthy eating?

Introduction: nutrition and health

Information on healthy eating is abundant, contradictory, and some-times misleading. Although the major thrust of nutrition advice has remained relatively stable over the past several decades, nuances in dietary recommendations paired with the vast power of food marketing tend to muddy the public's perception of what constitutes a healthy diet (Nestle 2007). At the same time, an increase in rates of overweight and obesity in many industrialized nations has fueled public concern about the links between diet and both individual and public health (Boero 2012; Kwan and Graves 2013; Saguy 2013). When you also consider the tendency for western cultures to equate beauty with thinness, especially for women (Bordo 1993), then it is no surprise that fad diets like the Special K Challenge, the Dole Banana Diet, and the Atkins diet thrive in such a context. This chapter examines the heightened public concern over diet, nutrition, and health.

In the first part of the chapter, we investigate the social construction of nutrition as exemplified in the United States Department of Agriculture's (USDA) dietary recommendations. Since the late nineteenth century, government agencies and health organizations have attempted to shape consumer foodways to improve population health by formulating nutrition guidelines (Nestle 2007). Additionally, the food industry promotes versions of healthy eating aimed at selling more of their products. We explore how "healthy" eating is socially constructed through a confluence of scientific, political, and corporate interests and how this shapes individual behaviors and public policies. Specifically, we explore how the USDA's dual mandate to protect US agriculture and simultaneously guide the American public on nutritional matters makes USDA dietary advice especially susceptible to corporate influence. We argue that what is considered "good to eat" is shaped as much by politics and profit as it is by nutritional science. While consumer taste preferences matter, we show how a variety of groups powerfully shape consumer preferences and, through them, dietary patterns, making what we eat both individual and social.

In the second part of the chapter, we investigate public concerns over growing rates of overweight and obesity in industrialized countries. Specifically, we explore the social construction of fatness as a disease that has reached "epidemic" proportions. The dominant perspective on fat frames it as an individual medical condition stemming from poor food choices and leading to a host of medical problems. Consequently, most public and private efforts to combat overweight and obesity are individual "downstream" efforts aimed at convincing individuals to adopt healthier eating habits and increase physical activity levels, which sets the stage for fad diets like the Special K Challenge. We interrogate this medical model, which critics charge perpetuates systems of social inequality. We conclude with a discussion of one structural or "upstream" effort to improve nutrition and reduce childhood overweight and obesity, specifically, attempts to limit the availability of junk foods in schools.

Throughout this chapter, we adopt a social constructionist perspective, focusing on how interest groups, often called **claims maker**s, attempt to constitute as "fact" a particular definition of reality that reflects and supports their own interests and beliefs (Spector and Kitsuse 1977). Using a social constructionist perspective, we do not attempt to determine which claims makers' definitions are correct. We do not, for instance, endorse any particular dietary plan as the best; nor do we take a position on the debate over overweight and obesity. Rather, our focus is on the social process through which prevailing definitions of healthy eating and healthy bodies are socially created. The definitions of reality that claims makers advance are called **frames**. Within any given frame, "claims makers articulate a root cause of an issue, identify a blameworthy culprit, and propose a solution of some kind" (Kwan and Graves 2013: 3). As this chapter shows, corporations attempt to shape nutritional advice to frame their products as healthy, while public health professionals have been extremely successful in framing overweight and obesity as medical problems.

Constructing nutrition advice

The USDA was established in 1862 as the chief federal agency responsible for "provid[ing] leadership on food, agriculture, natural resources, and related issues" (US Department of Agriculture "Mission Statement" n.d.: para. 1) and charged with two key functions: to promote and protect agriculture, and to offer dietary advice to the American public (Nestle 2007). The conflict between these two mandates was not initially apparent. Until the 1960s, nutrition advice followed what Nestle (2007) calls "**eat more**" messages, and displayed a reluctance to label any food unhealthy. Physicians, nutrition experts, and the USDA advised that the majority of Americans, especially growing children and working-class men, needed to consume more calories to combat nutritional inadequacy (de la Peña 2010; Nestle 2007). Additionally, nutrition advice promoted the idea that any food could be part of a healthful diet. For instance, nutritionists promoted the consumption of sugar "as a quick source of energy essential for working-class productivity," largely because it is calorically dense, "cheap, easy to digest, and palatable" (de la Peña 2010: 26). According to Nestle (2007: 34), "Food manufacturers and agricultural producers readily supported this emphasis because they grasped its marketing potential . . . Because all food animals and plants contain vitamins and minerals, all could be promoted on this basis." For decades, then, there was no conflict between government-sponsored nutrition advice and the interests of the agricultural industry.

By the late 1960s, however, growing awareness of the importance of nutritional properties in foods led to a shift in the emphasis of USDA-sponsored nutrition advice that increasingly came into conflict with the mandate to protect and promote agriculture. In the early 1970s, a congressional committee formed in response to alarming rates of hunger in the United States, held hearings and issued reports on dietary overconsumption and its link to obesity, diabetes, and heart disease. The committee highlighted scientific research on the links between animal fat, cholesterol levels, and heart disease and convinced some USDA nutritionists that "eat more" messages and promoting all foods as healthy were outdated (Nestle 2007). In 1977, the committee issued *Dietary Goals for the United States*, which encouraged Americans to consume more whole grains, fruits, vegetables, poultry and fish, but less meat, eggs, and other foods high in fat, sugar, and salt (Nestle 2007). The food industry, especially the producers of the foods that Americans were advised to eat less of, was incensed. They objected to the "eat less" messages contained in *Dietary Goals*, claiming that the science linking particular foods with health risks was shaky and that these new "eat less" recommendations would result in severe economic harm to the affected agricultural sectors (Nestle 2007). In response to this tremendous backlash, the committee significantly watered down the "eat less" messages contained in the original *Dietary Goals* (Nestle 2007).

Official USDA publications continued to downplay "eat less" messages, despite the growing consensus among health advocacy groups, like the American Heart Association and the National Cancer Institute, that they were both scientifically accurate and necessary to improve population health (Nestle 2007). USDA publications attempt to placate the food industry by "resorting to euphemisms, focusing recommendations on nutrients rather than on the foods that contain them, and giving a positive spin to any restrictive advice about food" (Nestle 2007: 3). Thus, the USDA's *Dietary Guidelines for Americans*, first issued in 1980 and updated at regular intervals, "replaced the unacceptable *eat less* phrases with the vague *avoid too much*" (Nestle 2007: 46). Further, while the 1980 and 1985 versions caution readers to "avoid" too much fat, saturated fat, and cholesterol, later editions more euphemistically advise consumers to "choose a diet low in" these elements. The difference may seem small, but "avoid" has clear negative connotations, while "choose" is more positive. Similarly, in the 1990 version, "choose a diet low in" replaced "avoid too much," while "have two or three servings of meat" replaced "choose lean meat" (Nestle 2007: 49–50). These changes were lauded by the affected food industries, but nutritionists have sharply criticized their obvious political posturing. P. J. Skerrett of the Harvard School of Public Health lambasted the 2010 *Guidelines* for their reliance on euphemisms and focus on abstract components:

> The new guidelines urge Americans to eat less "solid fat." What, exactly, does that mean – stop spooning up lard or Crisco? No. Solid fat is a catchphrase for red meat, butter, cheese, ice cream, and other full-fat dairy foods. But the guidelines can't say that, since they are partly created by the US Department of Agriculture, the agency charged with promoting the products of American farmers and ranchers, which includes red meat and dairy products. (Skerrett 2011a: paras 4–5)

Moreover, *Dietary Guidelines* continues to promote the idea that all foods can be part of a healthy diet. Thus, as Nestle (2007: 30) succinctly explains, because of the conflicting dual mandates of the USDA, "Dietary guidelines necessarily are political compromises between what science tells us about nutrition and health and what is good for the food industry." Why don't other government health agencies offer their own, clearer advice on diet and nutrition? The Food and Drug Administration (FDA), part of the US Department of Health and Human Services (DHHS), is an obvious candidate. However, US Congress has repeatedly affirmed that the USDA should be the lead federal agency advising the public on nutrition (Nestle 2007). Updating *Dietary Guidelines for Americans* continues to be mainly the responsibility of the USDA, although the DHHS works collaboratively with the USDA to prevent the two agencies from issuing conflicting advice or advice that might harm agriculture (Nestle 2007).

The USDA's graphical depictions of their dietary recommendations illustrate how nutrition advice is shaped by multiple claims makers through political compromises. In the 1950s, the USDA popularized the "basic four" food guide with four main food groups: (1) dairy/milk; (2) meat, fish, poultry, eggs, beans, and nuts; (3) fruits and vegetables; and (4) grains. According to Nestle (2007: 37), the "basic four," which was aimed principally at the public, "established minimum levels of daily servings to prevent nutritional deficiencies. Milk and meat producers appreciated its 'eat more' implication." The "Basic Four" is thus fully consistent with the "eat more" messages loved by the food industry.

However, as "eat more" messages shifted to "eat less," the graphics that the USDA created to illustrate these became more politically charged. The Eating Right Pyramid, slated for release in 1991, was withdrawn by the USDA amid food industry fury and replaced with the Food Guide Pyramid in 1992. Both were meant to convey three key messages contained in Dietary Guidelines for Americans: variety, moderation, and proportionality (Nestle 2007). USDA nutritionists chose a pyramid shape with distinct vertical layers depicting food groups and serving sizes, after years of research and development, to communicate that foods nearer the bottom of the pyramid (bread, cereal, rice, and pasta) should be consumed more frequently than those at the top (fats, oils, and sweets). The pyramid recommended that consumers should consume a variety of foods (via the various food groups listed) in moderation (by the number of servings) and in proportion to each other (according to each group's relative height on the pyramid).

Just prior to the release of the Eating Right Pyramid, the National Cattlemen's Association, a lobbying group for meat producers, "complained that the Pyramid would cause people to eat less meat and that meat should not be displayed so close to the fats and sugars" (Nestle 2007: 57). They were soon joined by the National Milk Producers Federation and the American Meat Institute, and the newly appointed USDA Secretary withdrew the graphic (Nestle 2007). The official explanation was that the pyramid needed to be tested with low-income groups and children, even though it had never been intended for use with these populations. It had always been aimed instead at high-school-educated adults with average incomes who ate an average American diet (Nestle 2007). Thus, critics of the pyramid's withdrawal were left to assume that the secretary put politics before population well-being by caving in to lobbying efforts by the meat and dairy industries. One year later, the USDA

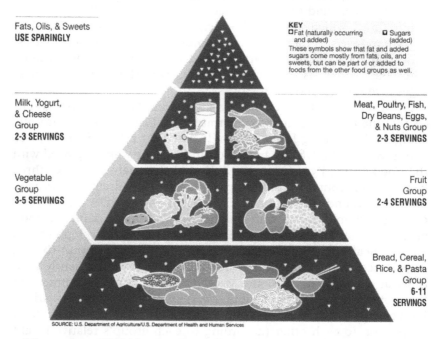

Food Guide Pyramid

A Guide to Daily Food Choices

Fats, Oils, & Sweets
USE SPARINGLY

KEY
□ Fat (naturally occurring   ▣ Sugars
and added)   (added)
These symbols show that fat and added
sugars come mostly from fats, oils, and
sweets, but can be part of or added to
foods from the other food groups as well.

Milk, Yogurt,
& Cheese
Group
2-3 SERVINGS

Meat, Poultry, Fish,
Dry Beans, Eggs,
& Nuts Group
2-3 SERVINGS

Vegetable
Group
3-5 SERVINGS

Fruit
Group
2-4 SERVINGS

Bread, Cereal,
Rice, & Pasta
Group
6-11
SERVINGS

SOURCE: U.S. Department of Agriculture/U.S. Department of Health and Human Services

Figure 4.1   USDA's 1992 Food Guide Pyramid was more acceptable
to the meat and dairy industries than the proposed Eating Right
Pyramid.

Source: US Department of Agriculture/US Department of Health and Human
Services. Retrieved February 29, 2012 from http://fnic.nal.usda.gov/nal_display/
index.php?info_center=4&tax_level=3&tax_subject=256&topic_id=1348&
level3_id=5729

released the modified Food Guide Pyramid (see Figure 4.1), which
differed from the Eating Right Pyramid "in at least 33 ways" (Nestle
2007: 63), including its name and the addition of "at least" in front
of all serving sizes. This latter change conveyed a minimum number
of servings, without implying a maximum. The new pyramid also
increased the recommended serving sizes for meat and dairy.

MyPyramid (see Figure 4.2), a later iteration debuted in 2005, differed substantially from the Food Guide Pyramid in that it required

Figure 4.2   USDA's MyPyramid icon, released in 2005, replaced the
Food Guide Pyramid

Source: US Department of Agriculture/US Department of Health and Human
Services. Retrieved February 29, 2012 from www.choosemyplate.gov/
print-materials-ordering/graphic-resources.html

the use of a USDA-sponsored website to make sense of it. As the addition of "my" suggests, the interactive website allowed users to construct their own individualized eating plan based on the more generic USDA recommendations. The icon itself, instead of being divided horizontally, was sliced vertically into color-coded sections representing the various food groups. The relative size of each slice conveyed the relative proportion of that group's daily allotment. Gone from the graphic were actual serving sizes, as well as the names of the food groups represented by each slice. Another new element was a human figure walking up steps on the left side of the pyramid, which represented exercise. The bottom of the pyramid listed the MyPyramid website and "steps to a healthier you." Predictably, the meat and dairy industries preferred this graphic to the previous one because the hierarchical arrangement of food groups was gone and the message of variety seemed to override the messages of moderation and proportionality. Nutritionists, however, lambasted the new icon, noting that it had been "stripped of any useful information" and constituted "a step backward" (Skerrett 2011b: para. 4).

The newest USDA graphic, MyPlate (see Figure 4.3), was released in 2011 amid much fanfare. First Lady Michelle Obama made healthy eating based on MyPlate a central focus of her Let's Move campaign, which aims to eliminate childhood obesity. The new MyPlate icon depicts a plate divided roughly into quarters, with the sections labeled "vegetables" and "grains" slightly larger than those labeled "protein" and "fruits." Alongside the plate is a circle

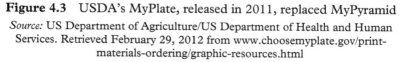

Figure 4.3   USDA's MyPlate, released in 2011, replaced MyPyramid

Source: US Department of Agriculture/US Department of Health and Human Services. Retrieved February 29, 2012 from www.choosemyplate.gov/print-materials-ordering/graphic-resources.html

labeled "dairy," its shape and placement calling to mind a glass of milk. While nutrition professionals favor some things about the new graphic, they also note that the MyPlate icon does not specify that fruits should be eaten whole, rather than as juices; that grains should be whole rather than refined (e.g., white bread, white rice); or that vegetables should reflect a palette of colors to ensure a wide array of nutrients (Skerrett 2011b). The "protein" category, the only section named for a nutrient (Nestle 2011), merely hints that protein comes from a variety of foods. People must understand what protein is and the variety of forms in which it is available to be able to select an appropriate portion. Moreover, critics charge that some popular protein sources, such as red meat, contain much higher proportions of fat and cholesterol than others, like chicken, beans, and seafood (Skerrett 2011b: para. 7). Even vegetables and grains contain some protein, but these are unlikely to register with most US consumers, who still largely equate protein with meat (Nestle 2011).

MyPlate also fails to address plate size. The same amount of food served on a small or medium-sized dinner plate looks bigger than when served on a large plate. Portions perceived as larger contribute to **satiety,** or how full we feel (Wansink 2007). By depicting only relative proportions – that half the plate should be fruits and vegetables, for example – MyPlate offers no guidance on what an absolute portion size should be, such as number of ounces or pieces of fruit. Also, MyPlate ignores snacking, a significant part of American food consumption. Finally, unlike its predecessor, MyPyramid, the new plate icon leaves out exercise completely.

Despite these criticisms, the new MyPlate icon is the basis for many school nutrition curricula, while the National School Lunch Program, the federal meal program that offers low- or no-cost lunches to children in participating schools, must meet nutrition standards outlined in the latest *Dietary Guidelines*. Therefore, shortcomings of MyPlate and compromises over the content of the *Guidelines* have real consequences, both with regard to the formal nutrition instruction children receive and to the food they eat.

Since the 1970s, most physicians and nutrition professionals agree that the healthiest diet is a varied diet low in fat, cholesterol, sodium, sugar, and other refined carbohydrates (Nestle 2007). Nevertheless, the idea that all foods can be part of a healthy diet and the USDA's mandate to protect agriculture leads to vague and conflicting advice presented with euphemisms designed to appease the food industry. Advice to "avoid added sugars" instead of the much clearer "avoid sugary beverages like soda and juice" perpetuates consumer confusion over what to eat. Paired with a constant barrage of contradictory news reports and clever marketing by food producers, it is no wonder that many consumers constantly wonder, "What should I eat?" Even "junk foods" like potato chips are increasingly marketed as potential health foods since the advent of natural, baked, low-sodium, low-fat, or fat-free varieties. While this section focused on the social construction of government-sponsored nutrition advice, the next section examines another key reason why consumers are so confused about diet and nutrition – food industry marketing.

Marketing Health, Manufacturing Taste

One key source of consumer confusion over healthy eating is the media. News outlets are quick to publicize research findings highlighting the benefits of single nutrients or ingredients, while food manufacturers attempt to capitalize on this attention through clever marketing. For instance, as whole grains gained attention, General Mills began promoting its Big G line of ready-to-eat cereals as "made with whole grain." Because ingredients are listed on labels in descending order beginning with the greatest by weight, General Mills argues that consumers can confidently choose any of the fifty varieties of their Big G cereals knowing that "there is more whole grain than any other single ingredient" (General Mills n.d.: para. 1).

Dannon's Activia brand yogurt offers an exemplary case of the promises and pitfalls of food manufacturers' use of health claims to increase sales. Yogurt is made by adding two bacterial cultures (*Lactobacillus bulgaricus* and *Streptococcus thermophilus*) to milk. The bacteria ferment the milk by breaking down its sugar (lactose) into lactic acid, which thickens it, imparting a distinctive tangy flavor, and making it digestible by persons with lactose intolerance. These "friendly bacteria," known as probiotics, are also what confer yogurt's supposed health benefits. They have been credited with alleviating digestive problems, boosting the immune system, and facilitating weight loss, among other benefits. Yet not all of yogurt's live and active bacteria cultures have demonstrated health benefits, and research findings are contradictory concerning how the cultures are delivered (i.e., in yogurt or in other mediums), what specific digestive issues they alleviate (Camilleri 2006; Szajewska et al. 2006; Wendakoon, Thomson, and Ozimek 2002), and how much one must consume to receive the health benefit (Schardt 2010).

Activia ads, including a series of highly recognizable television commercials featuring actress Jamie Lee Curtis, promote eating Activia as a corrective to "digestive issues like occasional irregularity" (Federal Trade Commission 2011b). More specifically, Dannon claims that a particular bacteria strain included in Activia, which Dannon trademarked as *Bifidus regularis*, "helps regulate your digestive system" (Dannon n.d.: para. 1). Marketing materials boast that "eaten every day, Activia is clinically proven to help regulate your digestive system in two weeks" and claim that Activia "helps slow intestinal transit," the time it takes food to pass through the digestive system (Federal Trade Commission 2011b). Health claims like these make Activia a **functional food**, one that purports to provide health benefits beyond its normal nutritional properties, typically because of added nutrients or other beneficial ingredients (Nestle 2007; Siró et al. 2008). Occupying a middle ground between food and medicine, functional foods offer endless marketing opportunities to health-conscious consumers and are a fast-growing, multi-billion dollar industry (Siró et al. 2008). As with all functional foods, Dannon cannot legally claim that Activia or the probiotics contained in it will cure or treat any specific disease such as irritable bowel syndrome or bacterial infections. Disease claims are heavily regulated by the US Food and Drug Administration (FDA). Instead, "By pitching itself as the cure to vaguely defined tummy troubles, Dannon's Activia has become a billion-dollar global brand," with US sales in its first year exceeding US$130 million and increasing by 50 percent in its second year (Sandler 2008: paras 1–2).

While its vague health claims clearly helped sell Activia, they also put Dannon on the defensive when those claims came under fire as a result of a class-action lawsuit alleging that the purported digestive health benefits were scientifically unsupported. Although admitting no wrongdoing, Dannon eventually settled the lawsuit in September 2009, agreeing to pay US$35 million to customers who had purchased Activia and to institute changes in how it labels Activia and DanActive, its yogurt drink (Parker-Pope 2009; US District Court 2010). Specifically, Dannon agreed to replace the phrases "clinically proven" and "scientifically proven" with the less precise "clinical studies show" on both Activia brand and DanActive brand products (US District Court 2010: 12).

Later, in December 2010, Dannon settled with the US Federal Trade Commission (FTC), the organization that regulates advertising claims, over similar charges that it had made scientifically unsupported health claims (Williams 2010). The FTC settlement prohibits Dannon from claiming "that Activia yogurt relieves temporary irregularity or helps with slow intestinal transit time, unless the representation is non-misleading and conveys that eating three servings a day is required to obtain the benefit" (Federal Trade Commission 2011a: 3). The settlement also stipulated that Dannon would need to produce two well-designed human trials conducted independently of each other to substantiate any health claims used in its marketing. Despite these legal setbacks, Dannon continues to tout Activia's health benefits in its marketing campaigns. In an interview published in September 2011, Sergio Fuster, a senior marketing executive for Dannon, noted that the company was already creating new marketing strategies to promote Activia's digestive health benefits "without necessarily having to speak about irregularity" (Schultz 2011: para 13), thus circumventing the FTC ruling.

By focusing on the healthful qualities of single ingredients or nutrients, marketers encourage consumers to overlook other less healthy characteristics of a food. Such marketing relies on what psychologists call the halo effect, "when an individual's evaluation of one attribute of an entity strongly influences or biases his or her perceptions of other attributes of that entity" (Lee et al. 2013: 34). By focusing attention on ingredients imbued with positive attributes (such as healthy, organic, and/or environmentally friendly), marketers create a **health halo** that influences consumers to regard the entire product in a positive light. Among the Big G cereals touting the health benefits of whole grains are kids' favorites Trix, Lucky Charms, and Cocoa Puffs (General Mills n.d.), which *Time* magazine rated among the top ten "sugary" cereal brands advertised to children. Although

General Mills has made an effort to reduce sugar in cereals advertised to children, both Trix and Lucky Charms are each 41 percent sugar (Rochman 2009). General Mills hopes that the health halo created by the focus on whole grains will lead consumers, especially parents, to view these cereals as healthy, despite their high sugar content. Likewise, most flavored yogurts, including Activia, contain so much sugar and other sweeteners that one leading nutritionist urges consumers to think of them as desserts, rather than health foods (Nestle 2006). Nevertheless, the health halo surrounding Activia and other yogurts leads consumers to regard them as healthy.

Similar to functional foods, some foods are now being hailed as **super foods** because of their high concentration of a particular nutrient and/or their overall dense nutritional value. More marketing lingo than accurate nutritional term, there is no widespread agreement on what actually constitutes a super food. One popular source describes them as fruits and vegetables "with more than their fair share of vitamins, minerals, and disease-fighting nutrients" (Gragg 2013: para. 2). A quick internet search for "super foods" will no doubt turn up blueberries, leafy greens such as kale and mustard, quinoa, chia seeds, acai, kefir, coconut oil, and many others. What these all have in common is a faddish popularity among middle-class health-conscious consumers in the global North. Quinoa, for example, a traditional food crop native to the high Andes in South America and lauded as a complete protein, high in B-vitamins and essential amino acids, has become especially popular among middle-class foodies in North America and Europe (Dobkin 2008). Like other super foods, the consumption of quinoa is important both symbolically and materially, as quinoa socially differentiates higher-class consumers from poorer ones in the global North. As described more in chapter 2, consumption of super foods, like quinoa and foods regarded as nutritious more generally, symbolically marks one as higher class. The irony here is that many so-called super foods such as quinoa were staple crops among indigenous peasants in their countries of origin (Brett 2010). (Chapter 7 explains how globalization facilitates production of food for global elites.)

Despite their value for increasing sales and leading consumers to overlook negative health qualities, health claims do not necessarily override palatability, especially with primarily taste-conscious consumers. Soy foods are a case in point. Although a staple of several Asian cuisines, soy is relatively new to most westerners. Soy product manufacturers claim that consuming 25 grams of soy protein a day can lower the risk of coronary heart disease when included as part of a healthy diet, a claim permitted on US food labels since 1999. Since then, sales of soy foods have doubled (Schardt 2006: 3). To include this claim on its label, a food must contain at least 6.25 grams of soy protein per serving, or one-quarter of the 25-gram daily total. Critics note that most people generally will not consume four or more servings of soy in a day (Nestle 2006; Schardt 2006), and, like the research on probiotics, results on the health effects of soy are contradictory.

Soy foods have the distinction of being perceived as both good to eat (i.e., healthy) and hard to stomach (i.e., unpalatable). In one experiment, participants were asked to rate the taste and nutritional qualities of a nutrition bar labeled as containing "soy protein," while others were asked to rate a bar labeled as containing just "protein." Both groups sampled the same kind of protein bar, which contained no soy. Nevertheless, those who thought they were eating a bar with soy rated it as less tasty but more nutritious than those eating the one labeled as containing just protein (Wansink 2003). In a similar study, soy labels had different effects for taste-conscious and health-conscious consumers. The soy label had no effect on the taste ratings of health-conscious consumers, while both taste- and health-conscious consumers felt soy labels made product health claims more believable (Wansink and Park 2002). Other research finds that nutritional claims on product labels are only effective for foods that consumers already perceive as healthy (van Trijp and van der Lans 2007).

Nutritionists claim that the health benefit derived from eating single foods, including so-called super foods, is likely to be small compared to the benefits of consuming a varied and balanced diet. In the case of soy, Nestle (2006: 134) cautions, "If you eat soy because you think it is healthful, you probably also follow other good health habits. If you follow other good health habits and do not eat soy, this omission is unlikely to make a difference. And eating soy is unlikely to compensate for whatever unhealthy habits you might practice." The same can be said for most single food items or nutrients, particularly when included in foods with other ingredients of dubious nutritional value. Nonetheless, attention to single ingredients and their health benefits persists because of the health halo such attention creates, because scientific research is designed to assess single components, and because the simplified results are easier to communicate to consumers (Nestle 2006, 2007). And, as the examples of quinoa and soy illustrate, health claims are especially likely to influence health-conscious middle-class consumers since class identity is linked symbolically to consumption of nutritious food.

In addition to clever marketing (discussed more in chapter 5), food manufacturers also heavily research the tastes people crave and scientifically engineer processed foods that cater to these tastes. The end result is foods laden with salt, sugar, and fat. When formulating a new sweetened beverage, for instance, food scientists will calculate its "bliss point," the point at which its concentration of sugar maximizes pleasure. Add too little sugar and you fall short of the bliss point, leaving consumers dissatisfied; but add too much sugar and you overshoot the bliss point, producing similarly dissatisfied consumers. In the latter situation, manufacturers will have also wasted money on unnecessary sweetener. Seen in this light, the high sugar content in foods marketed to children is no accident. As Michael Moss explains, "People love sugar, especially kids. And up to a certain point – the bliss point – the more sugar there is, the better" (Moss 2013: 16). Children have a higher bliss point than adults – their preferred optimal concentration of sugar is higher. When designing foods intended for children, such as ready-to-eat cereal, food scientists manipulate the sugar content to match children's higher bliss point. Such food engineering may also prime children to expect sweeter beverages and other foods throughout their lives, contributing to overweight and obesity (Moss 2013), the subject of the following section. Clearly, scientific, political, and corporate interests converge to create a confusing set of nutritional messages, while food companies tailor products and marketing efforts to appeal to health- and taste-conscious consumers.

Obesity: epidemic or epic delusion?

Just as there are competing perspectives on what constitutes a healthy diet, there are also competing conceptual frames on corpulence or fatness. Two competing claims makers framing popular discourses on fatness are anti-obesity researchers and activists, and fat acceptance activists (Saguy and Riley 2005). Anti-obesity researchers and activists, including medical doctors and public health and nutrition professionals, believe that overweight and obesity put affected people at risk for a wide array of health problems, including type 2 diabetes, hypertension, heart disease, cancer, and overall increased mortality (death). In this discussion, we refer to these claims makers as public health professionals and their framing of the issue as the **medical model of obesity**. This medical model constitutes the dominant cultural view of overweight and obesity in the global North (Saguy 2013; Saguy and Riley 2005), and advances the medicalization of fatness.

Medicalization refers to "the application and expansion of medicine and medical authority over increasing realms of human life" (Kwan and Graves 2013: 2). The medical model embraces medical understandings of fatness and endorses medical interventions like weight-loss drugs and bariatric surgery to treat it. This model "has become so pervasive and taken-for-granted . . . that most people do not even realize that it is a frame and that there are alternative ways of understanding fatness, as, for instance, beautiful, sexy, healthy, or a positive form of human diversity" (Saguy 2013: 5).

Fat acceptance activists, on the other hand, embrace these alternative understandings of fat. They promote the minority view that fat is just another kind of bodily diversity met with discrimination, and they question the view of obesity as a disease and health risk by focusing instead on the direct negative consequences of fat stigma (Kwan and Graves 2013; Saguy 2013; Saguy and Riley 2005). They charge that measurements of overweight and obesity are faulty, their links with disease unproven, and the resulting public health outcry more harmful than helpful.

Defining overweight and obesity

Overweight and obesity are calculated using the **Body Mass Index** (BMI), which divides weight in kilograms by height in meters squared. Adults aged 20 and over with a BMI of 30.0 or greater are considered obese, while those with a BMI between 25.0 and 29.9 are considered overweight (Ogden et al. 2014). The National Health and Nutrition Examination Survey (NHANES), based on a nationally representative sample of the US population, found that 33.5 percent of adult men and 36.1 percent of adult women were obese in 2011–12. The combined all-sex obesity rate of 34.9 percent for that same year showed no significant change in the prevalence of adult obesity compared to 2003–4 (Ogden et al. 2014). Although obesity rates increased throughout the 1980s and 1990s, rates leveled off in the 2000s (Flegal et al. 2012). Nevertheless, obesity rates are higher in the United States than in other affluent countries (Flegal et al. 2012). Moreover, obesity rates tend to correspond with forms of social inequality such as race and class. Rates are higher among non-Hispanic blacks and Latinos (47.8 and 42.5 percent, respectively) than among non-Hispanic whites (32.6 percent) (Ogden et al. 2014), and adults with more education tend to have lower rates of obesity (Himes and Reynolds 2005).

For children and youth, ages 2 through 19, overweight and obesity are assessed according to sex-specific BMI-for-age growth charts. Children and adolescents between the 85th and 95th percentiles of BMI-for-age are considered overweight, while those at or above the 95th percentile are considered obese (Ogden et al. 2014). By these measures, 16.7 percent of boys and 17.2 percent of girls were obese in 2011–12 (Ogden et al. 2014), with an overall prevalence of childhood obesity of 16.9 percent. According to Ogden et al. (2012: 490), "the rapid increases in obesity prevalence [among all children and adolescents] seen in the 1980s and 1990s have not continued in this decade and may be leveling off." In fact, the 2011–12 data show no significant changes in the overall rate of childhood obesity as compared to the 2003–4 data (Ogden et al. 2014). Still, as with adults, US childhood obesity rates are generally higher among particular racial and ethnic minorities (blacks and Hispanics), and US rates are higher than in other affluent countries (Ogden et al. 2014). Statistics like these have led public health professionals to declare obesity an "epidemic," despite the fact that the spread of obesity seems to have slowed or stopped.

Critics, including fat acceptance activists, question the use of BMI as a measure of obesity (Campos 2004; Oliver 2005). The World Health Organization, or WHO (World Health Organization 2011: para. 1) defines **obesity** as "abnormal or excessive fat accumulation that may impair health," not weight per se. As a simple ratio of weight to height, BMI does not measure fat accumulation because it cannot distinguish between muscle, bone, and fat (Campos 2004; Guthman 2011; Oliver 2006). People with high muscle mass like professional athletes or bodybuilders may have a BMI that classifies them as obese, showing that BMI does not reliably indicate physical fitness. Also, BMI does not account for sex differences in body mass or racial differences (Guthman 2011; Ross 2005). As Flegal et al. (2012: 495–6) explain, "At a given BMI, black men and women tend to have higher lean mass and lower fat mass than white men and women. As a result, race/ethnicity differences in the prevalence of obesity as defined by BMI do not always completely reflect body fatness." Even the WHO (n.d.: para. 1) calls BMI a "crude" measure.

Critics also question the range of BMI values that define overweight and obesity. Prior to 1998, the minimum BMI for an overweight adult was 27. When the National Institutes of Health (NIH) lowered the cutoff to 25, it increased the proportion of the population who were overweight overnight, fueling the perception that overweight and obesity are at epidemic proportions (Guthman 2011;

Oliver 2006; Ross 2005). Why, then, is BMI the measure most often used? Other techniques that measure fat more directly include "skin-fold measurements, underwater weighing, computerized tomography (in-body visualization), and the widely used but rarely admitted 'eyeball test'" (Guthman 2011: 27). With the exception of the highly subjective "eyeball test," these other measures are expensive and difficult to gather from large populations. BMI is both inexpensive and easy to measure.

In spite of the problems inherent in the use of BMI to measure obesity, the American Medical Association (AMA), the main professional organization representing US physicians, voted in 2013 to classify obesity as a disease (Pollack 2013), thereby reinforcing the medicalization of fatness. In doing so, the AMA's House of Delegates (the organization's policy-setting body) went against the recommendations of its own Council on Science and Public Health, which advocated against such a designation. The Council report was critical of the use of BMI to measure and therefore diagnose obesity, calling it "simplistic and flawed" (Pollack 2013: para. 12). Critics inside the AMA argued that obesity lacks specific symptoms and "is more a risk factor for other conditions than a disease in its own right" (Pollack 2013: para. 18). Moreover, they charged that designating obesity as a disease would redefine "one-third of the US population as ill" (Pollack 2013: para. 19), despite the fact that many obese people are healthy, while many normal-weight individuals are not (Pittman 2013; Pollack 2013), criticisms shared by many fat acceptance activists and discussed more in the next section.

Obesity – health risk or hype?

Fat acceptance activists question the medical framing of obesity. First, they point to flaws in the method used to calculate deaths attributed to obesity. Most research relies on the concept of excess mortality or **excess death** – the number of deaths over and above what would normally be expected in a population. In the case of obesity, researchers measure the "extra" deaths we see among obese persons compared to what we'd expect to find if obese persons had the same death rates as those of normal weight. Fat activists criticize this approach because the "extra" deaths are assumed to be caused by obesity, even though the actual cause of death is not determined (Guthman 2011; Oliver 2006). Public health professionals counter that reliance on excess deaths is a widely accepted tool in epidemiological research used to explore deaths from natural disasters to tobacco-related deaths (Klinenberg 2002).

Second, fat acceptance activists argue that, like all research based on associations among variables, correlation is not the same as causation. Even if obesity is associated with higher rates of type 2 diabetes, for example, the actual cause may be a different factor, such as lack of exercise or nutritionally poor diets (Guthman 2011: 35). They claim that only experimental studies, not population-based correlational studies like these, can definitively prove a causal link (Ross 2005). In short, while fat activists do not dispute the basic statistical claim that obesity and health problems tend to co-occur, they argue that the link between excess fat and increased health risks is much more complex than research to date suggests.

Third, in addition to criticizing the classification of obesity as a disease, fat acceptance activists maintain that classifying obesity as an **epidemic** is misleading (Campos 2004; Oliver 2006; Saguy and Riley 2005). Epidemic "originally referred to the rapid and episodic onset of infectious diseases and, as such, was historically associated with fear and sudden widespread death" (Saguy and Riley 2005: 892). Obesity is not infectious, and, if it leads to death at all, it does so slowly over many years. While the language of epidemic suggests that death rates climb directly with BMI, research shows that both extremely low and high BMIs are associated with a higher risk of death (Campos 2004; Flegal et al. 2007; Oliver 2006; Ross 2005). Moreover, the NHANES data indicate that, among the obese, only the extremely obese with a BMI greater than 35 have a higher mortality risk, and people who are overweight, with a BMI between 25 and 30, are actually less likely to die than those of normal weight (Flegal et al. 2007). Nevertheless, the public health approach to overweight and obesity promotes the simplified view that higher BMIs carry a higher mortality risk. For example, WHO (2006: para. 3) warns "the risk of health problems starts when someone is only very slightly overweight," and "the likelihood of problems increases as someone becomes more and more overweight." The persistence of such claims has led some fat activists to charge that public health organizations like WHO are intentionally distorting the truth about obesity (Campos 2004; Oliver 2006). Media coverage of the obesity "epidemic" has skyrocketed since 1995 but has not widely reported findings of the protective effects of overweight (Saguy and Riley 2005).

Impacts of the medical model of obesity

Fat acceptance activists maintain that the medical model of obesity justifies and disguises fat stigma, permitting discrimination against fat people under a rubric of health (Cogan 1999; Saguy and Riley 2005).The medical model generally frames overweight and obesity as the result of risky personal behaviors; it "assumes body weight is under personal control" and "that those who are fat have unhealthy lifestyles while the thin make good food and exercise choices" (Saguy and Riley 2005: 883). This view reflects dominant values of individualism and personal responsibility, which present obesity as the result of gluttony and poor morals (Kwan and Graves 2013; Oliver 2006; Saguy and Riley 2005).

Although the medical model exhorts overweight and obese persons to lose weight to improve their personal health and avoid future medical complications, according to Boero (2012), most overweight and obese individuals who pursue bariatric surgery do so in an attempt to feel normal. Being or feeling normal "meant not having to deal with the social and physical obstacles fat people deal with on a daily basis" (Boero 2012: 99). These micro-aggressions include, among others, dealing with rude stares or remarks, finding affordable clothes that fit, and physically fitting into a built environment made for thin people (e.g., bus or airplane seats that are too small). That the desire to feel normal was a more important motivator for weight-loss surgery than health concerns demonstrates the high cumulative toll these micro-aggressions take.

Additionally, fat people face more overt forms of prejudice and discrimination. In employment, fat people are discriminated against in both hiring and promotion decisions; in educational settings, obese women have lower college-acceptance rates than similarly qualified non-obese women, and parents are less likely to provide financial support for obese daughters than for normal-weight daughters attending college (Puhl and Brownell 2001). Moreover, rates of overweight and obesity map clearly onto other lines of social inequality, leading Saguy (2013: 20) to conclude that "in a context in which overt expressions of racism are decreasingly tolerated, and in which rates of 'obesity' are disproportionately high among the poor, African American women, and Mexican American men and women, condemnation of people for being fat may offer a socially acceptable way of expressing racism and classism." Given these findings, fat activists generally conclude that definitions of overweight and obesity, as well as the moral aspersions and stigma cast on fat people, function to perpetuate systems of social inequality.

Further, some fat activists charge that attempts to lose weight can be dangerous. The medical model promotes individual weight loss to address the medically defined problem of obesity and its attendant health risks (Campos 2004; Oliver 2005; Saguy and Riley 2005). The traditional strategies are to increase caloric expenditure through exercise, decrease caloric intake through diet, or both. Critics charge that such advice is useless for the unknown number of people whose weight is a result of genetics (Cogan 1999; Oliver 2006). Recall the Special K Challenge, discussed in the opening case study. The research supporting it only examined a two-week trial and therefore cannot address its effect on long-term weight loss. Fat activists point out that most meal replacement diets and food restriction diets lead to a pattern of **yo-yo dieting**: losing weight through dieting, regaining it, followed by more dieting, and so on. This weight fluctuation, some fat activists argue, may be more dangerous than persistent overweight and has not been accounted for in studies of the health effects of overweight and obesity (Cogan 1999).

Weight-loss drugs and surgeries may also be far more damaging than overweight, fat acceptance activists claim (Cogan 1999; Oliver 2006). For example, the combination weight-loss drug fenfluramine-phentermine, popularly known as "fen phen" and marketed under the brand names Redux and Pondimin, was removed from the US market in 1997 after reports of serious heart valve problems and deaths in patients using it (Kate Cohen 2003). More recently, Abbott Laboratories voluntarily removed Meridia from the market, due to an increased risk of heart attacks and stroke (Pollack 2010). Since 2012, the FDA has approved three new weight-loss drugs, Qsymia (formerly known as Qnexa), Belviq, and Contrave, all for use by overweight or obese patients with a weight–related medical condition such as diabetes, high blood pressure or high cholesterol (Painter 2014). All three have serious side effects. Side effects of Qsymia may include elevated heart rate, which can lead to stroke or heart attack, and birth defects in babies born to women who took the drug (Jaslow 2012), while Contrave may increase blood pressure, heart rate, and suicidal thoughts (Painter 2014).

Upstream approaches: food in schools

The medical model frames overweight and obesity as problems resulting from individual failings such as lack of self-control, laziness, or more neutrally, from poor diet and exercise habits. The proposed solution is typically to exhort overweight and obese individuals to lose weight. Because it focuses exclusively on individual behaviors, the medical approach is a downstream approach (McKinlay 2005). Upstream approaches, by contrast, focus on the social and structural context that shapes the food and lifestyle options available to different social groups (McKinlay 2005). In this section, we examine an alternative approach to the issue of overweight and obesity that takes on an upstream factor – specifically, attempts to ban soft drinks and other junk foods in schools.

Longitudinal studies that follow individuals over time find that body weight tends to be transmitted intergenerationally within families. Children with obese parents have a greater risk of being obese as young adults (Crossman, Sullivan, and Benin 2006). While part of this may reflect genetic factors, a great deal of research also suggests a link to childhood socialization within what are increasingly called **obesogenic environments** – settings such as families, neighborhoods, and schools that encourage overconsumption of foods believed to contribute to overweight and obesity. Families socialize children into particular foodways by example (Brown and Ogden 2004; Olivera et al. 1992) and by selecting and providing food for their children (Wardle 1995). The eating patterns they learn continue to influence children's weight into young adulthood (Crossman, Sullivan, and Benin 2006).

The growing awareness of the social and environmental influences on weight has led to new "upstream" approaches that attempt to prevent overweight and obesity by shaping children's social environments, such as schools, through public policies (Guthman 2011; Poppendieck 2010). For example, states, school districts, and parent associations have attempted to limit the availability of **competitive foods** in schools, so called because they compete with those available through the National School Lunch Program (NSLP) and the School Breakfast Program. Importantly, competitive foods do not have to meet the nutrition standards for school meals established by the USDA (van Hook and Altman 2012). Common competitive foods include soft drinks and other sugary beverages, candy bars, chips, and other snack foods that students purchase from vending machines, snack bars, or as à la carte items in cafeterias (Fried and Simon 2007; Poppendieck 2010; van Hook and Altman 2012). Although the types of competitive foods vary tremendously by school, "99 percent of high schools, 97 percent of middle schools, and 83 percent of elementary schools had one or more of such venues" where competitive foods were sold (Poppendieck 2010: 122). Cafeterias rely on competitive foods to make up for losses from their regular food service operations, and school clubs use them to fund trips and other activities (Fried and Simon 2007; Poppendieck 2010).

Here too the competing agenda of the food industry comes into play. In the late 1970s, the USDA attempted to put limits on the hours during which soft drinks and candy could be sold in schools, prompting strong opposition from the National Soft Drink Association (NSDA), which represents beverage manufacturers. The NSDA sued and the court ruled that soft drinks "could not be sold in the school cafeteria at lunchtime but were permissible in all other school venues and at other times during the school day" (Fried and Simon 2007: 1508). Since then, states have gotten involved. In 2003, a bill that would have banned soda sales in all public schools in California was met with strong opposition from the soft drink industry. The bill eventually passed, but with a key amendment that exempted high schools, where, not coincidentally, the bulk of school soda sales occur. In 2005, the state legislature finally passed a law banning soda in high schools, but it contained a key exemption for sugary sports drinks (Fried and Simon 2007: 1520–1).

Are these upstream strategies effective? Some research finds that restrictive policies on competitive foods promote healthier eating among students. Neumark-Sztainer et al. (2005) found that high-school students consumed fewer snack foods and soft drinks when they were less available, and Gonzalez, Jones, and Frongillo (2009) found that children consumed more fruits and vegetables in middle schools that restricted the availability of snacks. Other studies, however, find that such restrictions do not impact students' food consumption or risk for overweight and obesity. Blum et al. (2008) found no reductions in the consumption of sugar-sweetened beverages when restricted in Maine schools. Cunningham and Zavodny (2011) found that access to sweetened beverages at school was unrelated to BMI or obesity rates of fifth- and eighth-graders, and van Hook and Altman (2012) found no link between competitive food sales and students' weight. Authors of the latter finding explain that "Children's environments at home and in their communities may provide so many opportunities to eat unhealthy foods that competitive food sales in schools have little influence on children's weight" (van Hook and Altman 2012: 23–4). Thus, changes in schools may not be sufficient to counter the influence of other food environments and the broader structural context.

Conclusion

In this chapter, we explored the paradox that what is considered "good to eat" by health and nutrition professionals is often difficult for both the food industry and the public to swallow. The food industry objects to any nutritional advice that casts its products in a negative light and exerts political pressure on the USDA to frame advice in ways that cohere with industry marketing efforts. Food corporations also use information about single nutrients to tout the benefits of their products to consumers and shroud otherwise unhealthy foods within a health halo. The result of these competing scientific and corporate perspectives is nutrition advice that many consumers find confusing and contradictory. Moreover, we see again how foodways are both individual and social, shaped by the confluence of individual taste preferences, clever marketing, and nutrition advice.

Like nutrition advice, overweight and obesity are similarly contested issues, with the dominant medical model framing these as major health problems and fat acceptance activists framing them as elements of human diversity. Fat activists, in particular, hold that definitions of overweight and obesity, as well as the moral aspersions and stigma cast on fat people, function to perpetuate systems of social inequality. As in other chapters, we see how powerful individuals and institutions within public health have greater success in framing the issue of fatness as a medical problem that casts the eating habits of lower-status and less-educated persons as unhealthy, deviant, and in need of change. The next chapter delves further into the complex relationship between large corporations and individual consumers through a detailed exploration of branding and marketing.

Further reading

de la Peña, Carolyn. 2010. *Empty Pleasures: The Story of Artificial Sweeteners from Saccharin to Splenda*. Chapel Hill, NC: University of North Carolina Press. De la Peña offers a social history of artificial sweeteners, beginning with cyclamates and including modern-day alternatives such as aspartame.

This book includes an interesting discussion of the early vilification of saccharin and the valorization of sugar that accompanied it.

Guthman, Julie. 2011. *Weighing In: Obesity, Food Justice, and the Limits of
Capitalism*. Berkeley, CA: University of California Press. Guthman examines the obesity epidemic and the links between obesity and the current
food system, arguing that local and organic food may not be the cure-all
for contemporary food problems that some claim them to be.

Nestle, Marion. 2007. *Food Politics: How the Food Industry Influences Nutrition
and Health*. Berkeley, CA: University of California Press. Nestle outlines
how and why food is a political issue, addressing how special interests
shape nutrition advice, including the creation of the Dietary Guidelines
for Americans and the various food guide pyramids. Of special interest
are the chapters examining the rise of functional foods and the politics of
nutritional supplements.

Saguy, Abigail C. 2013. *What's Wrong with Fat?* New York: Oxford
University Press. Saguy explores the social construction of fat in the
United States through an examination of the primary frames through
which fat is viewed: as a moral issue; a medical issue; a public health crisis;
and a fat acceptance lens.

Wansink, Brian. 2007. *Mindless Eating: Why We Eat More Than We Think*.
New York: Bantam Books. Psychologist Brian Wansink distills hundreds
of psychological studies on eating into a highly accessible and interesting
volume. He addresses issues such as the effect of food labels on food palatability, effects of perceived serving size on satiety, eating scripts, health
halos and comfort foods, explaining why many people "are blissfully
unaware of what influences how much we eat" (p. 1).

Further exploration

1 FOR DISCUSSION: First, examine the Harvard School of Public
Health's Healthy Eating Plate and Healthy Eating Pyramid, both available at http://www.hsph.harvard.edu/nutritionsource/healthy-eating-plate/.
As a class, generate a list of the ways each graphic differs from its USDA
companion graphic pictured in the text. Why are the two pairs of graphics
so different? What objections would food industry executives likely have
to the Healthy Eating Pyramid and Healthy Eating Plate, and why?

2 IN CLASS: Bring in food labels with health claims, such as cereal boxes,
yogurt cups, or any other packaged or prepared foods making such a
claim. Using information from the chapter, in small groups, analyze the
health messages both in terms of why manufacturers include these specific messages on the labels, what groups they likely appeal to, and how
consumers are likely to view them. In your opinion, are any of the health
claims especially believable or especially outlandish? What makes them
so?

3 ONLINE: Listen to the podcast, "Who Killed Lard?" available from Planet
Money   at   http://www.npr.org/sections/money/2012/01/06/144806987/

the-friday-podcast-who-killed-lard. What are the main social and economic reasons for the declining popularity of lard among US consumers? How does the case of lard illustrate the confluence of scientific understandings of nutrition and corporate interests?

4 ONLINE: Watch the online video from CBS News featuring psychologist Brian Wansink discussing health halos and Subway, available at: www.youtube.com/watch?v=wKARlz2yq4Q&no redirect=1. How does Subway marketing aim to create a health halo around the entire restaurant chain? How do recent revelations of sexual misconduct by famed Subway spokesman Jared Fogle tarnish Subway's health halo?

5

Branding and Marketing: Governing the Sovereign Consumer

Case study

In 2003, the Pabst Brewing Company, maker of Pabst Blue Ribbon beer, faced a curious dilemma. At the time, Pabst accounted for about one half of 1 percent of the American beer market, but, because it was sold without expensive, splashy advertising, it yielded a small but dependable profit for its owner, a charitable trust that also owned other low-end, unheralded beers like Schlitz, Stroh's, and Old Milwaukee (Walker 2008). Then, around 2002, Pabst Blue Ribbon, or PBR for short, became popular among a rowdy subculture of punks, skaters, and bicycle couriers in Portland, Oregon (Walker 2008: 100). PBR suddenly became the fifth-most popular beer in Portland, a city renowned for its craft brews. Was it simply a blip of retro-chic, or perhaps an offshoot of the working-class fad that made plastic trucker-style baseball caps briefly popular?

A 27-year-old marketing director named Neal Stewart was dispatched to Portland to find out. Stewart chatted up PBR fans in bars and found that the brand appealed to this particular subculture because it was cheap and hardly ever advertised (Walker 2008: 101). He concluded that PBR drinkers were part of a youthful backlash against relentless corporate marketing and the consumerist lifestyle it represents. The Pabst Brewing Company was faced with a thorny question: how do you promote your product without visibly advertising? In other words, how do you market without marketing?

The answer was a set of practices that marketing journalist Rob Walker calls "murketing," a combination of "murky" and "marketing." Murketing refers to marketing tactics that "blur the line between branding channels and everyday life" (Walker 2008: xvii). They include strategies like placing products in movies or computer games, or recruiting popular teens to talk up their products to their peers. In Pabst's case, murketing meant sponsoring small-scale cultural events like bike polo tournaments, skateboard movie screenings, and indie art shows, without using signage or company representatives to publicize their support to attendees (Walker 2008: 105–6). Sales of PBR grew in other US cities, and other youth-culture networks increasingly sought out Pabst for these largely invisible sponsorship deals. Some questioned the effectiveness of this kind of marketing, but Stewart was convinced that more overt strategies, like placing ads on alternative radio stations or more visible sponsorships, would cause PBR fans to reject the brand as too commercial (Walker 2008: 105).

Walker also went to Portland to do his own informal research on the various values associated with the PBR brand within this outsider culture. On one hand, he met a skateboarder "who had recently gone through four tattoo sessions to get a Pabst logo about a foot square burned into his back" (Walker 2008: 107). The skater told Walker, "Pabst is part of my sub-culture. It's the only beer I think about. . . . The only thing that's going to stop me from drinking Pabst is when I die" (Walker 2008: 107). On the other hand, Walker also met the bike messenger who arranged PBR's first event sponsorship in Portland; he found PBR's new trendiness annoying. "Basically," he told Walker, "we're going to drink whatever beer costs a dollar" (2008: 107). Either due to or in spite of Stewart's clever murketing, PBR seems to have gained enduring hipster credibility. Pabst is now the fifth-largest beer producer in the United States, though it only accounts for 2.7 percent of beer sales, and the company was recently sold for US$250 million (Block 2010).

The PBR story reveals the complicated relationship between food corporations and the individuals who include or reject their products in crafting their foodways. When we think of brands and marketing, we tend to imagine companies formulating careful messages about their products and conveying those meanings to consumers at every available opportunity in the hope that they will respond favorably. The case of PBR illustrates that consumers rarely play such a passive, receptive role. Sociologist Douglas Holt (2006: 301–2) explains that branding contains an inherent dilemma for food corporations: brands "are more valuable to the extent that they enter the public" but when they do so they are "less under the control of their owners." Consumers actively ascribe their own individual and shared meanings to brands with greater or lesser influence from marketers. However, when brands enter the broader culture, culture itself becomes more commercialized and subject to corporate influence. Who is ultimately in control, then, the companies or the consumers?

Introduction: the myth of consumer sovereignty

Prior chapters explore many of the cultural processes and structures that shape what we eat, how we eat, and why. For most of us in advanced capitalist societies, our foodways include particular manufactured products, and even specific brands, leading some observers to describe the modern food marketplace as one that "provides consumers with an expansive and heterogeneous palette of resources from which to construct individual and collective identities" (Arnould and Thompson 2005: 871). Scholars of consumer culture explore the varied ways people pursue identity work within their broader cultural and historical contexts. These scholars examine consumer culture from a critical perspective, raising complex and important questions about power and inequality in the food system (Zukin and Maguire 2004). Simply asserting that people eat what they like ignores the powerful roles played by corporations and governments, as well as mediating factors of culture and geography. By the time a shopper is perusing a store shelf to decide among competing products, the interacting decisions of governments and corporations have largely determined the array of food stores in his or her area, the relative costs of the agricultural ingredients that make up the products, the nutritional information displayed on product labels, and the selection and presentation of products on the shelf. Consumer purchasing is just one component of a large and dynamic food system.

Going beyond an individualist perspective enables us to question what some observers call "the enchanting myth of **consumer sovereignty**" (Korczynski and Ott 2004: 575), the revered idea in capitalist culture that consumers should (and do) make their own free consumption choices based on their own unique tastes and wants, favoring the best and cheapest among competing selections. In capitalist culture, consumer sovereignty is assumed to guarantee fairness and efficiency because individuals are thought to act autonomously according to their basic (selfish) nature. In fact, the very idea of freedom is now frequently understood as a consumer's freedom of choice (Bauman 1992: 51). Market-oriented discourse denigrates any public constraints on consumption choices (and hence corporations' manufacturing and marketing choices) as an unjust abrogation of individual rights. One must put aside this myth of consumer sovereignty to explore how powerful organizations seek to shape foodways for their own benefit.

Corporate power certainly is not absolute, as the case of Pabst

Blue Ribbon demonstrates. They cannot force people to buy their products, and the spectacular flops of some heavily promoted products (purple ketchup, anyone?) illustrate the limits of advertising's persuasive techniques. Nevertheless, consumer decision making is conditioned in multiple ways, some more visible than others. To paraphrase Marx (2001 [1852]), consumers make the food market, but they do not make it as they please.

This chapter explores the interplay of marketing and consumer culture in shaping food systems. We explain first the key elements of the mass consumption system and, second, the social processes of branding and marketing, looking closely at the case of Coca-Cola. Next, we describe the origins of the self-service supermarket and recent shifts that have changed the relationships among food manufacturers, food retailers, and shoppers. Finally, we delve into the prominent role of consumer culture in our society and note critical perspectives on the commercialization of childhood. Throughout, we highlight the slippery, complex question of where power lies and how it works in food marketing.

The system of mass consumption

Most people in high-income countries (like the United States, Canada, and several countries in Europe) and, increasingly, middle-income countries (like China and India) participate in a system of mass consumption; that is, most people purchase most of their food and other basic needs with money (Frazão, Meade, and Regmi 2008). Mass consumption is one of the hallmarks of modernity, marking a sharp contrast to much of human history when most people met their basic needs by either producing food and other goods themselves or receiving them from kin or community (Slater 1999). While some people have been buying and selling food since the first urban centers emerged more than five thousand years ago, modern mass consumption has some distinct features that coevolved much more recently, features that illustrate the inseparable material and cultural dimensions of food and food systems.

A system of mass consumption requires a consumer culture that interacts with mass marketing. A society has a strong **consumer culture** when commercial products and practices of consumption are important symbols of values, norms, and identity. In other words, it is not just that people consume, but that their consumption choices strongly shape and communicate their sense of self in an increasingly commercialized cultural lexicon. **Mass marketing** refers to how food corporations, marketing firms, and retailers seek to encourage broad consumer desire for branded goods and then make those goods available for purchase. For our purposes, we focus on two key social phenomena involved in mass marketing. First, we discuss **branding**, which is the creation and promotion of meaning-laden symbols that represent particular products with compelling values and ideas (Holt 2006). As the story of Pabst Brewing illustrates, brands play a key role in how both consumers and firms engage with the food system. Second, we explore the emergence and impact of the modern self-service supermarket, an institution that shapes shopping behavior to maximize retail profit in distinctive ways (Dulsrud and Jacobsen 2009). We end by examining controversies about the impact of consumer culture on children.

Consumer culture

The enormous resources spent on branding and marketing reflect the central place of consumer culture in the societies of the United States and other wealthy countries. "Consumer culture," Slater (1999: 7) writes, "denotes a social arrangement in which the relation between lived culture and social resources, between meaningful ways of life and the symbolic and material resources on which they depend, is mediated through markets." In a consumer culture, most people consider it normal and desirable to meet their needs and cultivate their identities by purchasing branded products from mass retailers. Many contemporary readers who grew up within a strong consumer culture may find it difficult to imagine living in a society where branded products did not dominate the cultural landscape or in an era when limiting consumption (like during wartime) was presented as a patriotic duty. Many find it unsurprising to learn that a lot of two-year-olds have firm brand preferences (Schor 2004: 19).

It is important to note, then, that contemporary consumer culture is a particular phenomenon, no more or less natural than any other major social pattern. Some historians trace the modern rise of consumer culture in the linked societies of Britain and America to the late 1700s when manufacturing was expanding in Britain while colonial America was growing in both population and raw material exports (Breen 1988). It was in this era that we see consumption choices, such as tea or coffee, representing one's membership in the "imagined community" of the nation (Breen 1988: 76; see also chapter 2). Other scholars emphasize the unique global conditions following World War II, when US manufacturing that had boomed during the war found a ready global market in war-torn Europe and newly developing countries around the globe, fueling an unmatched and all-too-brief era of widespread prosperity in the United States (Lizabeth Cohen 2003). In the 1950s, historian Stephanie Coontz reminds us, "the average 30-year-old man could buy a median-priced home on only 15–18 percent of his salary" (1998: 33) leaving much of his income available for consumption. Consumption practices have reflected considerations of identity, values, and morality for centuries (Slater 1999), but the affluence of this post-World War II period explains much of the dominance of consumer culture today.

Some observers argue that consumers emphasize the symbolic and emotional content of brands, paying relatively little attention to the objective qualities of objects or the long-term impact of their consumption choices. For example, sociologist Richard Wilk (2006) sees bottled water as "the pure commodity in the age of branding." Generally, Wilk points out, we expect that a consumer good becomes popular when it offers higher quality at a competitive price. However, bottled water sales are growing the most in wealthy countries where substantial public investment has provided nearly everyone with safe, high-quality water that is conveniently and cheaply available at the kitchen sink. Wilk explains:

> Survey after survey shows that bottled water is generally no safer or purer than what comes from the tap. Though people claim they can easily taste the differences between tap and bottled waters, in blind tests many are unable to – especially because sometimes the liquid sold in bottles is tap water. . . . Clearly taste is not the central motivation behind the continuing inexorable increase in the bottled water trade. (Wilk 2006: 306)

For Wilk, the popularity of bottled water reflects, in part, consumers' doubts about how well governments can protect us from the myriad and complex environmental risks inherent in modern society (2006: 316). Increasingly, Wilk concludes, consumers look to the market, rather than governments, for solutions.

Some critics tracking the rise and intensification of consumer culture warn of the pervasive influence that corporations have in everyday life, while others note the dynamic opportunities for identity construction within a richly symbolized marketscape (Schor and Holt 2000). These two perspectives mark an ongoing debate about "whether consumption is a space of manipulation or freedom,

whether the consumer is sovereign or subject, active or passive, creative or determined" (Slater 1999: 32). That debate illustrates how
consumer culture can both challenge and reinforce inequalities of
power; no one group or institution created it or controls it, but some
participants in the system of mass consumption have more power
than others. To further illustrate, we return to brands as essential elements of consumer culture.

Brands and branding

A **brand** is simply a commercially developed symbol; as noted in
chapter 2, a **symbol** is anything that carries a shared meaning in a
culture. Words, gestures and images can all be symbols, and people
who share the same culture can use these symbols to communicate.
For example, consider an Oreo cookie. As Warren Belasco describes
(2008: 23–4), it is "one of America's best-selling, most cherished
brands." For many, it is a symbol of childhood, laden with images of
innocence, family, and fun. Competing chocolate-flavored sandwich
cookies do not taste exactly the same, nor do they carry the same
symbolic message. Whether a shopper chooses the classic Nabisco
Oreo, a more generic competitor, or an organic version has as much
to do with identity as with budget priorities. All food companies seek
to engage with the rich symbolic associations we have with food by
creating attractive, easily recognizable symbols and associating them
with compelling values. Figure 5.1, below, shows an example from
the 1950s in which the Dole fruit company sought to align its emerging brand with Hawaii, which was not yet a US state, and the back-
yard barbeque as a popular US pastime.

Brands are an important kind of capital owned by corporations,
which is to say they are profit-making resources in themselves,
distinct from the physical, human, and financial capital needed
to produce and market a product. Brands can be bought and sold
just like any other asset. For example, since 1990 Green Giant has
accomplished all its vegetable growing and processing by establishing contracts with farms and packing companies around the world
(Lyson 2004: 50–2). It owns no farms, processing plants, or other
tangible assets. In 2001, Diageo, a UK-based food corporation, sold
Green Giant (along with the rest of the Pillsbury division) to General
Mills for US$10.4 billion (Lyson 2004: 52). What did General Mills
actually buy if they did not buy any physical property? They bought
a powerful money-making symbol, together with access to a network

Figure 5.1   Dole was among the first companies to heavily promote a brand for relatively unprocessed fruits and vegetables. This 1956 magazine ad shows Dole branding their pineapple as specifically Hawaiian at a time when Hawaiian music and imagery were popular in US society.

Source: NW Ayer Advertising Agency Records, Archives Center, National Museum of American History, Smithsonian Institution.yplate.gov/print-materials-ordering/graphic-resources.html

of people and organizations that can produce the packaged products appropriate to the brand.

Coca-Cola as a food icon

As we have already seen, some brands, items, and rituals in food have special symbolic import. Brands or food items that constitute especially powerful symbols of group identity are referred to as **food icon**s. Vegemite, discussed in chapter 2, is a good example, as is the donut, which, as Penfold (2008) explains, has become a symbol of Canadian national identity. Research shows that food icons often emerge within particular historical and cultural milieus, much as the US ritual of Thanksgiving as explained in chapter 2.

One of the most well-known global brands, Coca-Cola, illustrates the interlinked material and symbolic practices which turn brands into food icons. For many in the United States, Coke and its familiar red and white symbol evoke comfort, familiarity, and an enduring sense of US identity. Outside the US, however, Coke may inspire resentment rather than admiration. For example, in March 2009, Venezuelan President Hugo Chavez, a fiery critic of America's global political influence, threatened to take over the Coca-Cola distribution plant in Caracas, symbolically draping the building with red banners – not as the color of Coke, but as the color of revolution (Carroll 2009). For Chavez, asserting ownership of a Coca-Cola plant marked a symbolic victory over US imperialism. In contrast, Miller (1998b) explains that the US associations of Coca-Cola were seen in a mostly positive light in Trinidad, as Trinidad and Tobago sought and gained independence from Britain in the 1960s. In both cases, we see that Coke is a symbol closely aligned with US identity but also enveloped in more localized meanings and debates.

Coke did not become a symbol of the United States by accident. Mark Weiner (1996) explains how the Coca-Cola Company purposefully made Coke into a national icon during World War II. By the time the United States entered the war in 1941, Coca-Cola was already a popular drink closely associated with the drugstore soda fountain, a lively site of social interaction among youth. In wartime, however, the company sought to align the brand with the deepest core of American identity, using many of the same visual methods as wartime propaganda to associate symbols of daily life with national and civic values (Weiner 1996: 117). In 1943, the company released an advertising campaign replete with warm images of service men and women enjoying an ice-cold Coca-Cola while home on leave, interacting with admiring civilians, or during relaxed times abroad. The company also made and distributed pro-America propaganda films and products for children like "Know Your War Planes" booklets (Pendergrast 2000: 203). The advertising and corporate gestures encouraged all to see Coke as the single most evocative symbol of home, country, and simple pleasures, and as a fully indispensable part of the American way of life.

Another remarkable part of the campaign was the company's efforts to integrate Coke into the daily lives of soldiers. In addition to sponsoring recreational programs and distributing "Coca-Cola Game Kits," the Coca-Cola Company collaborated closely with the US War Department to try to get Coke into the hands of as many soldiers as possible. In addition to shipping more than five billion cases of Coke to the military, which was a major feat during a time of sugar rationing and materials shortages, Coca-Cola sent 148 employees to accompany the forces. These "technical observers," dressed in military uniforms, established sixty-three bottling plants in cities worldwide to ensure soldiers' access to the drink (Weiner 1996). The military hoped that the presence of a familiar beloved product would improve soldier morale. The company was promoting deep brand loyalty and "laying the foundation for Coke's postwar expansion" (Weiner 1996).

It worked. Not only did soldiers come to enjoy Coke as a comfort food (see chapter 1), but they also began to describe their sense of American identity in the "language of commodities." For example, Weiner (1996: 122) quotes one soldier's letter to his parents in which he writes, "I've met and talked with some of the greatest men in the world, *real men who have gone through Hell and come out again, but would go back for a cold Coca-Cola*" (emphasis in Weiner). Mark Pendergrast, another historian of Coca-Cola, sees the near-religious importance of Coke in the lives of soldiers as described in their letters home (2000: 206). Some examples:

> It's the little things, not the big, that the individual soldier fights for or wants so badly when away. It's the girlfriend back home in a drug store over a Coke, or the juke box and the summer weather.

> You will probably think your son has had his head exposed to the sun too long. But the other day, three of us guys walked ten miles to buy a case of Coca-Cola, then carried it back. You will never know how good it tasted.

> This week, Coca-Cola came to Italy. Seemingly everyone had heard the rumor, but no one put much faith in it. How could it be true? Coca-Cola is some vaguely familiar nectar, reminiscent of some far-off paradise land. Italy is a land of C-rations and Spam and dehydrated food.

For these soldiers, Coke is not just a cold, fizzy drink; it is emblematic of a way of life. What is the American way of life, according to Coca-Cola? Weiner (1996: 110) sees it as "a democratic vision of consumer abundance." This notion is reinforced by the product itself: an inexpensive and simple beverage, requiring neither an experienced palate nor a big budget to enjoy.

It was also during the World War II era that Coca-Cola became a symbol of America, not just in the hearts of US soldiers and their loved ones at home, but also in the eyes of people across the globe.

On the negative side, Nazi press chief Otto Dietrich dismissively declared in 1942 that "America never contributed anything to world civilization but chewing gum and Coca-Cola" (Pendergrast 2000: 208). In contrast, Mary Churchill, the daughter and aide-de-camp of British prime minister Winston Churchill, christened a new destroyer with a bottle of Coca-Cola rather than the traditional champagne (Pendergrast 2000: 207). In multiethnic Trinidad, where Coca-Cola arrived with US soldiers in 1939, it became part of the national drink (rum and Coke), as well as a complex process of defining Trinidadian national identity and ethnic identities within (Miller 1998b).

We noted earlier Holt's (2006) insight that, as companies succeed in making their brands an important symbol in the broader culture, they lose control of how that brand is used. The complexity of the branding process is especially evident in how, after World War II, Coca-Cola became an important visual symbol in the civil rights movement (Weiner 1996). If sitting at the counter of a soda fountain to enjoy a cold Coca-Cola is a quintessential American experience, seeing black patrons systematically excluded from that practice (during lunch-counter sit-ins) exploded the myth that blacks and whites lived "separate but equal" lives in America. In context, Coke was not just a beverage; it was a symbol of the American way of life that soldiers, including many black Americans, fought for in World War II. Using powerful shared symbols like these, civil rights activists conveyed to other Americans the malignant injustice of Jim Crow laws.

More than one million people tour the 92,000-square-foot World of Coca-Cola in Atlanta, Georgia every year to see artifacts and films celebrating the company as a historic and global "Happiness Factory." Some might find it odd that so many people readily devote their vacation time and money to experiencing what is essentially a 90-minute commercial for a soft drink, but the narrative presented here explains how the symbolism of Coke has a cultural life beyond its material substance and, as such, is an object of cultural politics. Now we turn to the role of supermarkets, another major institution of mass marketing, in shaping the mass consumption system in both material and symbolic ways.

The retail revolution

To succeed in creating a large and enduring demand for their brands, food manufacturers must make them widely available to buyers.

Supermarkets emerged not just to meet demand, but also to create it. When we examine supermarkets as social institutions, we can see that they are remarkable feats of technological and social engineering that have played an enormous role in shaping the food system, both for those with access to supermarkets and, as we explain in chapter 8, those without. Overall, supermarkets embody a paradoxical arrangement in which we deeply value unfettered consumer choice as an expression of democracy while actually assigning a central controlling role to a handful of large food corporations. On one level, individual shoppers perform the role of the sovereign consumer, choosing among tens of thousands of products arrayed for their perusal, many of which traveled more than 1,500 miles to get there (Lang and Heasman 2004: 237). At the same time, these sovereign consumers are "governed" by the carefully designed layouts of stores and other techniques that influence shoppers' emotional states and physical behaviors (Dulsrud and Jacobsen 2009). Far away from the store aisles, corporate decisions largely determine which items are available to shoppers and which consumers even have access to supermarkets.

For most of American history, buying food from stores involved approaching the counter with a list of items to purchase. Storekeepers or clerks would collect your items from the shelves behind them and either take your payment or note the value of your purchase as a credit obligation. Depending on the time and context, they may also purchase items from shoppers, such as eggs, furs, or needlecrafts. In this system, the buyer chooses what kind of items to purchase and in what quantities, but few products, beyond tobacco and patent medicines, had a distinct brand identity. This system continued, even when the Great Atlantic and Pacific Tea Company (A&P) had grown into the country's first major chain of stores, with more than 200 locations nationwide by the beginning of the twentieth century (Ellis 2006). The first A&P stores were all structured in that traditional format.

In 1916, Clarence Saunders, motivated by a desire to save money on labor costs, pioneered the self-service model in his Piggly Wiggly store in Memphis, Tennessee, which he also grandly called "the Pink Palace." In a patented design that Patel (2007: 221) has termed a "consumption factory," shoppers would enter through a turnstile and walk through aisles laid out to create a single possible path all the way to the cashier. Many observers thought the self-service store was an unrealistic idea. Skeptics predicted that shoppers would not like doing uncompensated work themselves and that storekeepers using the self-service model would soon regret letting shoppers handle their carefully displayed merchandise (Shaw, Curth, and Alexander 2004). Obviously, the naysayers were wrong. The self-service model spread throughout the United States, and not just in food stores. Other retailers and, increasingly, restaurants began recruiting customers to do some of the tasks formerly accomplished by paid clerks. Sociologist Nona Y. Glazer (1993) calls this shift from paid to unpaid labor "the work transfer," and notes that it has had complex effects on both working life and private life, especially for women, who increasingly performed the labor previously performed by store clerks. The work transferred to shoppers also negatively impacts people who lack the requisite strength, endurance, or mobility to perform this role (Webber, Sobal, and Dollahite 2007).

The shift toward the self-service model accelerated during the Great Depression of the 1930s when shoppers, more than ever, sought the cheapest food prices. Michael Cullen, the proprietor of the King Kullen line of supermarkets in the 1930s, was among the first to make low prices the center of his business model (Tedlow 1990: 226–7). In the postwar boom, which also brought rapid suburbanization, supermarkets spread even faster, accounting for 70 percent of food sales by 1960 (Konefal et al. 2007: 270). The self-service model also spread to Britain after World War II in a government-sponsored effort to "Americanize" food retailing as part of the US-sponsored Marshall Plan (Shaw, Curth, and Alexander 2004: 568). In 1950, supermarkets captured 20 percent of grocery sales in the United Kingdom; by 1990, they had captured 80 percent (Lawrence and Burch 2007: 3). In this postwar era, the expansive, gleaming, low-price supermarket came to symbolize the impressive and forward-looking productivity of the American economy, which was booming, thanks in part to Europe's need to rebuild after the ravages of war. Among the high-profile visitors to the United States who specifically requested a tour of a modern supermarket were Britain's Queen Elizabeth II and Soviet leader Nikita Khrushchev (Ellis 2006).

As the industry became more competitive, bringing with it a stronger downward pressure on prices, supermarkets became more oriented toward expanding the volume of sales. That way, even if the store made less money per item (a smaller profit margin), it could still make more money by selling more items in a given span of time. One early invention to encourage shoppers was the wheeled shopping cart, first introduced in 1937 by Sylvan Goldman who noticed shoppers in his Oklahoma City store struggling with full baskets (Tedlow 1990: 231). At first, shoppers proved enormously reluctant to use them. Women found the carts ugly and men found them too feminine. In response, Goldman hired models to walk around the store "shopping" with the carts. It worked. Shoppers began using the carts and, consequently, buying more food at each trip, further reinforcing the car-dependent nature of supermarket shopping.

The in-store experience itself is designed to shape shoppers' behavior. Dulsrud and Jacobsen (2009) argue that in-store marketing techniques are a form of "discipline," in that they structure the shopper's possible actions in both overt and subtle ways. To understand how, they recommend we focus on shoppers' bodies and how they move. They explain, "On the one hand, shoppers were expected to spend as much time as possible inside the shop so as to be tempted to buy more goods. On the other hand, there was a need to prevent customers from taking too much time so as to avoid congestion or purposeless rambling" (Dulsrud and Jacobsen 2009: 206). Strategic traffic flow designs were created to "pull the bodies of shoppers through the store" while "'speed humps' – such as selling trays, end caps, and striking visual signs and lighting – were introduced to prevent consumers from rushing" (Dulsrud and Jacobsen 2009: 207). Visually, many supermarkets first present shoppers with a colorful array of produce, in which old standbys like apples, oranges, potatoes, and carrots are flanked by exotics like mangos, carambolas, cassavas, and sometimes even woody stalks of sugar cane. Do shoppers actually buy enough sugar cane to warrant its presence? No, but studies have found that the lush experience of abundance that these exotics create increases sales of other more common products (Hitt 1996). Another speed hump is achieved by displaying cans of soup in non-alphabetical order; that has been shown to increase sales of soup by 6 percent (Hitt 1996).

The particular arrangement of products on each section of shelving encourages shoppers to select some products over others, reflecting decades of behavioral research. For example, westerners tend to scan shelves from left to right, and items that are 15 degrees below eye level are the most readily seen and have the highest "grab factor" (Dulsrud and Jacobsen 2009: 208). Shoppers have to exert more thought and effort to get non-featured products, perhaps stretching up or crouching down in ways that are more physically demanding and risk the uncomfortable exposure of one's body. Additionally, they may have to find and ask store workers in order to locate less-favored items (Dulsrud and Jacobsen 2009: 212). While retailers cannot directly control the choices shoppers make in their stores, research shows that they can do a lot to condition shoppers' behavior through shoppers' own bodily experience.

The presence (or absence) and location of items in the store also reflects larger forces conditioning individuals. For one, the wide array of brands one sees on the shelves obscures the huge corporate concentration in the food industry. Overall, the largest ten food-processing corporations account for 60 percent of the US food supply (Lyson 2004: 49). For example, the Kraft Heinz Company, borne of the 2015 merger between Kraft and Heinz, is the third-largest food company in the United States and fifth in the world. It owns more than 200 brands, including such well-known ones as Oscar Meyer, Velveeta, Kool-Aid, Maxwell House, Planters, Ore-Ida, and Classico (www.kraftheinzcompany.com). And this is after Kraft spun off its global snack-foods division with brands like Oreo, Tang, Cadbury, Ritz, and Toblerone to a new company called Mondelez, a made-up name invoking the words "delicious" and "world" in several Romance languages.

In addition to controlling many products, the most powerful food manufacturers are also able to secure the prime shelf locations in supermarkets by paying "slotting fees" to retailers. This practice is part of a **category management** system, in which retailers and manufacturers together decide on the array of competing products that will be offered to consumers within a given category, such as pasta sauces, crackers, or frozen fruit juice concentrate, in order to maximize the profit of each unit of shelf space (Dulsrud and Jacobsen 2009: 212). This system is often called "efficient consumer response" (Kahn and McAllister 1997) though, paradoxically, it leads to a narrowing of shoppers' choices. Smaller food manufacturers, unable to pay slotting fees or demand retailers' attention, risk being excluded from supermarkets, even if they offer high-quality products that have a high potential demand.

As they collaborate in marketing, retailers and manufacturers also compete to capture a larger portion of food spending. In the 1950s and 1960s, food manufacturers had the upper hand. TV advertising was enormously effective for creating consumer demand because many Americans had ample disposable income and the great majority were all watching the same few television channels. Food manufacturers could advertise low prices and force retailers to sell those products at a very thin margin or even at a loss. Supermarkets, most of which were independently owned, simply had to carry the most popular brands to stay in business because it was these brands that pulled people into the store (Kahn and McAllister 1997). However, television advertising has become much less effective in more recent decades, as the number of television channels and other media forms has proliferated in ways that enable many to avoid conventional television ads (Kahn and McAllister 1997). In addition, independent grocery stores have given way to a small number of concentrated retailers who have a much stronger position in negotiating prices with manufacturers (Lawrence and Burch 2007). Walmart, the biggest corporation in the world, is also the biggest global food retailer. It accounts for between one-fourth and one-third of food retail in the United States and over half of food sales in 29 grocery market areas (Food & Water Watch 2012). Walmart and the next three biggest chains together control about 40 percent of food retailing nationally, but over 60 percent in most market areas (Martens 2008). In most European countries, the four biggest supermarket chains control over 50 percent of grocery sales (Vorley 2007), and the five largest Canadian food retailers capture 80 percent of food sales there (Fernando 2013). In Australia, only two retailers account for 70 percent of grocery purchases (Davey and Richards 2013).

Retailers have also captured more economic power by developing and promoting **private label** or own-brand products; that is, store-specific brands produced in supply chains managed by the retailing company itself. These are distinct from generic products, which were not branded, because the retailers develop and manage these brands much like other manufacturers do, seeking to associate them with positive emotions like quality, fun, and warmth. Walmart, for example, has a few of its own brands, including one called Great Value, a name meant to convey a straightforward message of savings.

Relatedly, retailers also emphasize **meal solutions**, that is, foods that are mostly prepared on site, requiring little attention at home to be ready to eat. Researchers find private labels and meal solutions remarkable because they show that supermarkets are entering directly into production and distribution, exerting much more control over the supply chain than they used to (Lawrence and Burch 2007). In addition, as private labels gain more market share, they reinforce the emerging role of supermarkets as food and lifestyle authorities, presenting themselves to consumers as active, benevolent mentors for a healthy and enjoyable life (Dixon 2007). In short, retailers now have unprecedented influence over both the economic and cultural aspects of foodways in advanced capitalist societies.

If retailers are now deeply involved in developing and managing supply chains, where does that leave food manufacturers? They have responded to these new pressures with creative marketing modes, such as product placement in movies, shows, and video games, as well as niche-specific products, such as children's yogurt or organic pasta sauce. Some industry thinkers encourage manufacturers to embrace the fact that they do not control the meaning of their brands and to actively enlist consumers as partners in a process of "value co-creation" (Zwick, Bonsu, and Darmody 2008). This notion inspires programs like PBR's nontraditional campaign, as well as those that recruit consumers as unpaid **brand ambassador**s; that is, people who spread the message about a branded item among their friends and family and log their contacts on a company website. Coca-Cola, for example, distributed "Coke cards" to "teen influentials," that is, youth who are popular among their peers and shape the tastes of their peer group (Nestle 2007: 185). Brand ambassadors are often offered some kind of point-based reward for their work. However, according to an article in *AdWeek* celebrating the growth in this kind of grassroots marketing (Voight 2007), many participate just for the fun of having an influence on others and, perhaps, being the first in their social circles to know about trendy new products. This practice marks an intriguing, and perhaps troubling, new twist in ever-changing consumerist foodways.

Children and youth

Questions about power and control in consumer culture are more urgent when it comes to the impact of advertising, particularly food advertising, on children and youth. In recent decades, food companies have set their sights on young consumers for two reasons. First, children in North America have more spending power than they used to. In the United States, for example, children's spending quadrupled between 1989 and 2002 (Schor 2004: 23). Second, food companies hope to turn children into loyal consumers of their products by embedding company brands into children's everyday emotional lives during powerful periods of socialization. Research has shown that even young children tend to have strong brand preferences (Nestle 2007: 177). Teenagers, and increasingly their younger "tween" siblings, are focused on identity construction, and as such are more persuaded by advertising that promises enhanced social status. In terms of food, the research shows that when children and youth purchase food with their own money, they most typically buy sweets, salty snacks, soft drinks, and fast food (Nestle 2007: 178).

Some countries, like Norway and Greece, as well as some states and provinces, like Maine and Quebec, have put limits on advertising to children, but most countries, including the US, UK, and

Canada, have few restrictions. Critics of food-industry marketing practices, like the American Academy of Pediatrics (2006), point out that most children – especially those younger than eight – cannot easily distinguish advertising from other kinds of programming (American Psychological Association 2004). Food manufacturers, for their part, argue that food marketing to children serves a public good. Nestle (2007: 179) quotes one representative statement from the food industry: "Advertising to children . . . is nothing less than primary education in commercial life; the provision, in effect, of free and elementary instruction in social economics – a passport to street wisdom. Far from being further restricted, as many suggest, this education course should in fact be supported, encouraged and enlarged." Apart from the health impacts of junk food marketing, many decry what they see as the general commercialization of childhood – the process by which children are increasingly drawn into the world of brands and trends at ever younger ages (Schor 2004).

Others are more sanguine, arguing that children and youth are more than capable of viewing marketing with a critical lens and balancing consumerist desire with other, more practical considerations. For example, anthropologist Elizabeth Chin (2001) studies low-income black children in the United States, a group often stereotyped as being excessively focused on status-seeking consumption, and finds their purchasing behavior to be largely pragmatic and often generous toward others. In addition, studies have shown that children can be educated to eat more fruits and vegetables (Knai et al. 2006) and that most kids understand the biased and persuasive nature of commercials by the time they are seven years old (John 1999). Consumer advocates have found it difficult to convince the US federal government to eliminate or sharply limit advertising aimed at kids, so some have turned to emphasizing media literacy education for children and their parents, raising further interesting questions about the nature of advertising and the extent to which individuals can effectively resist its messages.

Conclusion: manipulated or empowered?

Looking closely at marketing and branding reveals that neither corporations nor individuals exercise ultimate control over the success of advertised products or the meanings that brands take on in different social contexts. Individual consumers make their own choices, but they make them in an environment that reflects vast inequities in economic and cultural power. To claim that food manufacturers and retailers simply give consumers what they demand is to ignore all the obvious and subtle ways that these companies seek to create and direct consumer desires. As we have explained here, the branding process vividly illustrates the complex and dynamic interaction among individual consumers, the culture they participate in, and food corporations. Rob Walker (2008: xiii), informed by the case of Pabst Blue Ribbon, surmises that branding is the "dialog between consumer and consumed." Supermarkets, too, illustrate the paradoxical challenge that retailers face in giving shoppers an experience of consumer sovereignty while influencing their behavior to maximize profits. The questions that these complex processes raise cease to be simply academic when we consider their real or potential impact on children, a group of people generally considered in need of protection.

The next two chapters take this line of inquiry further back in the food system to examine the conditions of production and distribution that enable many of us to meet our food needs through an increasingly globalized mass consumption system. In doing so, it raises further questions about the idea of consumer choice: what do we choose when we choose what to eat? As this and the foregoing chapters make clear, food provides much more than a bundle of nutrients. We have seen how food also provides symbolic and emotional resources and the social experiences that ramify them. Forthcoming chapters also explore how food choices connect to the broader social and environmental impacts of the food system. Like the foods it produces, the modern industrialized food system delivers much more than calories and vitamins; it also delivers working conditions, environmental outcomes, economic forces, and structural influences on our everyday lives, raising interesting questions about the ability and responsibility of consumers to take those impacts into account.

Further reading

Dixon, Jane. 2007. "Supermarkets as New Food Authorities," in David Burch and Geoffrey Lawrence (eds), *Supermarkets and Agri-food Supply Chains: Transformations in the Production and Consumption of Foods.* Cheltenham: Edward Elgar, pp. 29–50. Dixon reviews direct and indirect ways that supermarkets seek to forge connections with their customers and position themselves as trustworthy authorities on food, health, and lifestyle.

Elliott, Charlene. 2011. "It's Junk Food and Chicken Nuggets": Children's Perspectives on 'Kids' Food' and the Question of Food Classification. *Journal of Consumer Behaviour* 10: 133–40. Elliott reports on focus groups with children to reveal how marketing has impacted how children classify some foods as kids' food, beyond particular brands or products.

Matejowsky, Ty. 2007. "SPAM and Fast-food 'Glocalization' in the Philippines." *Food, Culture and Society* 10(1): 23–41. Matejowsky offers a brief history of SPAM as an American-associated product and how it is employed and promoted within Philippine foodways in a simultaneously global and local (that is, "glocal") process. In this way, it makes an interesting comparison to Coca-Cola.

Miller, Daniel. 1998. *A Theory of Shopping*, 1st edn. Ithaca, NY: Cornell University Press. Miller provides a close ethnography of supermarket shopping in North London. The first chapter, "Making Love in Supermarkets," challenges the image of shopping as an individualized activity by emphasizing the ways shopping behavior enacts treasured social relationships.

O'Connor, Kaori. 2008. The Hawaiian Luau: Food as Tradition, Transgression, Transformation, and Travel. *Food, Culture and Society* 11(2): 149–72. With an expansive historical perspective, O'Connor explains the changing political context of the Hawaiian luau, including the now expected tourist experience that is part of Hawaii's brand. Together with the image in Figure 5.1, it raises interesting questions about the power in branding.

Further exploration

1 FOR DISCUSSION: What emotions, values, and messages do you see conveyed in the Dole advertisement shown in Figure 5.1? Given what you know about the United States in the 1950s, why would Dole brand its pineapple as specifically Hawaiian? How does O'Connor's (2008) historical analysis of the luau influence one's perception of that ad?

2 OBSERVATION: Visit a supermarket and pay close attention to the imagery, sensations, and messages presented to you. In what ways does the environment seek to influence your bodily experience and behavior? To what extent does this store present itself as an authority on living an enjoyable and healthy life?

3 ONLINE: Go to the "heritage" section of the website of the Coca-Cola Company (http://www.coca-colacompany.com/history), as well as the website of the World of Coca-Cola (www.worldofcoca-cola.com), and examine how the company tells the "story" of its brand. To what extent does it still emphasize Coke's association with American identity? To what extent does the company promote its association with the civil rights movement?

4 ONLINE: Choose a breakfast cereal marketed to kids (such as Froot Loops, Cap'n Crunch, or Frosted Flakes) and find its website. How do they seek to draw kids in? How do they present nutritional information? How do they seem to be responding to criticisms of their product and advertising practice?

6
Industrialization:
The High Costs of Cheap Food

Case study

In 2013, the US Centers for Disease Control and Prevention (CDC) published a startling report that confirmed what many scientists have been saying for years: the routine use of antibiotics in animal agriculture has accelerated the evolution of antibiotic-resistant pathogens that pose a significant threat to human health. The CDC estimates that two million Americans are sickened with resistant bacteria or fungi every year, and about 23 thousand die (CDC 2013: 13). Drug-resistant bacteria, fungi, and parasites are emerging in all world regions, which is especially worrisome, the World Health Organization points out, because no major new types of antimicrobial medicines have been discovered and developed in the last 30 years (World Health Organization 2014).

Antibiotic resistance occurs through a simple process, as illustrated in Figure 6.1 below. Whenever a person or animal is given antibiotics, it wipes out some (hopefully almost all) of the pathogens, leaving behind a few individuals that happen to be resistant to the medicine. Those resistant microbes may proliferate in the new, less competitive environment and then spread to new people or animals. With sufficient repetition, the resistant bacteria can outcompete the non-resistant bacteria. When a person or animal gets infected with resistant bacteria, conventional antibiotics won't make any difference. As the CDC explains "Simply using antibiotics creates resistance" (2013: 14), and they should be thought of as a "limited resource" that must be used responsibly according to principles of "antibiotic stewardship" (2013: 41).

A more complicated question is why the problem of antibiotic resistance is rapidly worsening. One issue, the CDC finds, is that "up to 50%

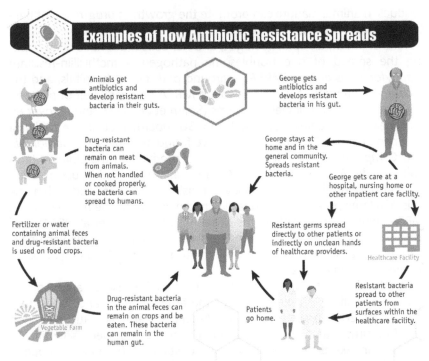

Figure 6.1 As this graphic from the US Centers for Disease Control and Prevention (CDC) explains, "Simply using antibiotics creates resistance." This image from their 2013 report illustrates how populations of antibiotic-resistant bacteria grow in human and animal hosts.

Source: The US Centers for Disease Control. Retrieved March 17, 2016 from http://www.cdc.gov/media/dpk/2013/images/untreatable/img2.jpg

of all the antibiotics prescribed for people are not needed or are not optimally effective as prescribed" (2013: 11). However, in the United States and worldwide, more antibiotics are given to animals than to people (World Health Organization 2014). They're sometimes used to treat animals that are sick, but most are given routinely to animals in food and water to prevent diseases amid crowded conditions and to encourage food animals to grow larger faster with less feed. A 2013 report by the United States' Food and Drug Administration (FDA) notes "from 2009 through 2013, domestic sales and distribution of medically important antimicrobials approved for use in food-producing animals increased by 20%" (19). Since then, additional studies have found that antibiotic residues in animal manure can promote the growth of drug-resistant bacteria in soils (Forsberg et al. 2012).

Tara C. Smith, an epidemiologist, and her colleagues have been tracking the spread of one troublesome pathogen – methicillin-resistant *Staphylococcus aureus* (MRSA) – around pork farms, hospitals, and the broader community in Iowa. She found MRSA on nearly half of pigs and pig farmers in two Midwestern farms (Smith et al. 2009) and on over 65 percent of pork samples collected from 36 supermarkets in the Midwest (O'Brien et al. 2012). Other studies have found drug-resistant *Salmonella* and *Campylobacter* in supermarket meat products in the United States and Canada (Agunos et al. 2014; Glenn et al. 2013). Colleagues of Smith have also found that patients in a veterans' hospital who lived within one mile of a large pork production facility had nearly triple the risk of carrying MRSA than other patients in the same hospital (Carrel et al. 2014), and people working on Iowa pig farms are six times more likely than an unexposed comparison group to carry the multi-drug resistant *Staphylococcus aureus* (Wardyn et al. 2015).

The food industry questions the claim that the use of antibiotics in animal agriculture is a key driver of the antibiotic-resistance crisis. In a September 2015 press release, the American Farm Bureau Federation (AFBF) claims that "antibiotic use in animals has not been scientifically linked to increases in human antibiotic resistance." The Bureau supports the voluntary initiative led by the US Food and Drug Administration (FDA) to phase out the use of antibiotics as growth-promoters but opposes any firm restrictions on their use. They prefer that the FDA, the US Department of Agriculture (USDA), CDC and other regulatory agencies focus on monitoring antibiotic resistance and food-borne illnesses and also promoting food safety measures and safe handling in homes and commercial kitchens. According to the AFBF's September 2015 press release, "Bacteria survival through food processing/handling is decreasing," and "food-borne illness is down."

Critics of industrial agriculture see the problem of antibiotic resistance as yet another sign of a fundamentally flawed food system enabled by inadequate regulation. "It's FDA's job to protect our food, our health, and our families," writes the Natural Resources Defense Council. "But all the agency has been willing to do is recommend that drug manufacturers and the meat industry voluntarily give up only some of their problematic antibiotics uses. Its voluntary guidelines are full of loopholes and leave action up to the industry" (http://www.nrdc.org/food/saving-antibiotics). Concerns about antibiotics have prompted some consumers to seek out organically produced meats because organic certification in the United States does not permit antibiotic use (Diaz-Sanchez et al. 2015).

The issue of antibiotic resistance and the ensuing debate raise important questions. How did the modern food system contribute to this frightening situation? Is antibiotic resistance a price we must pay for large-scale meat production? Does industrial food, in general, require that kind of trade off?

Introduction: the industrial food system

For nutritionists, food is a bundle of nutrients and energy. For food scientists, it is an arrangement of chemical properties. For economists, it is a commodity whose price is determined by supply and demand. For sociologists like Howard Becker (1998: 46), however, food, like any other thing, is "people acting together." Becker's insight is especially useful when we consider the industrialization of the food system, the focus of this chapter. We have already explored how people act together to establish and re-enact enduring patterns of procuring, preparing, and consuming food, all the while imbuing those processes with symbolic meaning. This chapter shifts our focus further up the chain to how those foods are produced, processed, transported, and marketed. Here, the notion of the food system – the vast set of interlinked institutions and processes that transform sunlight, water, and soil into the meaning-laden foods we find in front of us – provides an especially useful perspective because it draws our attention to the production and distribution of food, further removed from the consumption experience.

The food system is not designed and controlled by any one person or organization but instead is produced and continually reproduced through the interacting decisions of policy makers, producers, shoppers, and eaters. It is these interdependent elements that make it a "system," with its own complex and dynamic kind of unity. The American hamburger, for example, as both a material and symbolic object, is produced by tightly connected institutions and processes, including agricultural subsidies that promote the overproduction of feed grains and cheaper beef production (Fields 2004), a car-based settlement pattern that fosters ubiquitous fast-food restaurants (Dixon et al. 2007), and a petroleum-dependent economy that supports both industrial agriculture and suburbanization (Lang 2010a). Culturally, the common image of the hamburger as innocent, tasty fun interacts with these and other forces in making the burger emblematic of the food system that currently dominates in the United States and other wealthy countries of the global North.

The dominant food system is often characterized as industrial: that is, it emphasizes modern technologies to produce huge quantities of food sold at a relatively cheap cost. Proponents of the industrial food system, such as the American Farm Bureau Federation, are fond of saying that America has the cheapest, most abundant, and safest food supply in the world. It is true that, for most Americans, food is not a large expense. Americans now spend about 9.4 percent of their disposable personal incomes on food, and two-fifths of that is for snacks and meals away from home (US Department of Agriculture Economic Research Service 2011a). Comparatively, households in EU-member countries spend on average 15 percent of their income on food (Eurostat 2011), and, for the poorest in the world, food takes up more than half of their income: for example, 57 percent in Azerbaijan, 68 percent in Chad, and 71 percent in Cambodia (Food and Agriculture Organization 2011). Remarkably, the poorest Americans are now more likely to be overweight than underweight (see chapter 4).

It is also true that the American food supply is, on the whole, abundant. American farmers now produce 3,900 food calories per person per day in the United States (US Department of Agriculture Economic Research Service 2011b). That's nearly twice as many calories as most individuals need. And output is increasing even as the number of farms has been steadily dropping for decades. One US farmer produces enough calories to feed 155 people, compared to only 19 people in 1940 (American Farm Bureau Federation 2009). US agriculture currently produces 61 pounds of beef per person each year (down from a peak of 94 pounds in 1976), or the equivalent of 243 quarter-pound hamburgers for every man, woman, and child (US Department of Agriculture Economic Research Service 2011b). However, as the case of antibiotic resistance illustrates, there are costs associated with the industrial food system that are not captured in the shelf price. This chapter explores the food system's contradictory outcomes and the questions they raise.

How did the dominant industrial food system come to be? Here, it is helpful to introduce two linked concepts that reveal its key features. First, the policies and practices that shape the industrial food system reflect **productivism**: an ideology promoting ever-increasing output and efficiency with the assumption that it ultimately benefits everyone (Lang and Heasman 2004). Second, the system depends on **commodification**; that is, the process of shaping products to be interchangeable mass-produced goods that take their value from the prices they fetch on the market. Overall, the industrial food system reflects deeply held, though increasingly contested, assumptions about the most just and efficient ways to accomplish food production and distribution.

The next part of the chapter illustrates the industrialization of the food system with the fascinating case of fluid milk. Next, we review some of the major criticisms of the conventional industrial food system, highlighting the negative social and environmental impacts. Finally, we explore ongoing debates about how to respond to these problems: new, higher-tech solutions or a radically different paradigm? This chapter focuses on the United States, where many of these industrial practices originated. Chapter 7 examines the industrialization of food in its global context.

The industrialization of milk

Over the last few millennia, some human societies forged a close partnership with ruminant animals; humans provided protection and assistance with foraging, and animals, in exchange, converted cellulose-heavy grasses (which humans cannot eat) into useful products like meat, milk, traction, manure, fiber, skins, and companionship. Milk played an important symbolic role, and sometimes a nutritive one, in some societies of biblical-era Eurasia, including Egypt, India, Greece, and Mesopotamia, providing a compact source of scarce fat and protein, as well as a rich symbol of creation and femininity (Valenze 2011). Still, fluid milk consumption was sharply limited because milk is highly perishable, difficult for many adults to digest and, in many societies, associated with infancy and early childhood (Valenze 2011). In the current age, we tend to see milk drinking as the modern adaptation of an ancient practice and one particularly authentic to Euro-American traditional foodways (DuPuis 2002: 4). Many are surprised to learn that the idea of milk as a healthful beverage for everyone originated in the modern era. The construction of a modern milk industry illustrates the conjoined imperatives of productivism and commodification.

Looking at conditions in the mid-1800s, it seemed unlikely that milk would become a major staple food. Sociologist E. Melanie DuPuis (2002) sets the scene: cities were growing rapidly, and accelerating immigration raised questions about the meaning of national identity in a young nation. Meanwhile, a remarkable surge of religious fervor, known as the Second Great Awakening inspired organized efforts to improve and modernize American society through movements like temperance, abolition, and urban reform. Before this time, urban Americans consumed relatively little milk, less than six ounces (two-thirds of a cup) per person per day, and that was usually in coffee, tea, or baked goods (Freidberg 2009). Farm families with dairy animals incorporated fresh milk into beverages and dishes more often, but generally turned raw milk into longer-lasting products like cheese and butter (Valenze 2011). As a beverage, fresh milk was almost exclusively for infants and very young children (DuPuis 2002).

Even more surprising is that much of the fresh milk that nineteenth-century city-dwellers drank in the densely settled north-eastern United States was from within the city itself. Geographer Susanne Freidberg (2009: 203) explains that "until the 1870s, much of [New York City's] milk came from 'swill dairies,' where cows lived off the slurry waste of adjacent distilleries and breweries." In addition, it was not unusual for landless urban families in the nineteenth century to own a dairy cow that was fed and milked right outside the back door and left to wander the environs between milkings (Freidberg 2009: 202). Urban consumers often bought milk from corner stores or early-morning peddlers, bringing their own containers to be filled (Freidberg 2009: 203). Predictably, in this era before reliable refrigeration or pasteurization, the milk was frequently contaminated at the source and made worse through handling (Block 2005). In fact, physicians warned against drinking fresh cow's milk, drawing on several studies that confirmed that babies fed cow's milk were much more likely to die from diarrhea than breast-fed babies (DuPuis 2002). Conditions for babies were already challenging enough. In the 1840s, babies born in New York City had only a 50 percent chance of surviving until age five (DuPuis 2002). Nevertheless, breast-feeding had become an infrequent practice, as poorer women had to return to work as quickly as possible and wealthier women subscribed to Victorian ideals of feminine vulnerability and norms of propriety that discouraged nursing (Freidberg 2009).

DuPuis explains (2002) that, despite this unpromising situation, fresh fluid milk came to be seen as an indispensable food for physical, social, and moral integrity. One of the first proponents was religious and social reformer Robert Hartley, who argued in the 1840s that New York City must have a reliable supply of fresh country milk for its social and moral betterment; his argument was well received. Hartley argued that fresh cow's milk was nutritionally complete and that drinking it was a biblically sanctioned, universal human practice. Historians now know that he was wrong on both counts: few people outside of northern Europe or the Sahara ever drank milk, and the "milk" mentioned in the Bible was actually cultured products like yogurt. But Hartley's idea took hold, in large part because most urban reformers were also part of the temperance movement. Milk was a healthful and moral alternative to alcoholic beverages like ales and ciders which most men, women, and children consumed every day (DuPuis 2002). In an era also obsessed with hygiene, several popular movements demanded a highly regulated milk industry in order to assure a safe, consistent, affordable supply. This was an ambitious goal in pursuit of a perfect society (Atkins 2010; Valenze 2011).

The means chosen for creating a modern urban milk supply reflected notions of purity drawn from the religiously informed movements of the time (Block 2005; DuPuis 2002). Between 1860 and 1900, major cities in the northeast United States banned swill dairies, and New York instituted a city-managed licensing and inspection system, staffed by veterinarians and other scientists, to bring country milk into the city by rail. To assure consumers little inclined to trust milk from such distant sources (Freidberg 2009: 204), company advertising gradually used more images of uniformed men milking cows in a modern-looking facility and fewer of winsome barefoot milkmaids in dreamy pastoral settings (Block 2005; DuPuis 2002). While ice-cooled railroad cars helped protect country milk, what finally made it safer was a higher-tech solution: pasteurization. Freidberg (2009: 217) explains that, despite misgivings about the safety or nutritional value of pasteurized milk, "by the mid-1920s, about 75 percent of New England's milk supply was pasteurized." Through this era, milk, once a feminine pastoral product, became a modern commodity controlled by science and planning, realms associated with masculinity (Block 2005).

Just as urban milk policies rejected imagined traditions in favor of modern technologies, dairy farmers in the countryside were encouraged to make their farms into milk factories, producing milk (and only milk) year round with ever-increasing production. As railroads threaded their way through the northeast United States in the late nineteenth century, small-town creameries producing cheese and butter opened in the countryside, which encouraged farm families to focus on selling more milk rather than processing it at home (Freidberg 2009: 207). Meanwhile, the same rail systems carrying milk were bringing in huge quantities of grains, pork, and wool from the Great West, making those traditional products less lucrative for New England farmers (Freidberg 2009: 205).

As dairy farmers faced these growing constraints on diversified agriculture, they also found inducements to focus on industrializing milk production. Researchers at state universities found ways to increase production through selective breeding and high-protein diets provided in confined conditions, rather than on pasture. Gains in production accelerated over the course of the twentieth century. In 1926, the average dairy cow in the United States gave a little less than 5,000 pounds of milk per year; by 2009, the average cow was giving almost 21,000 pounds, more than four times the 1926 figure (National Agricultural Statistics Service 2009). Some individual cows can produce an astonishing 70,000 pounds each year (Fyksen 2006), which is more than forty times the body weight of a typical lactating cow. University Extension services in all states were charged with bringing university-developed technologies to farmers and encouraging their adoption, along with a productivist mindset. Industrial agricultural technologies were presented as not just opportune, but wholly necessary.

As DuPuis (2002) explains, the productivist vision driving the industrialization of dairy farming was especially apparent in government efforts to transform the landscape itself. In the late nineteenth and early twentieth centuries, before the high point of industrialization, dairy farms were divided into two distinct groups. Dairy farms close to railroads and cities were "intensive producers," using high-protein feeds to ensure year-round milk production for fluid milk markets, with more cows in total and more cows per acre. Dairy farms in more remote areas, and especially those on hills, were "extensive producers," relying more on pasture to feed their cows and often milking only in the spring and summer, bringing their milk to the local cheese plant. Production levels were lower per acre in these "summer hill dairies," but so were costs, enough so that they were consistently profitable (DuPuis 2002: 148). However, policy makers still saw them as unproductive, marginal, and even a "social pathology" (DuPuis 2002: 191). New York State, among others, set out to dismantle the summer hill dairy system by offering to buy hill farms with one hand and denying hill-farm families electrical service and other amenities with the other. Hill-farm families moved into the valleys and their former farmlands became state and national forests. What's important about this story is that the summer hill dairy system did not succumb to abstract economic forces like many people assume; rather, it was deliberately undone according to a productivist ideology.

The industrialization of milk also entailed creating quality grades and pricing systems to create orderly regional markets and a predictable, standardized product. What Freidberg (2009: 218) calls "the mind-numbing details of federal milk-market policies" show that commodification is a social achievement rather than a spontaneous economic process. Milk, like any product of nature, varies in quantity and quality from month to month and from place to place. Cows tend to produce significantly more milk in the spring and summer; without market controls, the milk market would vacillate between summer gluts and winter shortages, making pricing wildly unstable. Economists call a situation like that a "disorderly market" (DuPuis 2002: 172). In the first decades of the twentieth century, a constellation of city-managed permit systems and dairy cooperatives, together with geographic patterns, controlled which farmers could sell fluid milk and which could only sell to cheese plants. However, as trucks replaced rail, the barrier between the two markets broke down and they ceased to function well during the Great Depression (Freidberg 2009). In response, the federal government created strict milk-marketing orders to serve specified urban markets. Farmers who belonged to a milk-marketing order benefited from a consistently higher price, which fomented troublesome conflicts between members and non-members for several decades (DuPuis 2002).

The complex government regulations needed to turn milk into a predictable, orderly commodity were matched by an equally involved set of price supports needed to keep the system functioning. For decades now, the US federal government has paid subsidies directly to farmers and has also propped up the market by buying excess milk, encouraging exports, and, at times, buying and retiring dairy herds to shrink supply. Surplus milk is turned into powdered milk for export, as well as the famed "government cheese" of comedic lore, which, as we explore in chapter 8, is then distributed through nutritional assistance programs, school lunches, and overseas food aid. Currently, milk production per cow continues to rise, but demand for milk is slowly dropping off as "cholesterol-conscious, cola-drinking consumers" continually reduce their consumption (Freidberg 2009: 225), adding economic pressure to the industry and its public supports.

The regional structure of the US milk market and the image of milk as a fresh product lead many to underestimate just how industrial fluid milk really is. Fluid milk in the supermarket may look like the substance that comes from the cow, but it has been highly processed: separated into components, reassembled into standardized products, shaken until the fat no longer separates (homogenized), and then cooked at a high temperature (pasteurized). The final product is as consistent and predictable as a fast-food hamburger. The thicket of government regulations and support programs have maintained surprisingly strong regional links between the production and consumption of milk; however, those who want to purchase unprocessed milk directly from dairy farms often have a difficult time doing so due to these strict regulations (Freidberg 2009). Consequently, even though mainstream milk drinkers may be geographically proximate to their sources, they are still socially distant.

The story of modern milk illustrates that the dominant, industrial food system was not created by immutable economic laws. Rather, "people acting together," in Becker's sense, as individuals and institutions, created both the cultural value placed on fluid milk as a wholesome beverage and an industry structured according to productivist values and commodified processes. Few modern consumers know that, when the drive to create a milk market began, milk was a recognized danger to health, disruptively perishable, stubbornly seasonal, promoting both economic instability and political upheaval. It is remarkable that by 1940 people in the United States were drinking, on average, a pint per day (DuPuis 2002: 6), embracing their role as eaters within the emerging industrialized food system and accepting the image of milk as an indispensable source of nutrition, especially for children (Wiley 2011). The practice of milk drinking has spread globally, with particularly notable spikes in India and China, two large countries engaged in vigorous modernization programs (Wiley 2011). To be an industrial eater, one must place one's trust in particular technologies and the governments and corporations that wield them to produce a specifically defined kind of quality.

The industrial food system has benefits and costs that are distributed unequally among different social groups. Critical analysts argue that these inequalities are not simply by-products of industrialization; rather, they are fundamental to the system as a whole. Unsurprisingly, they do not go uncontested, as we illustrate in the following survey of some major social and environmental costs of industrial food.

Social costs

Sociologist C. Wright Mills (1958: 8) famously described the sociological imagination as the ability to understand the connections between "personal troubles" and "public issues," that is, the connections between individual experiences and the broader social forces that produce them. Increasingly, critics fault the industrial food system for problems like farm failures, water shortages, pesticide exposures, food-borne pathogen outbreaks, and overnutrition (see chapter 4) and encourage us to view the industrial food system in a more holistic way. As agricultural economist Jules Pretty (2002: 281–2) explains, "we actually pay three times for our food – once at the till in the shop, a second time through taxes that are used to subsidize farmers or support agricultural development, and a third time to clean up the environmental and health side effects." When food system critics look at industrial food, they see beyond the shelf price to assess hidden costs, such as the depletion of aquifers, the objectionable treatment of animals, the health and safety risks faced by farmers and food system workers, and the poor health status of some industrial eaters.

Returning to the example of milk, we see that many social costs of the industrial food system are borne by farming people themselves and that their private troubles reveal a pattern and, hence, an important public issue. One troublesome pattern is the **technology treadmill**, in which falling unit prices force farmers to adopt costly new technologies to garner higher yields and, they hope, equal or greater income. However, even when farmers successfully increase production, the new oversupply pushes prices down, further erasing potential gains. Farmers are left with a higher debt load and a stagnant or reduced income. This process was identified in the 1950s (Cochrane 1958) but, in the ensuing decades, the US government, public universities, and corporations have continued to develop and promote high-yielding genetics, high-production feeds, and more mechanized systems, ignoring both the falling consumption of milk in the United States and the treadmill pattern in general. These burdens became unsustainable in the 1970s and 1980s when the sudden onset of high inflation caught heavily indebted farmers in a bind. While the decline of farming has been ongoing throughout the twentieth century and beyond, the decades of the 1970s and 1980s came to be publicly defined as the farm crisis, inspiring high-profile benefit concerts and documentary television specials but, unfortunately, little change in public policy.

Research shows that by the time a dairy farm fails, the farm family is often deeply in debt and understandably demoralized. Anthropologist Janet Fitchen (1991) studied the personal and community impact of the farm crisis in dairy-dependent communities and found that, in the face of chronic financial straits, affected families tended to isolate themselves from one another. In this way, the chronic farm crisis differed enormously from a temporary crisis, such as a barn fire or transient illness, which tends to draw neighbors together to help out until things return to normal (Fitchen 1991). Fitchen (1991) also found that, as more and more farms faced failure, the organizations and institutions that upheld community life in dairy regions, like the Grange, 4-H, the Farm Bureau, and cooperatives, found it hard to recruit sufficient participants. Many of Fitchen's research participants recounted that the personal cost of dairy-farm failure hits its peak on the day the cows leave the farm. Without the rituals of milking and tending the herd, men and women experienced an intense **role loss**: a painful readjustment of one's personal identity due to the disappearance of an important social role. Some argue that these shifts, though painful, simply reflect the necessary march of progress. However, it is also clear that incentivizing farmers to produce more and more milk in the face of stagnant or falling demand contributed directly to the slow-rolling disaster in US dairy farming.

The dairy industry of New Zealand shows an alternative path. New Zealand farmers focused on using pastures to feed cows rather than adopting the US model of confining cows to barns to eat pre-mixed, grain-based feed. In New Zealand-style rotational grazing systems, the herd grazes on a fenced-off section of pasture for a couple of days before moving to fresh grass in the next small section. By the time the cows come back to the first section, it has completely recovered. Rotational grazing requires close management but entails much less expense for machinery and fuel, fewer visits from veterinarians, and sharply reduced risks of soil erosion (Logsdon 2004). New Zealand farmers have received fewer subsidies than their American counterparts and face similarly low prices for their milk, but they enjoy a more stable income level due to lower costs of production (Harris and Kolver 2001). Beginning in the 1990s, more and more dairy farmers in the United States and elsewhere have looked to New Zealand-style grazing as a way to cut costs, improve cow health, and escape the technology treadmill. Contemporary graziers have developed and adopted new technologies like improved portable fencing and watering mechanisms, but, these technologies tend to accommodate, rather than obliterate, the unique variations of each farm and the herd therein (Hassanein 1999; Lyon et al. 2011).

The ideological nature of productivism is especially apparent to those who choose a different direction. Social research has shown that the initial adopters of rotational grazing have borne a social cost, as their neighbors, friends, and relatives found their rejection of productivist approaches utterly inconceivable. Marked as "dairy heretics," they formed organizations and networks both to share information and to collectively cope with the stigma of deviating from such strongly held social norms (Hassanein 1999: 114–15). More recently, grazing has become a more legitimated choice, but, as we explain in chapter 9, moving from conventional to alternative practices entails a challenging shift in identity.

Just as modernism and productivism held out an image of a proper, modern farm, they also held out a standard image of the farmer as a white male owner-operator, marginalizing many others engaged in agriculture. Gender issues are explored in chapter 9; here, we explain how racial discrimination plays a pervasive role in shaping the industrial food system. In the 1930s, the federal agencies that were resettling northeastern hill farmers into valleys were, at the same time, "modernizing" agriculture in the south by purchasing large farms that rented parcels to sharecroppers, evicting these renting farmers (disproportionately black) from those lands and then selling the best parcels to farmers who were disproportionately white. As in the later farm crisis, these interventions often destroyed thriving communities. Adams and Gorton (2009: 330–1) describe one such case: the 10,000-acre Transylvania Plantation, a tenant-farming community of mostly freed slaves "in which residents forged strong networks based on kinship, economic and social exchanges, fraternal organizations, churches, cemeteries, a Rosenwald school, and shared work on the plantation." The Farm Security Administration (FSA), arguing that farming on rented land was a kind of social pathology (similar to summer hill dairies), purchased the property from its corporate owner in 1938, removed about 250 farming families, and sold parcels to landless whites, all despite vigorous protest. The families displaced from Transylvania Plantation were to be resettled on other lands, but the move was poorly planned, and the community, sadly, dispersed. While the FSA justified its actions by focusing on ownership status, racism clearly permeated the process. Only white men could play the role of the modern farmer in the popular imagination.

Black farmers who succeeded in purchasing their own land still did not escape racist policies. In 2000, a class-action group of thousands of black farmers won a landmark settlement with the USDA for several decades of discrimination against black farmers who were offered less favorable terms on loans and more often foreclosed upon. While the number of farmers in all groups shrank through the twentieth century, the decline in black farmers was especially steep. In 1920, there were more than a million black farmers; by the time the lawsuit succeeded, there were fewer than 18,000 (Parker 2000).

The legal victory has only been partial; in 2008, eight years after the ruling, the Government Accounting Office accused the USDA of mishandling the process of settling claims, unnecessarily delaying payouts as more and more black farmers face bankruptcy (Fears 2008). Meanwhile, while about 13,000 black farmers received some compensation from the original lawsuit, an additional 70,000 people, who attorneys failed to reach, sought to make a claim after the first deadline in 2000. In December 2010, the Claims Resolution Act funded the US$1.15 billion settlement of this larger group of black farmers nationwide. Overall, most awards were very modest, with few more than US$50,000, which hardly compensates for the loss of landed wealth and a whole livelihood. Nevertheless, the black farmers' campaign has encouraged other groups, including Hispanic, Native American, Asian American, and women farmers, to seek redress for discriminatory practices as well.

Relatedly, an even larger group of people doing critically important work in agriculture are denied the admiring title of "farmer" and kept socially and politically marginalized as a poorly paid labor force. Industrialized agriculture depends on low-paid seasonal labor to be profitable because labor-intensive crops like fruits and vegetables are grown in specialized single-crop systems rather than on mixed farms. Thus, a farm growing thousands of acres of strawberries, for example, needs a huge work crew at harvest-time, but only a small crew at other times of the growing year. In California, which produces more than half of all the fruits, vegetables, and nuts grown in the States, large growers have always relied on contractors to bring work crews for these critical periods. As early as 1850, large American growers were employing farmworkers from China, Japan, and Mexico, as well as European immigrants and low-income whites and free blacks (National Center for Farmworker Health 2010). Until 1952, immigrants of color could not become citizens, which limited the ability of this large immigrant population to establish themselves economically and accumulate wealth, perhaps becoming farm owners themselves. White immigrants, in contrast, could aspire to that path.

Throughout the twentieth century, laws specifically maintained the marginalized status of the farmworker population. In 1917, the US federal government established a legal basis for bringing in migrant workers from Mexico on a temporary basis. Later, with the economic downturn of the 1930s, hundreds of thousands of Mexican workers were rapidly deported, enabling dust-bowl refugees to take their place on California farms. After the economy recovered, the 1943 Bracero Agreement between the US and Mexican governments restored Mexican farmworker migrant streams. The Bracero program was abolished in 1964, and industrial growers have since used other immigration programs that tend to be slower and more cumbersome. The National Center for Farmworker Health (2010) estimates that currently 52 percent of farmworkers are undocumented and that 81 percent of farmworkers, citizens and non-citizens alike, speak Spanish as a first language. Despite working long hours and moving eleven to thirteen times a year, most farmworkers earn less than US$12,500 per year. From the beginning, agricultural businesses have been exempted from labor laws that pertain to minimum wage, work hours, and benefits. Similarly, the 1935 Social Security Act specifically excluded farmworkers and domestic workers (another largely non-white population) from protections. Existing laws to protect their safety and health on the job are often poorly enforced, in part due to their marginal status and high mobility. An ongoing farmworkers' movement has had some notable successes but still struggles with changing economic and legal terrain amidst these fundamental disadvantages. Though they bear the brunt of the social costs in an industrial food system that could not function without them, farmworkers are a largely invisible population to most US eaters, hidden behind the commodity systems they sustain.

Environmental costs

While the social impacts of the industrial food system may seem subtle, the environmental impacts are anything but. Certainly, all human activity has an impact on the rest of nature, and premodern societies were more than capable of ruining their environment through overgrazing, over-tilling, and unsustainable irrigation. However, critics see a modern pattern in which the environmental problems created by industrial agriculture are addressed with industrial solutions that then bring new, larger-scale risks. Lyson (2004: 19–20) summarizes the industrialization of the food system in terms of three "technological revolutions": the "mechanical revolution," beginning about 1900, the "chemical revolution," beginning at the end of World War II in 1945, and the "biotechnology revolution," beginning in the 1980s. In unequal societies, the benefits and burdens of these risks are unequally distributed as well.

A chemical revolution in agriculture began in World War I and continued in World War II. During World War I, German chemist Fritz Haber learned how to synthesize the nitrogen needed for bomb making. Before that, bombs needed natural sources of concentrated nitrogen, such as that found in bat guano. Farmers also needed soil nitrogen, but, because these mined sources were scarce and expensive, they relied on nitrogen-fixing microbes living on the roots of leguminous plants like beans and peas. Planting legumes (such as soybeans) one year would build up soil nitrogen for a non-legume (such as corn) the next. The invention of synthetic nitrogen enabled farmers to skip these rotations and focus on the most high-value crops. Other wartime chemicals, including nerve gases and plant-killing defoliants, became the insecticides and herbicides that chemical companies and agricultural extension agents encouraged farmers to use after the wars were over. As early as the 1970s, there were more than 100 factories in the United States producing more than 1,000 different pesticides (Lyson 2004: 20). Meanwhile, the use of synthetic nitrogen fertilizers increased sevenfold between 1945 and 1980 (Lyson 2004: 20).

These chemicals indisputably boost agricultural production per unit of land, but they also carry risks. A first wave of concern about agricultural pesticides followed the publication of Rachel Carson's landmark book *Silent Spring* in 1962. Through a painstaking review of complex scientific findings, Carson, an aquatic biologist, explained how persistent pesticides like DDT were building up in animal tissues throughout the food chain. For example, insects covered in DDT were consumed by other insects, which were then eaten by frogs hunted by birds and other predators. DDT accumulated in the tissues of these longer-living predators. As birds became poisoned, they laid eggs with shells too thin to protect developing embryos. The "silent spring" of Carson's title described a future without songbirds, made extinct by this inability to reproduce. Carson's book was an immediate best-seller, galvanizing an environmental movement that has pressed for stronger environmental protections and, as we explain in chapter 9, launching a growing movement to generate alternative systems of food production and distribution. DDT was banned in 1972, and some other persistent pesticides have similarly been taken out of use; but environmentalists and consumers are still concerned about ones that remain. For example, the widely used herbicide atrazine has been linked to the increase in deformed and hermaphroditic frogs (Lydersen 2009), and some pesticides are linked to cancer.

Chemical fertilizers have also created a paradoxical problem called **nutrient pollution**. When runoff from fertilized farm fields carries excessive nitrogen and phosphorus (important nutrients for plants) to bodies of water, algae and some aquatic and marine plants grow too vigorously. When these plants die, they reduce the amount of dissolved oxygen in the water (a process called **eutrophication**), stifling other aquatic life and creating a dead zone. There are now more than 400 identified oceanic dead zones, including one in the Gulf of Mexico of about 8,000 square miles caused by fertilizers washing down the Mississippi River (Achenbach 2008). Appropriate nutrition management on farms can greatly lessen these risks; but, while the process is well understood, nutrient pollution is still a problem. From a productivist perspective, the benefits of chemical pesticides and fertilizers are clear. Costs like oceanic dead zones are harder to see and account for.

The "biotechnology revolution" was developed, in part, to address the problems of agricultural chemicals (Lyson 2004). Genetic engineering entails manipulating genetic codes in the lab, rather than through conventional plant and animal breeding. As such, it enables biotech engineers to bring genetic code from one species to another, using specially developed viruses. The uses of genetic engineering are limited because very few important traits are controlled by a single gene or identified by a single marker. However, technologies that manipulate single-gene traits have had a huge impact on the two most important crops in the United States: corn and soy.

Some varieties of corn (along with cotton and potatoes) have been genetically engineered to produce a protein that is toxic to many caterpillars (which are the larvae of butterflies and moths) but not to humans or other mammals. The protein is made by a soil bacterium called *Bacillus thuringiensis*, and pesticide companies have used the bacteria to manufacture popular pesticide sprays that are highly effective against troublesome insect pests like the European corn borer. More recently, Syngenta, a Swiss biotech company, used genetic engineering to insert a gene from the bacterium into corn, cotton, and potatoes, creating so-called "Bt" varieties of plants that make the toxic protein themselves, killing larvae that burrow into the plant. Meanwhile, non-pest species of butterflies and moths in the vicinity of the field are less likely to be exposed than they would be through spraying the same toxin. Currently, 93 percent of cotton and 86 percent of corn planted in the United States is genetically engineered (US Department of Agriculture Economic Research Service 2010).

One problem with Bt corn is that it exacerbates **pesticide resistance**. As more European corn borers are exposed to Bt, the individuals immune to Bt outlive the ones who succumb, passing on their immunity to their offspring. With overuse, the majority of the pest population becomes immune to the pesticide. Federal rules dictate that farmers using Bt corn must plant 20 percent of their acreage in non-Bt varieties to forestall pesticide resistance; but a recent study found that one-quarter of farmers using Bt corn do not comply (Pollack 2009). As a result, pesticide resistance is growing, reducing the usefulness of this once relatively benign chemical.

Another predominant biotechnology is embodied in Roundup Ready varieties. Roundup is a popular herbicide (weed killer) produced by Monsanto. Its main ingredient, glyphosate, is taken up by the plant's leaves and quickly transported to the roots where it kills the plant. Glyphosate is thought to break down quickly into inert ingredients, though some research contests that view (Relyea 2005; Richard et al. 2005). Monsanto's genetic engineering arm developed special varieties of soybeans, canola, alfalfa, and other crops that contain a gene from the Brazil nut that makes them immune to glyphosate. Farmers using these Roundup Ready varieties can plant their crops and then spray Roundup a few weeks later when weeds emerge. The young crops are immune but the weeds around them quickly die. Farmers can plant their rows closer together and get more yield per unit of land because they no longer have to leave space to spray or mechanically dig up weeds. Currently, more than 90 percent of the soy grown in the US is a Roundup Ready variety (US Department of Agriculture Economic Research Service 2010).

In addition to some environmental risks, this technology carries a social one in that it gives a single corporation ownership over critically important food resources. Farmers purchasing Roundup Ready seeds are contractually prohibited from saving some seed from one year's crop to plant the next year, effectively forcing them to purchase seed every year. In fact, farmers who choose not to plant Roundup Ready soybeans but whose fields have been contaminated by Monsanto's Roundup Ready genetics are also, as a result of recent lawsuits, legally prohibited from saving their own seed. Many farmers save seeds for generations to select those that thrive best on their particular farm. Rather than requiring Monsanto or Roundup Ready farmers to prevent genetic contamination, the burden has been placed on those who do not stand to benefit from the technology (Kenner 2008). Non-Roundup users also have to deal with glyphosate-resistant "superweeds" emerging in the wake of expanded Roundup spraying.

Environmental groups concerned about genetic engineering are also raising the alarm about **genetic pollution**, especially in relation to "pharming," which uses genetically modified crops to produce chemicals used in medicines. The Union of Concerned Scientists, for example, advocates banning pharming in corn because corn pollen can travel by air for many miles, contaminating cornfields destined for the food supply. In Pretty's (2002) terms, the costs of addressing pollution, pesticide, and herbicide resistance, and corporate control of agricultural genetics comprise the third time we pay, individually and collectively, for industrial food (after public farm subsidies and the shelf price). Critics see the maldistribution of costs and benefits as not simply unfortunate, but wholly unjust and avoidable.

Conclusion: why is cheap food so costly?

Given the high technological investments we have made in agriculture and food processing and the vast distances that most of our food travels before arriving in our pantries, it is all the more remarkable that we pay so little – less than 10 percent of disposable income on average for Americans – for our food. How we have arrived here is a complex but consistent story of the industrialization of the food system and the particular cultural and material arrangements therein. Productivist ideologies guided agricultural research and policy, as well as farming culture, leading to an ongoing crisis in farm viability as well as new arenas for racial and gender discrimination. Commodification encouraged eaters to focus only on the edible thing before them, making it difficult to know its attendant benefits or costs. Critics argue that the many costs of "cheap" food, experientially removed from the product on the shelf, are largely borne by individuals and the public sector, while the profits accrue disproportionately to food corporations. The patient struggling with a multidrug resistant *E. coli* infection may not be aware of how the use of antibiotics in chicken farming has set the stage for her predicament and the shopper choosing among different products in the store has little information with which to act on his environmental or social values.

The dominant food system is not only industrial; it is also global. The next chapter explores the global food system, with a particular focus on the corporation as an economic and social institution. With relatively loose ties to any particular place, global food companies can seem a lot like global food: everywhere but nowhere in particular. However, global institutions and processes are instantiated in local practices and effects. Similarly, the histories of Coca-Cola (chapter

5) and milk consumption (this chapter) reflect particular historical confluences of local and transnational processes.

Further reading

Freidberg, Susanne. 2009. *Fresh: A Perishable History*. Cambridge, MA: Harvard University Press. Geographer Susanne Freidberg offers a highly engaging account of how long-distance commodity chains of perishable foods came to be. Particularly germane is Freidberg's chapter 1, "Refrigeration: Cold Revolution," which describes initial skepticism about cold storage. In addition to her analysis of milk, cited above, other chapters provide fascinating case studies of beef, eggs, vegetables, fruits, and fish.

Guptill, Amy and Welsh, Rick. 2014. "The Declining Middle of American Agriculture: A Spatial Phenomenon" in C. Bailey, L. Jensen, and E. Ransom (eds), *Rural America in a Globalizing World: Problems and Prospects for the 2010s*. Morgantown, WV: West Virginia University Press, pp. 36–50. In this short chapter, Guptill and Welsh explain why the largest and smallest farms are growing in number while mid-size farms continue to decline. They also and describe some innovative ways to rebuild the agricultural middle.

Laudan, Rachel. 2001. "A Plea for Culinary Modernism: Why We Should Love New, Fast, Processed Food." *Gastronomica* 1(1): 36–44. In this now-classic essay, Laudan, a historian, reminds us that "If we romanticize the past, we may miss the fact that it is the modern, global, industrial economy . . . that allows us to savor traditional, peasant, fresh, and natural foods" (42).

Striffler, Steve. 2005. *Chicken: The Dangerous Transformation of America's Favorite Food*. New Haven, CT: Yale University Press. Anthropologist Steve Striffler brings a Latin American studies perspective to a wide-ranging critical account of the broiler industry and its impact on workers, communities, and eaters. Chapter 2, "An American Industry," recounts the history of industrial American chicken, and chapter 6, "Inside the Poultry Plant," describes his own experience working in a processing plant.

Further exploration

1 FOR DISCUSSION: What other areas of social life have been industrialized over the last century? For example, to what extent can we apply the concepts of productivism and commodification to describe broad shifts in education, health care, or the entertainment or fashion industries?

2 FOR DISCUSSION: Go to soylent.com and read about the meal-replacement food product developed and promoted by Robert Rhinehart. Also watch the brief video available at https://www.youtube.com/watch?v=SGkLWjuiakQ. In what ways is Soylent an industrial food? In what ways is Soylent a rejection of industrial food?

3 IN CLASS and ONLINE: Watch *Food, Inc.* (a film by Robert Kenner,
   Magnolia Pictures, 2008), and find some positive reviews of the film
   online. Then read Monsanto's response to the film found at http://www.
   monsanto.com/food-inc/pages/default.aspx. How do the rhetorical strategies of the two sides differ? How does each define "safe" food or "quality"
   food? Who should eaters trust, according to each side of the debate?

7

Global Food:
From Everywhere and Nowhere

Case study

The McDonald's in Beijing is abuzz with the noise and energy from a child's birthday party. Watson's (2005) and Yan's (2005) research sets the scene. Small children unwrap their individually chosen foods (like little presents!) and eagerly await the appearance of Ronald McDonald. Parents and grandparents smile at their "little emperors" and "little empresses," though they remember the time before birthday parties, when children were not the focus of such spirited celebration but were instead expected to display reverence for their elders. These days, however, after 30 years of China's one-child policy, many urban families have only one grandchild for every four grandparents, and such Confucian norms have weakened. The children's parents, anxious to prepare their child for an increasingly globalized world, are willing to pay the considerable expense of a meal at McDonald's, even if they themselves eat at the cheaper noodle houses next door. For the parents, McDonald's seems an exotic American import and a way to portray one's cosmopolitan sophistication. For the children, McDonald's is simply a part of the everyday landscape, no less "Chinese" than any neighboring eatery.

Across the world, as Helene Brembeck (2005) describes, middle-class families with young children in suburban Sweden are also gathering at McDonald's for a leisurely meal. It is not a special event like a birthday party, just the end of a day of shopping, errands, and activities that have cut into dinner-preparation time. These parents are not trying to educate their children in the ways of a globalized world; instead, they are maintaining the daily ritual of a family dinner by eating together at McDonald's. One could easily mistake the scene for a party, though, because many of the patrons are acquainted with one another from living in the same neighborhoods, having children in the same schools, and participating in the same activities.

While there are notable contextual and experiential differences, patrons in Seoul, São Paolo, and Stockholm are all eating fries from the same carefully managed sources. French fries account for the largest share of North American potato production, and McDonald's is, by far, the biggest buyer at more than 3 billion pounds a year. Consequently, the Potato Variety Management Institute (a multi-state collaboration of potato commissions) understands that new varieties must cater to McDonald's to be commercially viable (Miller 2009). All of the French fries served in 33,000 McDonald's restaurants in 119 countries come from three suppliers: JR Simplot, McCain Foods, and Lamb Weston (owned by Con-Agra) which, among them, have frozen potato product plants in at least 14 countries: Argentina, Australia, Canada, China, France, India, the Netherlands, New Zealand, Poland, South Africa, Spain, Turkey, the United Kingdom, and the United States (Kirkman 2007: 33). Overall, these three companies control about 80 percent of the total frozen French-fry market (Schlosser 2002: 116). They purchase processing and seed potatoes from farmers around the world, and make contracts with growers that stipulate seed sources, production methods, and quality criteria for the crop (Cheng 2005; Pritchard and Tonts 2011; Singh 2008). Later, "fast food companies purchase frozen fries for about 30 cents a pound, reheat them in oil, then sell them for about $6 a pound." From the US$1.50 that a consumer spends on an order of fries, about two pennies accrue to the farmer (Schlosser 2002: 117).

With so much market power, it is not surprising that McDonald's headquarters have become an important target for environmental activists. In 1999, the Organic Consumers Association, Friends of the Earth, Greenpeace, the Center for Food Safety, and other organizations banded together to pressure the largest food corporations not to buy genetically modified products. McDonald's, along with Frito-Lay and Procter & Gamble, quietly eliminated genetically modified potatoes from their supply chains, effectively killing the market for that technology (Kilman 2000; Phillips 2007). More recently, ethical investor groups working through shareholder agreements successfully goaded McDonald's into exploring potato varieties that require less water and fewer agricultural chemicals than the finicky, delicate Russet Burbank (Miller 2009). Mitch Smith, McDonald's agricultural products director, explains, "If we can find a variety that [meets consumers' taste expectations] with less inputs, water or whatever, that's something we're looking for. To date, there are not a lot of varieties that perform consistently enough" (Miller 2009). The result is that one corporation has a lot of influence in how farmers and others balance productivity concerns with environmental ones. Activists have, at times, succeeded in changing corporate policies to bring out good outcomes; some warn that the very effectiveness of these tactics reflects excessive corporate power.

Experientially and structurally, McDonald's is emblematic of the globalizing food system. On one hand, a McDonald's hamburger tastes more or less the same everywhere, and affluent consumers can increasingly buy many fruits and vegetables year round, regardless of the season. In this way, the foods that come from "everywhere" seem to come from nowhere in particular. On the other hand, all aspects of global food chains, from land to mouth, are grounded in – and have consequences for – particular people and locales. This paradox of placelessness raises important questions: How have these global food chains become such a prominent part of foodways around the world? And how do individual choices and experiences relate to these broad global forces?

Introduction: international versus global

On the one hand, there has been international trade in food for centuries. As far back as the thirteenth century, Eurasia and northern Africa were linked through a vibrant integrated trading system (Abu-Lughod 1989). Despite differences in languages, currencies, and cultures, these societies traded spices, olive oil, honey, nuts, dried fruits, cotton, wool, silk, leather, livestock, and other agricultural products, contributing new flavors and symbols to the foodways of participating countries. Within this multi-continent system were eight distinct zones, defined by trading routes that were controlled by locally dominant societies whose rulers were eager to tax the commerce of their realms. Surprisingly to historians, however, no one empire controlled the system as a whole (Marks 2007: 35). Until the Portuguese made armed incursions into the Indian Ocean and the South China Sea in the early 1500s, the system was largely decentralized but still impressively stable.

On the other hand, cross-national trade in food today is much more extensive and is characteristically global rather than simply international. It is not just that the food is grown in one country and eaten in another; rather, it is that the food is produced through a transnational network constructed and managed by transnational corporations and institutions (Hughes 2006). In a classic essay, political scientist Steven E. Sanderson (1986) claims that we have arrived at the era of the "world steer," which, like the "world car," transcends national borders and, importantly, national policies. He writes, "We now face an epoch in which the meat on consumers' tables will have been developed in Europe and North America, bred in Latin America, fed with export grains from the key producing countries (which itself is processed by multinational corporations), slaughtered under international standards, and consumed in communities most removed from their point of origin" (Sanderson 1986: 147). The global cattle complex Sanderson describes – the set of interlinked processes of grain growing, feed production, breeding, finishing, slaughter, quality grading, and marketing – is global in two ways. It connects places around the globe, and it is shaped by global institutions like development lending and transnational corporations. As illustrated in the opening case study, global firms like McDonald's and McCain do not just buy and sell across borders. Rather, they coordinate diverse economic activities in multiple and shifting sites around the globe. All told, about 30 percent of international trade is between parent companies and their subsidiaries, and almost half of US imports are accounted for by this intra-firm trade (Lanz and Miroudot 2011).

While the contemporary era of global food is unique in the breadth and complexity of these sourcing networks, it is important to remember that transnational food has been a major feature of all modern world history (Lechner 2009). Through the last few centuries, the **global North** (Europe, North America, and other "first world" countries) has forged economic links with the **global South** (low-income countries in Africa, the Americas, and Asia that were formerly European colonies) that have been decidedly unequal. First, modern colonialism (roughly 1600s to 1940s) instituted an **international division of labor**, with primary products (from agriculture, mining, and other nature-based industries) sourced from colonies and then transformed into manufactured products at the seat of the empire for local and international sale. After World War II, former colonies gained political independence and entered into a development era (1950s to 1980s); however, as we explain, much of development policy failed to ameliorate global inequalities and instead reinforced them. A third era began in the 1980s, as global institutions like the World Trade Organization sought to promote global trade with less regard for the enduring economic foundations of member countries (McMichael 2011). While these three eras are distinct in the technologies and institutions of global food trade, they are connected by the persistent inequality between North and South as well as the central role of transnational corporations, an organizational form that was born in the colonial era and has played a major role in the global economy ever since.

Two concepts formulated by Goodman, Sorj, and Wilkinson (1987) help explain how corporations have come to wield so much power in the food system. The first is **appropriationism**, which refers to the practice of corporations selling inputs to farmers that were previously produced on the farm itself, such as manufactured fertilizers instead of manures, or purchased seeds instead of those saved from prior harvests. Farmers trapped on a technology treadmill (see chapter 6) or farming on contract may find themselves compelled to purchase these inputs, even if such purchases are expensive. The other is **substitutionism**, where corporations seek "to reduce the rural product to a simple industrial input" (Goodman, Sorj, and Wilkinson 1987: 58). For example, when cane sugar, beet sugar, and high-fructose corn syrup can be used interchangeably in manufactured foods, it is easier for corporations to negotiate lower prices for any one of those products. Together, Goodman, Sorj, and Wilkinson (1987) explain, appropriationism and substitutionism enable corporations to avoid the risks of farming – plagued as it is with the vagaries of weather, pests, weeds, and sometimes volatile prices – and instead control the segments of the production chain that yield more profit and lower risk.

As this chapter explains, transnational corporations have played a major role in shaping the global food system throughout modern history. We discuss three eras in turn, beginning with modern colonialism and the emergence of the limited liability corporation, highlighting the case of sugar production and trade. We next turn to the development decades to explain how food aid and the terms of international lending shaped developing countries' engagement with global food trade. After that, we take a close look at the case of cocoa production in Ghana to illustrate how a colonial production system was recreated, rather than dismantled, through development policies. We next draw distinctions between the vision of development in the mid-twentieth century and the neoliberal ideologies that underpin global trade governance today. We lastly look at the consumption of globally sourced foods to further show how individual foodways connect to global food systems and can reinforce or contest social inequalities.

The colonial division of labor

Empire building is as old as civilization, but the modern era of colonialism, from roughly the seventeenth century to World War II, set the stage for the contemporary global food system. In that time, as industrialization unfolded in Europe and the United States, overseas colonies supplied raw products for European factories and, increasingly, food energy for industrial workers (Mintz 1985). As growing populations in Europe overwhelmed their natural resource base, there was even more pressure to source the raw products of nature from colonies at low prices (Marks 2007). This new **international division of labor**, in which colonies produced raw materials and metropoles (i.e., seats of empire) produced finished goods, modified foodways on both sides of the colonial relation in complex and dynamic ways.

Anthropologist Sidney Mintz (1985) broke new intellectual ground when his study of global sugar showed how plantation agriculture in the colonies enabled industrialization in the North. He begins historically, explaining that from the Crusades to the late 1600s, sugar was seen as a spice in Europe: an exotic delicacy used by the elite in small quantities to improve the flavor of their food. Sugar was enormously popular. Entrepreneurs involved in developing overseas colonies, particularly those in the Caribbean, were drawn to sugar, especially as the European market for tobacco, another addictive product of the Americas, became saturated. Colonists developed slave-based plantation systems on a model pioneered by the Portuguese in the Canary Islands off the coast of Africa (Marks 2007). The growth of sugar plantations drove the economic demand for African slaves to work in the Caribbean, which had been largely depopulated by disease, violence, and, for the relatively lucky, escape. Mintz (1985) argues that these sugar plantations were an early form of agricultural industrialization, in that sugar cane (and nothing but sugar cane) was grown and processed in vast quantities for a commodity market.

The global sugar chain shaped foodways in both the metropole and the colony (Mintz 1985). In Britain, sugar became an important source of food energy as the quantity increased and, predictably, its price dropped. New coal-fired factories drew men, women, and children into industrial workplaces during the first half of the eighteenth century, and they came to depend on the cheap and portable energy of sugar, dissolved in tea (another tropical commodity moving through colonial channels) or in fruit jams, to fuel their long work days. Sugar became a key part of the purchased shelf-stable foods whose consumption grew relative to the fresher food prepared at home.

On the other end of the colonial relation, workers in the Caribbean toiling in what Mintz calls "factories in the field" also came to depend on imported staples like salted fish and rice that were carried on merchant and slave ships, as well as molasses and sugar produced on site. Many plantations included provisioning grounds or kitchen gardens on which slaves were allowed or compelled to produce some of their own food (Carney 2008). However, sugar plantation slaves in the British Caribbean worked, on average, 76 hours per week in the cane fields or mills, which left little time and even less energy to grow food (Higman 1995). On both ends of the sugar commodity chain, Mintz (1985) explains, we find people coerced by violence or circumstance into working under impoverishing and life-shortening conditions. In both places, long-distance industrial food chains provided a larger part of food supply and shorter-distance ones (growing one's own or buying locally) less so, yielding poorer diets for working people (Brown 2008; Carney 2008; Mintz 1985). On an international scale, England became a wealthy industrial country while Caribbean colonies remained persistently poor. The story of sugar is mirrored in that of other tropical commodities that many countries of the global South still depend on, such as tea, coffee, chocolate, and bananas, as well as non-food crops like cotton and rubber.

To develop and manage these long-distance value chains, colonizing countries depended on a relatively new form of economic organization and governance: the **corporation**. In modern form, the corporation has four key characteristics: (1) "limited liability," which means that individual investors may lose all their invested money but are not individually liable for debts accrued by the corporation; (2) "transferability of shares," which means that shares can be freely bought and sold; (3) legal "personhood," which means that the corporation can do some things a person can do, such as own property, enter into contracts, sue and be sued; and (4) "indefinite duration," which means that the corporation can persist even when the original founders are no longer involved ("Corporation" 2010).

While some forms of limited-liability businesses date back 2,300 years to the Mauryan empire (Khanna 2005), these types of organizations took on an unprecedentedly large role during modern European colonialism. In this era, monarchs and governments chartered private companies to explore, exploit, and govern colonies abroad because the expense of these undertakings demanded more capital than the crown or state could muster. Among the first was the "Governor and Company of Merchants of London, trading into the East Indies," more popularly known as the East India Company. Queen Elizabeth I chartered the East India Company in 1600, empowering it to manage a trading monopoly with colonial territories and to enact and enforce laws in those territories. Other similar semi-public monopoly ventures followed, like the Hudson's Bay Company, the Dutch East India Company, the Dutch West India Company, the Portuguese East India Company, and the Royal African Company. While they cooperated at home to garner favorable terms, they competed fiercely with one another to control lucrative trade flows and productive resources (Adams 1996). While the precise forms of these companies and their relationships to governments have changed over the last 400 years, the role of corporations in global food chains has persisted and grown.

Decolonization and development

At the end of World War II, growing social movements against colonialism, together with the wartime devastation of Europe and the ascendancy of the United States, marked the end of the colonial era. Former colonies declared independence, the financial ministers of wealthy countries founded global economic organizations, and the United States contributed to the rebuilding of Europe and Japan. All these efforts took place in an atmosphere of modernist optimism (see chapter 6). The path for industrial development was clear (because the United States and Europe had already blazed it), achievable (thanks to modern science and scientific management), and inevitable (because progress was assumed to be linear and natural) (Rist 2002). Many assumed it was only a matter of time before the so-called third world countries broke their economic dependence on raw, primary products and took their place among the industrialized countries of the world. However, the terms of what McMichael (2011) calls the **development project** reflected multiple priorities, with only some of them stemming from the needs of developing countries. Development, a global effort to modernize the societies and economies of the South, was as much about creating a global economy as meeting the needs of the world's poor. As a result, development policies often reproduced the unequal structure of global food chains forged under colonialism.

One key shaper of global food in the development era was the United States' goal to be an agricultural powerhouse as well as an industrial one. After the war, the United States was in a unique position to substantially and effectively subsidize exported grain. The US dollar had become the key global currency, agricultural subsidies had fostered persistent overproduction in the United States, and war-torn

Europe needed to import grain in the wake of war (Friedmann 1982: S260). A major part of the Marshall Plan to aid Europe and Japan was a food aid program that sold the United States' growing stockpile of surplus grain to Europe at subsidized prices. Cash aid was disbursed in US dollars to encourage the purchase of American exports. While meeting immediate needs, the goal of the Marshall Plan was to lay the foundation for continued exports of American agricultural products in the postwar era.

In 1954, the focus of food aid shifted to the global South, in part because farmers in Europe successfully pressured their governments to protect national agricultures with trade barriers (Patel 2007: 90). The US Congress passed Public Law 480 (PL-480), giving ongoing authorization to the USDA to purchase surplus commodities and ship them overseas as aid. Some development theorists at the time argued that an inexpensive food supply fuels economic growth: when food is cheap, workers can live well on less pay and, thus, the things they produce will be more competitively priced in the world market. At the same time, the bags of grain bearing symbols of the United States were thought to serve a rhetorical purpose in countries potentially seduced by the communist bloc; the visible abundance would demonstrate the agricultural prowess of capitalism (Friedmann 1982). As in the Marshall Plan, the longer-term goal was to use food aid to cultivate a future market. Sociologist Harriet Friedmann (1982: S252) explains, "The penetration of self-sufficient agricultural societies by commodity relations was part of the project to incorporate them within the open world economy. Nationalist movements threatening to restrict trade and capital movements thus seemed as dangerous to the free world as Soviet political influence." As we explain in chapter 8, food aid contributed to the weakening of domestic food production, increasing risks of food insecurity.

Together, food aid and development policy pushed countries in the global South toward producing for export rather than for their own food needs. The flood of food aid encouraged many countries in the South to abandon efforts to promote food self-sufficiency. Also, the terms of the development loans made by the World Bank and similar regional lenders, such as the Inter-American Development Bank, promoted commodity production for global markets, even those commodities like tea and sugar that seemed like distasteful holdovers from the colonial era. To understand why, consider that the World Bank made loans for development in so-called G-7 currencies, the currencies of the seven countries with the largest economies: the United States, the United Kingdom, France, Germany, Japan,

Italy, and Canada. Loan money was spent, logically, in G-7 countries to purchase industrial infrastructure and agricultural technologies, such as irrigation systems and packing and processing facilities. Those loans had to be repaid in G-7 currency, so debtor countries had to export products to G-7 countries to get the dollars, pounds, francs, deutschmarks, yen, or lire they needed to service their debt. While most countries of the South sought to develop modern manufacturing sectors to replace colonial industries, many countries ended up relying on the same commodity exports that developed under colonialism. The landscapes, workforce, facilities, and markets for these export industries were already in place and needed to be mobilized to ensure earnings for these short-term loans. To this day, Costa Rica, El Salvador, Guatemala, and Nicaragua continue to export coffee and sugar (industries established under colonialism) and have added new export sectors like beef (Paige 1997: 91); West African countries like Senegal, Guinea, Nigeria, and Cameroon are still significant world producers of peanuts, a crop introduced during the colonial era. The following case study of cocoa production in Ghana illustrates how postwar international development policies tended to recreate the international division of labor established under colonialism in which export industries were prioritized over the food needs of people in the global South.

Case study: cocoa in Ghana

Anthropologist Gwendolyn Mikell (1989: 24–7) explains that, for three centuries before late nineteenth-century colonialism, rural people in what is now Ghana (then the Gold Coast) produced food for local consumption as well as palm oil and kola nuts for the extensive trans-Sahara trade system. Later, European and American traders purchased gold and slaves from Ghana, which drew Ghanaian merchants into contact with the global capitalist economy. When Britain established firm colonial rule in 1895, they introduced the cacao tree. The high prices paid for cocoa made cacao farming immediately popular, even though chocolate was not (and still is not) part of the local traditional diet. By 1911, cocoa was a major export crop and shaped the everyday lives of many Ghanaians. Cocoa was so lucrative that people from northern Ghana, traditionally a center of food production and trade, migrated to the cocoa-producing region in the south, a pattern which persists today (van der Geest 2011). Cocoa taxes were the main revenue source for the colonial administration (Mikell 1989: 83–4).

As cocoa expanded, subsistence agriculture suffered. Ghanaians had been importing rice to supplement locally grown foods like plantains, maize (introduced from the Americas), yams, and garden vegetables for at least six decades prior to the first cocoa boom in the early part of the twentieth century (Mikell 1989: 58–9). But cocoa trees take up a lot of land and nutrients, so food production, primarily an activity of women, was pushed to even more marginal spaces (Grier 1992). For the first three decades of the twentieth century, cocoa farmers made good incomes from cocoa (Berry 1993), and the decline in food production was matched with increased purchases of imported food. When world prices for cocoa collapsed during the Great Depression, however, it became clear how vulnerable Ghana had become by depending so heavily on a single export crop that requires extensive processing to eat.

The impact of the Depression was magnified by the fact that much of Ghanaian cocoa in the 1930s was purchased by only three British firms: the United Africa Company (or UAC, now part of food-giant Unilever), Cadbury Brothers Limited (later purchased by Kraft) and John Holt and Company. The UAC and Holt bought and sold unprocessed cocoa, while Cadbury manufactured chocolate and purchased cocoa for other manufacturers (Milburn 1970: 57–8). These companies met regularly from 1936 to 1937 to set prices for West Africa and quotas for buyers. They wanted to avoid bidding against one another and driving up the price. They argued to the colonial government that such price-fixing would reduce the role of intermediaries and bring a fairer and more stable price to the farmer (Milburn 1970: 60–1). When the agreement was published in Ghana, the world price fell precipitously. Ghanaian farmers, in protest at what they saw as a European monopoly, successfully organized a "cocoa hold-up," and the British governor of the Gold Coast also protested the agreement (Milburn 1970: 63). Despite the governor's support, cocoa farmers added their numerous voices to calls for national independence (Mikell 1989: 139–44). Independent Ghana was founded in 1957 under the leadership of the charismatic Kwame Nkrumah.

During the development decades, Ghana found it difficult to reduce the nation's dependence on cocoa exports. Ghana's hope, like that of many other developing countries, was to develop a robust industrial sector and move away from exporting raw products that are prone to boom–bust cycles. In the 1950s, cocoa accounted for almost two-thirds of Ghana's export earnings, and Nkrumah's administration sought to amass tax revenues through a newly established Cocoa Marketing Board in order to fund industrial development. However, volatile world prices for cocoa made earnings hard to predict, which meant that the government had to borrow internationally to finance ambitious industrial development

projects in sectors like pharmaceuticals, furniture making, and food processing (Mikell 1989: 175–6, 186). Earnings from these initial industrial
projects were insufficient, however, and Ghana continued to depend on
cocoa exports to pay back development loans. The government has also
sought to increase domestic production of food staples such as rice and
poultry, particularly since the cocoa crisis of the 1980s, but the low price
of imported foods has hampered efforts to cultivate a sustainable competitive industry (Field, Masakure, and Henson 2010).

In Ghana, as in many other places, economic development policies
reproduced the nation's dependency on this colonial export crop. Despite
an ongoing series of crises, Ghana is still a major cocoa exporter (though
now second to the Ivory Coast), and most cocoa is still grown by individual smallholders whose livelihoods are vulnerable to plant disease
and the vagaries of international markets and politics. In 2000, Ghana,
Nigeria, Cameroon, and the Ivory Coast, who together account for 70
percent of world production, announced that they would destroy a
quarter-million tons of cocoa in an effort to raise world prices to sustainable levels ("Ghana; Cocoa Crisis" 2000), but cocoa revenues continue
to disappoint. Despite efforts to diversify the economy, "agriculture
accounts for about 40 percent of Ghana's gross domestic product and 75
percent of its export earnings and employs 55 percent of its labour force"
(Field, Masakure, and Henson 2010: 262). Nevertheless, Ghana continues to import "100 percent of its wheat and sugar, two-thirds of its rice,
half of its beef and one-third of its chicken" (Dzanku and Sarpong 2010:
192). Despite stable governance and the recent discovery of offshore oil
reserves, nearly 30 percent of Ghana's population is living on less than
US$1.25 per day, which is one of the United Nations' key indicators of
absolute poverty (United Nations Development Program 2015). These
problems persist, despite Ghana's role as a major exporter of a high-value
commodity, one it produces at a consistently high quality (Gilbert 2009).

Clearly, the low prices Ghanaian farmers receive are not due to declining consumer demand, as chocolate consumption has been stable, even
through the recent recession. Rather, Goodman, Sorj, and Wilkinson's
(1987) concepts of substitutionism and appropriationism help to explain
why chocolate companies can earn steady profits while farmers languish.
First, the handful of European corporations that buy almost all of the
cocoa produced in West Africa are able to turn cocoa grown in markedly
different conditions worldwide into standardized commodities: cocoa
butter and cocoa powder (Gilbert 2009). This substitutionism sets independent West African growers in competition with cocoa plantations in
Asia and Latin America to offer the cheapest prices, forcing them all to
subsist on the thinnest profit margins. Meanwhile, after more than 200

mergers and acquisitions between 1970 and 1990, only a handful of corporations control the chocolate industry, giving growers few options for marketing (Fold 2001: 408). In consumers' minds, the quality of finished chocolate is associated with where it is manufactured, rather than where the main ingredient was grown (Cidell and Alberts 2006).

Second, the companies that profit most from chocolate have stayed out of farming and instead focused on controlling more profitable aspects of the industry, such as cocoa grinding, currently controlled by three "transnational giants": Cargill, ADM, and Barry Callebaut (Fold 2001: 411). This appropriationist strategy largely shields these companies from the economic risks of farming while garnering the rewards of steady consumer demand. They can stockpile cocoa beans when prices are low and purchase less when prices are high, while farmers must sell their products, regardless of the world price, to earn any income at all. Because smallholder cocoa production reflects agroforestry systems and skills developed over generations, these farmers cannot easily shift into new products. Purchasing corporations are assisted by the terms of international lending that have required some West African countries (though not Ghana) to dismantle the national marketing boards which purchased beans from farmers and marketed them collectively (Gilbert 2009). From colonialism to the development era to globalization, the case of Ghanaian cocoa illustrates the multiple forces at work in shaping the global food system and inequalities therein.

The globalization project

Just as colonialism set the context for the development project, development policies set the stage for what McMichael (2011) calls **the globalization project**, the effort to expand the global economy. Rather than developing interlinked industries and agricultures within each country, the globalization project sought to promote production and marketing networks that transcend national boundaries. For example, Renato Ruggiero, the first director-general of the World Trade Organization (WTO), declared, "progress in resolving the challenge of the new century will hinge on our ability not just to build a coherent global architecture, but to build a political constituency for globalization. . . . Without the WTO, we will go back to a world of national barriers, protectionism, economic nationalism, and conflict" (McMichael 2011: 126). In the development project, tariffs and other trade barriers were accepted means to help countries of the South grow fledgling industries, but, under this globalization regime, any barriers to trade are also seen as needless barriers to growth, progress, and peace. That view is called **neoliberalism**. Neoliberalism is an ideology, like productivism (chapter 6), that presents its vision as inherently positive and inevitable.

The WTO is the central institution of the globalization project. It was founded in 1994 to replace the General Agreement on Tariffs and Trade (GATT). The GATT was a treaty organization; if a country enacted a tariff or quota in violation of a GATT agreement, there was little that another country could do. The WTO, in contrast, is a membership organization that has the authority to enforce its rules. One member country can bring a complaint against another for imposing artificial restraint on trade. WTO member countries are not allowed, for example, to privilege products from their own businesses over those of foreign companies. If a member nation passes a law limiting imports due to a food safety concern, they may be accused of a restraint on trade and required to show that the food safety risk is high. For example, in 1989, the European Union banned the sale of hormone-treated beef and veal for human consumption; as a result, imports of American-grown beef fell 94 percent between 1982 and 1990 (Kastner and Pawsey 2002: 50). In 1996, Canada and the United States brought a complaint against Europe under the recently established WTO, arguing that this law was an unfair restraint on trade. The WTO ruled against the EU, concluding that they had insufficient scientific evidence to show that hormone-treated beef was known to be harmful; the EU was ordered to lift the ban by the fall of 1999. The EU refused, and the United States and Canada got permission from the WTO to levy their own retaliatory tariffs against the EU. The standoff continued until 2009, when the United States and EU hammered out a provisional agreement to modestly expand imports of hormone-free US beef into the EU; Canada struck a similar deal in 2011 (van Puyvelde 2011). A similar dispute erupted in 2003 when the EU banned food made from genetically modified organisms. The EU can afford to take a hard line on some of these issues, but many other countries, especially those with large development debts, cannot.

Another revealing case illustrates how global trade rules can directly hamper countries of the global South. In 1996, the United States complained to the WTO about the Lomé Convention, a trade deal founded in 1975 in which former European colonies in Africa, the Caribbean, and the Pacific (the so-called ACP countries) enjoyed preferential access to the European markets for the sale of bananas and a few other minor products. Bananas grown in the participating

ACP countries are produced primarily on small, independent farms; thus, the Lomé Convention was an easy way for the EU to support the economies of former colonies and many households within. Analysts find this dispute especially interesting because neither the United States nor the EU has banana industries, so neither is acting on behalf of their own farmers (Alter and Meunier 2006). The American beneficiaries of the US action are corporate giants Dole, Chiquita, and Del Monte, which have acquired and maintained huge banana plantations in Central America since the beginning of the twentieth century and already, at the time of the initial dispute, controlled about 85 percent of the global banana trade (Raynolds 2003: 37). Critics of the US action note that Chiquita Brands (at the time called United Fruit) helped engineer a bloody coup in Guatemala in 1954 that replaced a democratically elected president with a dictator (Raynolds 2003: 26) and admitted guilt in 2007 in funding paramilitary forces during Colombia's civil war (Forero 2007). The WTO ruled against the EU, and the whole Lomé Convention was phased out, which has devastated banana growers in the eastern Caribbean (Fridell 2011).

The WTO has instituted parts of the neoliberal dream of a borderless world market, but agriculture and food have been the most sharply contested sectors. In multiple rounds of negotiations, the countries of the North have strenuously pressured southern countries to reduce their agricultural tariffs, while refusing to reduce the agricultural subsidies that push global prices down (Patterson 2001). The conflict came to a head in the 2003 meetings of the WTO in Cancún, Mexico, when the negotiators representing many countries of the South walked out of the negotiations. They were perhaps inspired by the dramatic protest of Korean farmer and activist, Lee Kyung Hae, who, days before, had climbed the fence surrounding the meeting site in Cancún, "flipped open his red penknife, shouted 'the WTO kills farmers' and stabbed himself high in his chest. He died a few hours later" (Patel 2007: 35). While the WTO resolved in 2005 to resume negotiating about agricultural issues in 2006, no progress was made, and the negotiations have been largely stalled ever since (de Paula and Pessali 2014).

Since the worldwide economic downturn beginning in 2007–8, analysts of the global food system have noted another troubling trend: the **financialization of food**, which refers to the growing power of financial institutions in shaping the global food system. In 2007 and early 2008, world prices for basic agricultural commodities shot way up, pushing millions of households in the global South (and more than a few in the global North) into terrible food insecurity. In late 2008, world commodity prices dropped just as dramatically, but food prices for consumers did not necessarily follow. Meanwhile, farmers and food businesses around the world struggled as well (Clapp and Helleiner 2012). The usual economic models of supply and demand didn't explain these volatile shifts; rather, they were largely driven by global speculation in agricultural derivatives, which are financial products through which investors can make bets about the future price of an agricultural commodity. Large US investors became more interested in agricultural derivatives (such as forward-contracts, futures, and swaps) after the dot-com bust in the early 2000s and successfully lobbied the US federal government to ease the rules about their sale and purchase. As a result, world agricultural prices were determined by the actions of short-term investors responding to volatility in fuel prices and financial markets more generally, rather than by classic supply-and-demand forces (Clapp and Helleiner 2012).

Relatedly, observers are noting that global investors have increasingly purchased or leased prime agricultural lands in poor countries since the economic downturn of 2007–8, a phenomenon termed the **global land grab**. Some buyers are food or energy corporations, seeking to exert more direct control over some of their supply chains for food or biofuels, but others are simply financial firms treating land like any other commodity (Zoomers 2010). While systematic, reliable data on the extent and types of land grab are hard to come by, it is clear that these transactions are displacing many small-scale producers around the globe who may not have secure title to the land that they depend on (Cotula 2013). The data made available by LandMatrix.org, mapped in Figure 7.1, indicate that vulnerability to land grabbing is concentrated in Latin America, Central Europe, Africa, and Southeast Asia.

Food for global elites

The economic and legal framework of globalization, together with new technologies, has enabled global sourcing networks that would have been unimaginable a generation earlier. Farmers in some countries have been able to develop high-tech production and transport systems to export specialized perishable products to the North. Dole, Chiquita, and Del Monte source "counter-seasonal" vegetables from different climate zones throughout the Americas, enabling

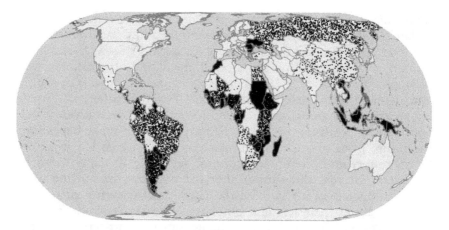

Figure 7.1 This map shows deals in which land, in units of 200 hectares or more, has been or will be purchased or leased by investors in order to convert small-farming or community land into commercial production. These data, downloaded from The Land Matrix (landmatrix.org) in April 2016, were reported by collaborating observers from around the world combing newspaper reports and public announcements. Each dot represented about 10 square miles of land involved in a deal since 2000.

Source: Created with data from landmatrix.org, retrieved April 3, 2016 from http://www.landmatrix.org/en/get-involved/.

privileged consumers in the North to buy some fresh vegetables year-round rather than just in their local season (McMichael 2011: 100). Eaters in the United States can enjoy a serving of fresh green beans at any time of year, a serving that has traveled perhaps 1,500 miles (Pirog and Benjamin 2003) to provide the eater with a whopping 25 calories of food energy. Similarly, most Europeans can eat baby vegetables grown in Zambia to exacting aesthetic standards (Freidberg 2009: 195), while Zambia imports staple food crops and depends, periodically, on food aid to meet its needs (del Ninno, Dorosh, and Subbarao 2007). To many consumers in the North, a meal at McDonald's or a Chilean-grown apple hardly seem like a significant luxury, but, from a global perspective, this consumption is a marker of extraordinary privilege.

Sushi, as a highly perishable food, illustrates the reach of today's global food chains. A generation ago, most sushi was eaten as a quick street snack in Tokyo. Any sushi served in the United States rarely included raw fish. Beginning in the 1980s, the sushi craze began to spread from major cities like Los Angeles, São Paolo, New York, Singapore, and London to smaller cities and towns in the global

North. As a result, the oilier species of tuna, which before 1970 were considered good only for pet food and sport fishing, have become, in journalist Sasha Issenberg's (2007: xii) words, fish that are, "on a per-pound basis, the most expensive food [many people] have ever consumed." The energy-intensive cold chain that enables this trade to exist begins on ocean fishing boats and ends in the restaurant, supermarket, or home cooler. Nowadays a sushi-grade bluefin tuna caught off the Spanish coast is quickly chilled, shipped to Madrid, and then flown to Tokyo (via Bangkok) to be auctioned off to global buyers (Issenberg 2007). A single fish might cost as much as US$100,000, and pieces of it will end up in maki, sushi, or sashimi bites around the globe (Issenberg 2007). Given raw tuna's high value and perishability, this trade depends on seamless global telecommunication and financial infrastructure, both fairly recent phenomena.

Similarly, the quinoa craze discussed in chapter 4 illustrates the ties between consumers and producers around the globe. A traditional crop among poor farmers in the Andes Mountains of South America, quinoa was largely unknown to the average consumer in the United States and Europe. "In 1993, NASA researchers recommended it as part of a potential space-colony diet," explains journalist Jean Friedman-Rudovsky (2012). "Over the following decade, the food gained wider appeal, going from hippie hype to Costco convenient practically overnight." Increased demand helped convert quinoa into a "major export crop generating much needed hard currency and income for peasant farmers" (Brett 2010: 28). But as Brett (2010: 28) reports, quinoa's international market success had unintended consequences for Andean producers, including "steep local price increases resulting in a highly nutritious traditional food source becoming largely unavailable to the majority of the population." Quinoa's popularity as a profitable export crop also fueled a land grab among farmers and raised numerous environmental concerns. Much of the land now used for quinoa cultivation was once used for llama grazing, which provided a natural fertilizer. However, to meet the international demand for quinoa, more and more land once used for grazing was converted to exclusive quinoa cultivation, creating soil quality and soil erosion problems (Friedman-Rudovsky 2012).

Conclusion: food from everywhere or somewhere?

Food has been crossing seas and borders for centuries, but now we see a food system that is "global" in a deeper sense. It is not just that food travels the globe; rather, the whole system of producing, processing, and marketing is globally organized and governed by transnational corporations, global trade institutions, and, increasingly, global financial markets. More and more people, spread around the globe, rely on this system for their livelihoods and their sustenance. As classical social thinker Emile Durkheim explains, one key characteristic of modernity is that we have come to rely on people far beyond kin or acquaintanceship to meet our most fundamental needs. Under the current wave of globalization, that web of interdependence has reached unprecedented levels, shaping the continually changing foodways of the people and places that engage with these chains as growers, workers, sellers, or eaters. To be clear, not all the world's population shops at the great global supermarket or refuels at McDonald's. As the elite around the world (including most citizens of the global North) forge tighter links through investments, work lives, and consumption patterns, much of the world's population is incorporated into this web on marginalized terms (Patel 2007). Though global food sometimes appears to come from nowhere, it always comes from several, sometimes shifting, "somewheres" and has tangible consequences in those places.

While most consumers want to make food choices that cohere with their deeply held values, the breadth and complexity of global food chains means that they cannot easily see their relative privilege or the impacts of their choices on people and environments. The next chapter explores another key facet of the current globalized food system: the persistence of food scarcity. Even in a world that produces more than enough food calories for everyone and, as the sushi example illustrates, has enormous technical capacity, more than 1 billion people struggle to meet their nutritional needs (Patel 2007). As chapter 8 explains, decades of effort to eradicate hunger have failed, largely because they have approached this complex social justice problem as if it were merely a technical one. Chapter 9, the concluding chapter of this text, surveys diverse movements to solve these and other food-system problems, in part by reconnecting producers and consumers on different, and more equal, terms.

Further reading

Bezner Kerr, Rachel. 2010. "The Land is Changing: Contested Agricultural Narratives in Northern Malawi," in P. McMichael (ed.), *Contesting Development: Critical Struggles for Social Change*. New York: Routledge, pp. 98–115. This is one of several excellent chapters on how ordinary people are rejecting the precepts of global economic development and forging alternatives. In this chapter, Bezner Kerr analyzes the "Soils, Food, and Healthy Communities" project, in which small-scale farmers in more than a hundred villages promote food security through ecologically sound and socially just agriculture.

Brown, Vincent. 2008. "Eating the Dead: Consumption and Regeneration in the History of Sugar." *Food and Foodways* 16(2): 117–26. In this essay, Brown responds to the pathbreaking work of Sidney Mintz to explore the social dimensions of sugar production in the Caribbean in the face of its devastating impact on enslaved sugar workers. Calling sugar "a murderous commodity" (p. 117), Brown argues that sugar consumption is, in some ways, an act of cannibalism.

Genoways, Ted. 2015. "Corn Wars." *The New Republic*, August 16. Retrieved August 27, 2015 (http://www.newrepublic.com/article/122441/corn-wars). Genoways provides a thorough and fascinating account of how the intellectual property of commercial hybrid corn has become a matter of national security and global geopolitics. He puts some recent cases of alleged corn-related espionage into their broader historical context.

Konefal, Jason, Mascarenhas, Michael, and Hatanaka, Maki. 2005. "Governance in the Global Agro-food System: Backlighting the Role of Transnational Supermarket Chains." *Agriculture and Human Values* 22(3): 291–302. These authors explain the large and growing, yet hidden, role of global food retailers in shaping both the processes and geographies of food production.

Lee, Jennifer 8. 2008. *The Fortune Cookie Chronicles: Adventures in the World of Chinese Food.* New York: Twelve. Lee offers a historically informed journalist's account of the construction of Chinese food interwoven with the experience of immigration, an aspect of globalization not covered in this chapter. Her eighth chapter, entitled "The Golden Venture: Restaurant Workers to Go," offers a compelling glimpse into a robust labor market that few are even aware of.

Further exploration

1 FOR DISCUSSION: Keep a log of everything you eat in a typical day, and do some research on where, geographically, its major ingredients come from. How global is your diet? How would your consumption practices change if you ate only foods from a 300-mile radius of where you live?

2 IN CLASS: View *Life and Debt*, Stephanie Black's 2001 documentary film (Tuff Gong Pictures) about the impact of international debt and globalization on the Jamaican economy. What drove the changes in policy? What impacts did they have on local food production? How have people coped with the changes?

3 ONLINE: Break into groups to research collaboratively a major global

commodity. Where is it produced? What are the major steps in processing? In what forms is this commodity finally consumed? When, in history, did this product become global? Which corporations dominate processing, manufacturing, and marketing stages? To whom is the product promoted? Is it a good deal for farmers? Is it a good deal for consumers? How difficult is it to uncover this information? Some major global commodities that work well for this exercise include wheat, farmed shrimp, soybeans, coffee, bananas, beef, corn, oranges, peanuts, and sugar.

8

Food Access: Surplus and Scarcity

Case study

Sociologist Janet Poppendieck argues that "fighting hunger [in the US] has become a national pastime" (1998: 24): millions of Americans volunteer at food banks, pantries, or soup kitchens or, more often, participate in food drives. Church groups, youth groups, workplaces, schools, and other institutions often value food drives because they are bounded, concrete, accessible events that, ostensibly, transcend political or religious differences. Also, as Poppendieck (1998: 41) explains, because food is richly symbolic of our shared humanity, "it makes sense that imagining people without food makes us intensely uncomfortable, and that providing food for people who lack it is intensely satisfying." If each participant spends a few dollars at the supermarket or a few moments rummaging through the cupboards, a drive can quickly yield hundreds of pounds of food, providing an attractive visual symbol of nourishing abundance and abiding generosity. Because food in the supermarket is relatively cheap in the United States (see chapter 6), many can participate in food drives, garnering an emotional boost at a low economic cost.

Food drives also serve as moral training for the young. For example, in the United States the annual Scouting for Food project dispatches Cub Scouts, Boy Scouts, their parents, and other volunteers to collect food from local households and then sort the items for delivery to local food pantries. The program is one of the signature events of many local troops and packs, fulfilling, in part, the Boy Scout Oath to "help other people at all times." Projects like these in schools and clubs are thought to help privileged youth appreciate the advantages they enjoy, as well as develop a deeper sense of solidarity with those less fortunate (Kawecka Nenga

2011). The hope is that youth realize that they, unlike others, often have more than they need.

The food-drive model assumes that households have surplus food to donate, food that might otherwise go to waste. A recent study by the US Department of Agriculture estimates that "31 percent – or 133 billion pounds – of the 430 billion pounds of the available food supply at the retail and consumer levels in 2010 went uneaten" (Buzby, Wells, and Hyman 2014: 11). About one-third of that waste happens at the retail level, and two-thirds at the household level. That figure doesn't include food that never made it to stores or restaurants because it was damaged, misshapen, or unharvested due to oversupply. Including those farm-level and farm-to-retail losses brings the estimate up to 50 percent of potential food that is lost in the United States between farm and plate (Hall et al. 2009). While this may seem like a reflection of the United States' agricultural abundance, global studies of food waste conducted by the United Nations' Food and Agricultural Organization estimate global food loss at about 30 percent, and attribute much of the loss in medium- and high-income countries to the habits of consumers who buy too much and eventually throw it out (Gustavsson, Cederberg, and Sonesson 2011).

While donating surplus food from households does lead to reduced waste, it also contributes to one of the well-known downsides of food drives: the variability and uncertain appropriateness of donated food. Staff members of a food bank in the San Francisco Bay Area listed some memorable products of food drives: mango-chutney-flavored corn pappadums, Jufran banana sauce, salted duck eggs, meatless Nuteena peanut loaf (made with soy, corn, and rice), blood pudding with raisins, and chocolate body paint (Jacob 2003). Even less exotic donations often have questionable nutritional content, working against the public health missions of some anti-hunger organizations.

We can see another connection between surplus food and anti-hunger efforts in the Pound-for-Pound Challenge sponsored by the hit reality show, *The Biggest Loser*, in collaboration with General Mills, Subway, and Feeding America (formerly America's Second Harvest), the leading national network of food banks. In the challenge, individuals and teams pledge to lose weight and select a Feeding America-member food bank to be their beneficiary. For every pound they pledge before the deadline, the Pound-for-Pound challenge will donate 11 cents to the designated food bank, to represent the cost of about 1 pound of food. In 2011, the challenge would donate up to US$1,040,000 nationwide, or about 9.5 million pounds pledged (see www.pfpchallenge.com/). Weight Watchers recently had a similar program, called Lose for Good, which donated money to national anti-hunger charities based on pounds lost and encouraged local groups to mount food drives. In these interesting cases, the transfer of food from the non-needy to the needy is symbolic, as if eating less food (or at least pledging to) left more for those facing hunger.

Food drives and other charitable anti-hunger activities seek to draw from surpluses of food and privilege to address the scarcities faced by others, to turn inequality of circumstance into a felicitous coincidence. However, looked at another way, one has to ask why there is persistent hunger in affluent societies or, from a global perspective, why there are now about as many overweight people as underfed ones: roughly one billion of each (Patel 2007). To heighten the paradox, people experiencing food insecurity also have a higher risk of overweight and obesity (Dinour, Bergen, and Yeh 2007). The eagerness of so many to fight hunger shows that this kind of deprivation makes many well-fed people profoundly uncomfortable (Poppendieck 1998). So questions arise: Why does the global food system produce both surplus and scarcity? And how are they related?

Introduction: poverty and social exclusion

What we eat, how, and why (i.e., our foodways) reflect our material circumstances. The lack of food is, quite obviously, a sign of poverty. But what is poverty? Social scientists use two concepts to be more precise: **absolute poverty** and **relative poverty**. Absolute poverty refers to the extent to which a person or household lacks the basic needs for survival and well-being, things like food, shelter, health care, and freedom from violence or threats. Relative poverty refers to the extent that a person or household is deprived of the comforts and privileges that most people in their society enjoy. That is, a person who is protected from harsh absolute poverty by a social safety net could still experience relative poverty if he or she does not have access to a quality education, a safe and fairly compensated job, and critical public and private services. Global institutions like the World Bank or the United Nations tend to focus on measures of absolute poverty, while those in the United States or other countries of the global North emphasize relative poverty.

Social thinkers tend to view poverty as **social exclusion**. That is, to be poor is to be excluded from many of the key social institutions in mainstream society. For example, many living in poor communities beset by substandard elementary and secondary schooling struggle to gain college degrees or a stable career at a living wage. With meager support from the public safety net, they also have limited participation in the consumer economy, which, as chapters 2 and 5 discuss, is a very important source of identity and belonging in American society. Further, the destructive impacts of crime in poor communities mean that people in poverty are also more likely to experience ruptures in family and community structures, both critically important institutions for achieving and maintaining well-being (Edin and Kefalas 2005).

The scarcity of food as a consequence of poverty is a much more complicated problem than it seems on the surface, especially when examined through a food system lens. The intertwined problems of surplus and scarcity reveal new ways that food can reproduce or contest relations of inequality on local, national, and global levels (Allen and Wilson 2008). While contexts change, some themes persist. Both surplus and scarcity are human creations and, as such, are political rather than technical in origin (Bello 2008). Perhaps more than any other major topic within food studies, patterns of food deprivation clarify power inequalities in the food system and the broader society.

In the rest of this chapter, we explain the social origins of food-access problems and their surprisingly close links with the problem of surplus production. The first half of the chapter focuses on the US picture. We first explore how the lack of food comes to be defined as a social problem rather than an individual one and then analyze how the government and charity groups have responded. In doing so, we explain why the overproduction of some agricultural commodities actually exacerbates the conditions that lead to food insecurity. In the latter half of the chapter, we look at the global picture of scarcity and surplus and explain why some observers contend that interventions meant to address food scarcity problems sometimes make them worse.

Defining a social problem

Hunger is considered a **social problem** in US society, that is, a pattern in society that is widely regarded as both undesirable and changeable, making it an appropriate target for policy or other interventions. As we noted in chapter 6, not all individual troubles are understood as social problems within mainstream cultures. For example, researchers have found startlingly strong evidence that left-handed people have a slightly lower life expectancy than right-handed people (see Ellis and Engh 2000), but we never see politicians demanding a thorough investigation or activist groups advocating southpaw liberation. Even with life and death consequences, it is not considered a social problem. On the other hand, discrimination against people with disabilities is coming to be seen as a social problem, one that demands attention from policy makers and people in general. Just a few decades ago, few thought about the rights of people with disabilities to be active shapers of their own lives, focusing instead on basic welfare and care (Thomas 2002). Nowadays, the social barriers faced by people with disabilities are considered an urgent social problem, not just an individual one.

As noted in the opening case study, hunger in the United States counts as a social problem, in that few are untroubled by the fact that there are people, especially children, needlessly going hungry (Poppendieck 1998). However, it is also important to examine how social problems are defined because those definitions help determine appropriate solutions. In the past, the more common term used to describe a pervasive lack of food was **hunger**, a term that focuses our attention on an individual's immediate physiological discomfort. Since about the late 1980s, however, activists have sought to deepen popular understandings of food scarcity by emphasizing the term **food insecurity**, a state in which consistent access to nutritionally sound and culturally appropriate food from reliable mainstream sources is lacking (Poppendieck 1998: 9). For example, a family that just ate supper at a soup kitchen is no longer hungry, but they are still food insecure because they are not sure to have access to food for their next meal and beyond. The distinction between hunger and food insecurity helps explain why food insecurity is actually a risk factor for overweight and obesity in the United States (Dinour, Bergen, and Yeh 2007). Framing the problem as food insecurity highlights the chronic nature of the issue for most of the affected people. The solution to "hunger" is to feed people. Resolving "food insecurity," however, demands more fundamental changes.

Analysts have explored the causes and consequences of food insecurity at various levels of social life, including households, communities, and countries. In the United States, the Department of Agriculture has developed a method for measuring **household food security**, which it defines as "access by all people at all times to enough food for an active, healthy life." The survey asks 18 questions about access to food (see Figure 8.1) and uses the results to classify households into three main categories. In the most recent survey, 86 percent of American households were found to be food secure throughout the year, 8.4 percent to have "low food security," meaning they had some difficulty obtaining food, and 5.6 percent to have "very low food security," indicating that some household members have had to reduce their food consumption (Coleman-Jensen et al. 2015). Global organizations, such as the United Nations World Food Program, measure household food insecurity in similar ways, but adapted to national contexts.

Activists in the United States have developed a distinct concept of **community food security**. The Community Food Security Coalition, founded in 1997, defines it as "a condition in which all community residents obtain a safe, culturally acceptable, nutritionally adequate diet through a sustainable food system that maximizes community self-reliance and social justice" (www.foodsecurity.org/views_cfs_faq.html). While many of the descriptors are the same, the community approach shifts the focus from characteristics of households to the systemic forces shaping the community at large (Johnston and Baker 2005). To measure it, activists and researchers collect community-level data that include the number of food-insecure households, as well as factors like the location and offerings of full-service grocery stores and convenience stores and the availability of garden plots and locally grown produce. In defining the problem this way, activists encourage the food secure to get involved in promoting social change that would make high-quality foods available to all (McCullum et al. 2005). More recently, a **food justice movement** has emerged within the community food security milieu to focus more squarely on "dismantling racism as part of [achieving] food security" (Morales 2011: 158).

Some communities in the United States are termed **food deserts** because they lack full-line supermarkets, forcing low-income residents of those areas either to make do with fast-food restaurants and convenience stores or travel long distances to access a supermarket. In the absence of efficient public transportation, travel will be costly or impossible, especially if the shopper has impaired mobility due to a disability (Webber, Sobal, and Dollahite 2007). In one recent study of two neighborhoods in Chicago, Block and Kouba (2006) found that residents in a lower-middle-class neighborhood had fewer supermarkets and more corner groceries than an upper-middle-income suburb. By collecting data on the prices and availability of a list of goods, the researchers found that packaged food in the lower-income neighborhood was more expensive than in the upper-income community. The lower-income community actually had cheaper produce, but selection was very limited and the quality very low. Another study in Detroit found that poorer black neighborhoods were significantly

1. "We worried whether our food would run out before we got money to buy more." Was that often, sometimes, or never true for you in the last 12 months?
2. "The food that we bought just didn't last and we didn't have money to get more." Was that often, sometimes, or never true for you in the last 12 months?
3. "We couldn't afford to eat balanced meals." Was that often, sometimes, or never true for you in the last 12 months?
4. In the last 12 months, did you or other adults in the household ever cut the size of your meals or skip meals because there wasn't enough money for food? (Yes/No)
5. (If yes to question 4) How often did this happen – almost every month, some months but not every month, or in only 1 or 2 months?
6. In the last 12 months, did you ever eat less than you felt you should because there wasn't enough money for food? (Yes/No)
7. In the last 12 months, were you ever hungry, but didn't eat, because there wasn't enough money for food? (Yes/No)
8. In the last 12 months, did you lose weight because there wasn't enough money for food? (Yes/No)
9. In the last 12 months did you or other adults in your household ever not eat for a whole day because there wasn't enough money for food? (Yes/No)
10. (If yes to question 9) How often did this happen – almost every month, some months but not every month, or in only 1 or 2 months?

(Questions 11–18 were asked only if the household included children age 0–17)
11. "We relied on only a few kinds of low-cost food to feed our children because we were running out of money to buy food." Was that often, sometimes, or never true for you in the last 12 months?
12. "We couldn't feed our children a balanced meal because we couldn't afford that." Was that often, sometimes, or never true for you in the last 12 months?
13. "The children were not eating enough because we just couldn't afford enough food." Was that often, sometimes, or never true for you in the last 12 months?
14. In the last 12 months, did you ever cut the size of any of the children's meals because there wasn't enough money for food? (Yes/No)
15. In the last 12 months, were the children ever hungry but you just couldn't afford more food? (Yes/No)
16. In the last 12 months, did any of the children ever skip a meal because there wasn't enough money for food? (Yes/No)
17. (If yes to question 16) How often did this happen – almost every month, some months but not every month, or in only 1 or 2 months?
18. In the last 12 months, did any of the children ever not eat for a whole day because there wasn't enough money for food? (Yes/No)

Figure 8.1 The survey questions used to assess household food security in the United States

Source: Coleman-Jensen et al. 2015.

less likely to have a supermarket nearby than poorer white neighborhoods. Well-off neighborhoods, in contrast, had similar access to supermarkets, regardless of racial composition (Zenk et al. 2005).

As these studies indicate, urban places defined as food deserts often have a lot of retail food outlets. For that reason, some advocates argue that the term "food desert" is misleading, suggesting that a term like "food swamp" would better highlight the limited and often undesirable food choices available in poor neighborhoods (Kolata 2012). Food justice advocates, on the other hand, reject both "food desert" and "food swamp" because both metaphors invoke natural processes. To make a more pointed critique of the public and corporate policies that shape starkly unequal food environments by race, they use the powerful term **food apartheid**. As the founder of the People's Grocery, a food justice organization in West Oakland, CA put it, "we may live *in* food deserts, but we live *under* food apartheid" (Ahmadi 2009, quoted in Sbicca 2012: 461).

The desert metaphor may be more apt for rural areas which may, indeed, lack many food outlets at all. Blanchard and Matthews (2007: 201) cite a recent study that found that "over 70 percent of the low-income population in the [rural Lower Mississippi Delta] traveled thirty or more miles to purchase groceries at supermarkets in an effort to avoid high-priced smaller grocers and inadequate quality food sold at convenience stores and gas stations." They identified food deserts across rural America and noted a similar pattern as that found in urban areas: when supermarkets are lacking, convenience stores and other smaller outlets fill the gap. Paradoxically, many farm towns or former farm towns are today's rural food deserts. Some research indicates that rural food-desert residents are more likely to have access to produce from a home garden than their urban counterparts (Morton et al. 2008). But, overall, people living in food deserts are likely to pay more for food of lesser quality and experience negative health effects as a result.

Putting a name to food deserts raises questions about the processes that produce them. Like other analysts, Blanchard and Matthews (2007) emphasize the role of the concentration of food retailing (see chapter 5). The number of independently owned grocery stores has shrunk over the last 40 years while large supermarket chains and discount merchandise superstores like Walmart capture more and more of the market. Several studies have focused on Walmart in particular because it is the largest food retailer globally and has spread through rural areas and suburbs in North America. Research shows that, when a new Walmart opens in a rural area, the number of retail establishments shrinks (Blanchard and Matthews 2007). Smaller or poorer population centers are likely to lose their own medium-sized grocery stores, forcing those residents to travel as much as 30 miles to shop at a supermarket. While some community food-security activists focus on recruiting full-service grocery stores to underserved areas, others focus on promoting alternative sources of quality food such as urban farming and community gardens.

Analyses of **national food security** take the broadest view, measuring both the number of food-insecure households and systemic threats to the food security of a nation or a distinct population within a nation, specifically to head off hunger crises. The United Nations' Food and Agriculture Organization (FAO), for example, defines its mission as "fighting hunger" and sponsors a Special Program for Food Security. That program collects donated funds from member nations and uses them to help food-insecure countries improve food-related infrastructure and increase food production, such as promoting more efficient irrigation systems and so-called "short-cycle animals," like goats or rabbits, which demand fewer resources to yield meat (www.fao.org). The main strategy of the FAO is to assist countries to develop a National Food Security Plan or, in collaboration with neighboring countries, a Regional Food Security Plan.

Some observers and activists have argued that defining national food problems as ones of "food security" is misleading because it treats the lack of food as a technical problem rather than a justice issue (Rosset 2008). La Via Campesina, a major international coalition of 148 farmers' organizations from 69 different countries, was the first to advocate a different paradigm: **food sovereignty**, which they define as "the right of peoples to healthy and culturally appropriate food produced through ecologically sound and sustainable methods, and their right to define their own food and agriculture systems" (La Via Campesina 2008). While both the FAO and La Via Campesina want to see everyone get fed in a sustainable way, their differences in wording reveal fundamentally different approaches. The FAO approach sees the roots of food insecurity in the lack of technology among farmers in food-insecure countries; La Via Campesina sees the fundamental problem as unfair international trade rules and, relatedly, the power of transnational biotech and food corporations to profit at the expense of farmers (see chapter 7). From this viewpoint, a nation that has an accessible, well-distributed supply of food (and, thus, is food secure) will nevertheless lack food sovereignty if that nation does not manage its own resources in a stable, democratic way. This distinction shows that efforts to address hunger may challenge inequality or actually reinforce it.

The scarcity fallacy

One assumption that critics repeatedly condemn is the notion that the prevalence of hunger indicates that there is simply not enough food to go around. Drawing on productivist themes, proponents of new agricultural technologies (like genetic modification) celebrate them as new solutions to an age-old problem of food scarcity. Food sovereignty activists call this assumption **the scarcity fallacy**. As we explain in chapter 6, the industrialization of the food system led to huge gains in agricultural productivity in many countries. In the United States, for example, wheat yields grew from 13 bushels per acre to 44 bushels per acre between 1926 and 2009, while corn yields grew from 22 bushels per acre to an astounding 165 bushels per acre in the same period. Even though farmers comprise less than 2 percent of the US population, they produce enough to provide every person in the United States with 3,800 calories per day of food energy, which is more than one and a half times what an average person needs (Kantor et al. 1997). Nevertheless, in a "fact sheet" produced by the Cattlemen's Beef Board and the National Cattlemen's Association, they claim, "Today, the US population is more than 310 million people and is expected to reach 458 million people by 2050 – meaning we need to produce more food in order to meet the needs of a growing population" ("Cattle Farmers and Ranchers Fighting Hunger" 2010).

On a global level, hunger persists for many of the same reasons it persists in the United States: poor people must purchase food and do not have the money to do it. More than enough food calories are currently produced to feed the world – over 2,800 calories per person per day (Scanlan, Jenkins and Peterson 2010). Globally, the hungry are almost all in the developing world (96 percent) and about one-fourth of them are children (Scanlan, Jenkins, and Peterson 2010). The poorest citizens of poor countries must often spend 60 percent or more of their incomes on food (Scanlan et al. 2010). Despite these well-documented patterns, some persist in presenting global hunger as a problem of underproduction. For example, the Alliance for Better Foods, a pro-biotech advocacy group sponsored by major food-industry associations, subtly invokes the scarcity assumption when the organization writes, "World hunger and malnutrition are global problems that are not readily or easily solved. However, the use of biotech plants and foods is increasingly seen as providing part of the solution. Agricultural biotechnology has tremendous potential as a tool for producing more and better foods on existing farmland" (www.betterfoods.org/Promise/Hunger/Hunger.htm).

Critics of the scarcity fallacy also point out that major modern famines have taken place in countries with enough food to meet everyone's needs. In 1943, for example, a famine in the Bengal region of India killed 3 million people, even though there was plenty of food in the region to feed everyone (Patel 2007: 129). In the wake of that famine, the Indian government began a system of stockpiling surplus grain to distribute to people in need during a crisis. While not a perfect system, it did prevent widespread famine during a major drought in 1987 (Patel 2007: 129). In 2002, however, many of India's 350 million hungry were succumbing to starvation, and anti-poverty activists sued the Indian government to try to force the release of some of the 53 metric tons of stockpiled grain (Waldman 2002). The government was reluctant to release the surpluses; they wanted to keep local grain prices high to benefit farmers and to satisfy the terms of international lending agencies, which demanded lower expenditures on social services; they chose instead to export the grain at low prices or let it rot in storage (Waldman 2002). This story is not unique to India; it is, in fact, dishearteningly common. Ethiopia, for example, was exporting food in the 1980s as many Ethiopians starved, and, "even Ireland during the Great Famine exported vast quantities of food" (Scanlan et al. 2010: 36). Thus, even during acute national-level crises, lack of supply is rarely the root of the problem.

A recent rise in hunger has followed from a global food crisis, marked by a spike in food prices in 2007 and 2008 (McMichael 2009). The rise in prices was due in part to increased demand for resource-intensive animal products among new members of the global middle class in places like South Korea, Mexico, Turkey, Poland, China, and India. That demand, as well as the subsidized growth of ethanol production, diverts grains from human food to animal food and fuel, making all food more expensive. As explained in chapter 7, however, the financialization of food, in which investors make bets on whether the world prices of major commodities will rise or fall, has set the stage for volatile food prices. At the same time, when the global price of oil rises, all farm inputs (including manufactured fertilizers) become more expensive, raising the price of food. The situation has become untenable for many low-income people, prompting riots over the high price of food around the world; Italy,

Uzbekistan, Morocco, Guinea, Mauritania, Senegal, West Bengal, Indonesia, Zimbabwe, Burkina Faso, Cameroon, Yemen, Jordan, Saudi Arabia, Egypt, Mexico, Argentina, and Haiti all saw popular unrest (McMichael 2009: 282). Rosset (2008: 460) notes a bitter irony: "It seems odd that we are in a crisis of high food prices when the past 20–30 years have seen a crisis of low prices, prices so low that millions of peasant and family farmers around the world were driven off the land and into national and international migrant streams." From a critic's perspective, the scarcity fallacy is a rhetorical device deployed to mask the deep inequalities embedded in food problems.

Anti-hunger efforts in the United States and Canada

Anti-hunger programs in the United States and Canada that address the lack of food can be usefully classified into three types: entitlement programs, emergency (charity-based) programs, and empowerment programs. While all share the basic goal of providing food to people who need it, they differ remarkably in philosophy, approach, and impact. The form that entitlement and some emergency programs take reflects popular views of what social scientists call the **culture of poverty thesis**. This theory, emerging in the 1950s, claims that families and communities become trapped in poverty because they have developed cultural traits that work against bettering their situation. Chief among them, the original theorists argued, was an inability to delay gratification and plan for the future. The theory, with little evidence to support it, was later roundly condemned as a "blame the victim" approach, so much so that social scientists refrained from investigating any cultural contributors to social marginalization for decades (see Cohen 2010). In comparing anti-hunger programs, we see that the form these practices take reflects, in part, these and other assumptions about the people they serve. We also see that the recipients of food aid are only one of the groups that benefit from these anti-hunger programs, and it is not necessarily their needs that carry the day.

In the United States, several government programs exist to prevent hunger. These are all called **entitlement programs** because anyone who meets the eligibility requirements is entitled to receive these services. The broadest is the Supplemental Nutritional Assistance Program (SNAP). This program is still commonly referred to as "food stamps," even though it now disburses debit cards rather than paper scrip. Other major programs include Women, Infants, and

Children (WIC), school food programs (for low-income students), and the Commodity Supplemental Food Program, which disburses surplus agricultural commodities (such as peanut butter) to qualifying elderly residents. The practice of distributing electronic equivalents of food stamps or food stuffs, rather than simple cash, appeals to those who believe that the poor are prone to shortsighted decision making, as the culture of poverty thesis asserts. The debit-card system and the commodities program, though, require administrative expenses that could be avoided by simply distributing money.

The history and operation of these programs show that they serve purposes beyond addressing hunger. The commodities program, for example, got its start in a rather colorful episode during the Depression era when the federal government announced a special program to purchase young pigs from farmers in order to prevent an overproduction of pork that threatened to drive prices down. Slaughterhouses meant for full-sized hogs could not process the small pigs, so many of them were killed and ground into fertilizer. Some escaped to run "squealing down the streets of Chicago and Omaha," which brought vivid imagery and popular attention to the program (Poppendieck 1998: 143). Given widespread unemployment and hunger, the slaughter and disposal of pigs for non-food uses drew major public criticism. In response, President Roosevelt announced a new federal agency to purchase surplus agricultural products and deliver the food to the poor. Some celebrated the new program while others criticized it as cumbersome and unnecessary; now the government would have to develop and maintain an infrastructure to amass and distribute these commodities, in essence duplicating the existing food industry. The federal school lunch program, much criticized for unappetizing or unhealthful fare, is similarly an outlet for surplus agricultural commodities (Levine 2010).

The food-stamp program, founded in the 1960s, was celebrated by anti-hunger activists as a marked improvement over commodity distributions and an end to the breadlines and soup kitchens of the Great Depression era, which many saw as a national shame (DeVault and Pitts 1984). As Poppendieck (1998: 12) explains, "Food stamps permitted their recipients to shop with the same convenience and almost the same degree of consumer choice as their non-poor neighbors. In a society where the consumer role is of paramount importance, they 'mainstreamed' participants, making their lives, or at least their shopping trips, as much as possible like those of their non-poor neighbors." In addition, the program is highly efficient in that recipients simply buy food from the existing private-sector retail system rather than through duplicate channels. Shopping (compared to breadlines) also mitigates the social marginalization that is a part of the experience of poverty in a wealthy nation. Critics on the right decry food stamps, like other welfare programs, for allegedly perpetuating dependency. Some states have made them extremely difficult to obtain by, for example, requiring birth certificates of all household members, or requiring that participants have almost no assets such as, problematically, a relatively new car. Recipients living in food deserts also find that benefits do not go very far when used in convenience stores and other high-priced outlets.

When people cannot get enough food through mainstream channels and entitlement programs, they turn to the **emergency food system**: the network of food banks, food pantries, soup kitchens, and other organizations that provide food to the needy on a volunteer, charitable basis. **Food banks** serve as wholesalers, amassing donations from food drives and corporate sources and distributing them to member organizations that are the "frontline" food providers. These include **food pantries**, where recipients receive unprepared foods to take home, and **soup kitchens**, where prepared meals are served. The names can be misnomers; some food pantries have "food bank" in their names even though they do not perform wholesaling functions, and soup kitchens serve much more than soup. Sources of food for the emergency system include corporations, especially retailers who donate near-expired foods to avoid dumping fees; individual donations; **food rescue programs**, which transport prepared food from catered events and food services to soup kitchens; and **gleaning**, where volunteers harvest crops that would otherwise rot in the fields or orchards. These crops may come from the spaces in the field that the machinery cannot reach or may be unsalable due to low prices or a harmless cosmetic flaw. The labor in the emergency food system is largely performed by volunteers as a moral practice (Allahyari 2000).

Those who have grown up contributing funds, goods, or hours to the emergency food system are often surprised to learn that its modern form has quite recent origins (Tarasuk and Eakin 2003). As Poppendieck (1998) explains, there were few pantries and soup kitchens until a deep recession and a wave of factory closings in the 1980s prompted concerned people to organize responses to the widening crisis. Food became a popular focus for several reasons. It was an accessible problem, in that starting a food pantry is much easier than tackling larger issues like homelessness and access to health care; it was emotionally satisfying to provide food to those who needed it;

and it cohered with a growing conservative ideology that valued voluntarism over government programs (Poppendieck 1998). While once a distasteful symbol of a weakened national economy, soup kitchens came to symbolize entrepreneurial community partnership and Christian charity (DeLind 1994; Tarasuk and Eakin 2003).

Analysts highlight two fundamental problems with the emergency food system in wealthy countries. First, societies have come to rely excessively on a system that is unplanned, incomplete, and only partly about feeding the poor. For example, Tarasuk and Eakin (2003: 1511) note that food bank operations are "disassociated from clients' needs" in that the amount and kind of assistance they receive are "driven not by their needs for food so much as by food bank policies and practices designed to maintain operations in the face of a limited, highly variable, and largely uncontrollable supply of food donations." Poppendieck (1998) also notes a geographic mismatch: the communities most in need of emergency food are often the ones least equipped to start and maintain a food pantry or soup kitchen. The second major problem with relying on emergency food to feed the food insecure is that it marginalizes recipients from mainstream institutions. Despite the best efforts of providers to acknowledge and promote the dignity of recipients, the simple fact that recipients have such little choice in foods, Poppendieck (1998) argues, further marks them as failures in our consumer-driven society. Given these fundamental, inevitable shortcomings, Tarasuk and Eakin (2003: 1505) characterize food giving within the emergency food system as "essentially a symbolic gesture."

Why has the "emergency" food system come to serve chronic needs for which it is not designed? Critics note that recipients are only one group to benefit from their operations. Federal and state governments, for example, save money on entitlement programs, and their court systems rely heavily on food pantries and the like as sites for community service sentences (Poppendieck 1998). Many volunteers enjoy the sociability and good feeling they get from feeding the needy and preventing waste, and, as we described in the opening case study, youth development organizations value anti-hunger efforts as grounds for moral training. Corporate donors benefit from having a tax-deductible outlet for unsalable foods and the opportunity to boost their reputations (DeLind 1994). Perhaps most importantly, the emergency food system enables the non-poor to feel better about poverty in our midst, believing that this system effectively prevents hunger. In Poppendieck's (1998) words, it functions as a "moral safety valve."

The creative and caring anti-hunger activists who developed the emergency food system are not blind to its shortcomings (Tarasuk and Eakin 2003; Poppendieck 1998). Many who opened food pantries and soup kitchens during the economic downturn of the 1980s thought they would simply close their doors when the economy recovered (Poppendieck 1998: 259). Staff and volunteers report being distressed by the inability of the system to fully meet clients' needs. As a result, some have looked to develop approaches focused on empowerment, helping people engage with the food system on more favorable terms. It is these activists who have termed and promoted the concept of community food security. As one example, the *New York Times* profiled "what may well be the country's hippest food bank" in Forestville, California, where volunteers harvest sorrel, pea shoots, heirloom tomatoes, amaranth, lemon verbena, and more well-known vegetables and herbs from a garden alongside a food pantry for people with HIV and AIDS (Brown 2006). Most of the garden volunteers are also clients, who enjoy the tasty food and the time outdoors as a kind of "horticultural therapy." One volunteer explained that he used to go to a different food pantry that offered "government-issued spaghetti sauce, old and tasteless" that seemed to convey the message that "You're not worth much, somehow." He finds the food pantry and garden in Forestville a revitalizing experience, in part because he is actively involved in meeting his own needs. Other programs have developed new food distribution schemes, urban farming projects, and other food-related enterprises that earn resources for the organization and provide clients with income, job training, and work experience. Proponents of empowerment programs also advocate a seamless, dignified social safety net, arguing that charitable programs cannot systematically address food needs and other poverty-related problems (Allen 1999; Johnston and Baker 2005).

With the exception of food stamps, domestic food assistance programs at first seem to be outside the mainstream food system. However, the research summarized here shows how both entitlement and emergency programs serve an important function in absorbing surplus foods from subsidized agriculture, major food manufacturers and retailers, and household cupboards. In that sense, these programs are an essential element of the industrial food system as a whole. Like other aspects of foodways, these programs have both material and symbolic dimensions and shape relations of inequality in broader society.

Food aid and the Green Revolution

On a global level as well, responses to hunger are shaped by more than just the needs of recipients and, as a result, can do significant harm. For example, major agricultural countries like the United States routinely send surplus food to low-income countries, a practice that seems like a global win–win. Critics, however, note that this practice does more harm than good when cheap donated grain drives local farmers out of business and deepens the country's dependence on imported and purchased foods. The American food aid program PL-480 (see chapter 7) was founded in the 1950s with the explicit goals of disposing of surplus commodities and laying the groundwork for lasting export markets for US agricultural products (McMichael 2011). Many international anti-hunger organizations, like Oxfam International, argue that a better response to short- and long-term food crises is to help people in crisis buy agricultural products from within their regions; this approach would meet immediate needs while promoting a robust agricultural sector and enduring food security (Scanlan et al. 2010).

Other international programs do seek to increase agricultural production in the global South but on terms that may further threaten food security. A landmark effort in the 1960s and 1970s, called the **Green Revolution**, used funds from charitable foundations to develop high-yielding varieties of staple crops like wheat and rice that were packaged with modern technologies to maximize their yield: irrigation, chemical fertilizers, pesticides, and machinery. In this terminology, "green" does not refer to environmentalism; rather, it refers to the fact that the program dealt with biotechnology rather than something like manufacturing. The "green" descriptor also made clear that it wasn't a "red," which is to say socialist, revolution. Norman Borlaug, one of the main figures in defining and establishing the Green Revolution, was awarded the 1970 Nobel Peace Prize and 1997 Presidential Medal of Freedom for his efforts.

The Green Revolution has had mixed results. In Mexico, India, and Pakistan, for example, a new short-stemmed strain of wheat, together with a package of agricultural technologies, brought astounding gains in yields, turning Mexico, for example, from a wheat-importer to a wheat-exporter. Similarly, six Asian countries (India, Indonesia, the Philippines, Bangladesh, Burma, and Vietnam) became major producers of Green Revolution rice (McMichael 2011). Some countries successfully adopted Green Revolution technologies, reduced their imports of staple grains, and were better able to feed growing urban populations to support economic development (Evenson and Gollin 2003). However, outside of the few agricultural zones where irrigated, mechanized, and chemical-intensive agriculture works well, Green Revolution technologies were sometimes counterproductive because they displaced local varieties of crops, bred over generations, that were much better suited to local conditions and grew success-fully without industrial inputs. The use of fertilizers, pesticides, and irrigation also turned out to be environmentally problematic in many places (Conway 1997). Less often analyzed is how the new farming procedures demanded by Green Revolution technologies sometimes disrupted traditional social practices. The following case study illus-trates one such instance.

Case study: irrigated rice in Gambia

Jennie Dey's (1981) account of a Green Revolution-style intervention in Gambia illustrates the problems that come from ignoring the social context of farming. As Dey (1981: 110) explains, men and women in the Mandinka farming system traditionally had "reciprocal rights and duties which are complementary, fairly balanced, and sanctioned by custom." Both men and women produce crops for consumption by the extended-family household, as well as for sale, though they grow different crops for each of these purposes. Women and men each control the cash income earned from their cash crops, and both are responsible for purchasing food for household consumption if their own consumption crops fail to yield sufficient quantities (Dey 1981). Also, women and men each control the land that they cleared and prepared for planting. They do not own the land in the western sense, but they have clear, indisputable use rights. While men typically (though not always) head these complex households, they do not traditionally control either the labor of female household members or the fruits of that labor. If a wife, for example, agrees to perform some work for her husband's crops, he would pay her for her time.

Three separate international projects, sponsored by Taiwan, the World Bank, and China, sought to develop irrigated rice production in the newly independent Gambia between 1966 and 1979. Rice was both a food crop and a cash crop, and irrigation meant that it could be grown during the dry season, offering potentially spectacular yields that could increase both the self-sufficiency and cash incomes of participating households. However, the international project teams, ignorant of local social customs, assumed that Mandinka men directed household labor and the use of other resources. Women had always been the rice growers in this culture, but project leaders recruited and organized men to clear and prepare fields for irrigated rice, giving men exclusive control of these lands. The men were also given the diesel-powered water pumps, power tillers, threshing machines, seeds, and fertilizers called for by this intensive production model (Dey 1981: 118).

Problems arose when the men, given their other customary farming obligations, had neither the time nor the knowledge to effectively germinate, transplant, weed, and harvest rice. They desperately needed women's skilled labor. Women, who did not have access to the irrigated rice plots, were pressured to work for low pay in the men's plots, and many did, in part because they anticipated that the irrigated rice would flood the local market, driving down the market price for their own rice. Overall, the project failed to increase rice yields significantly; fields were poorly located, the irrigation equipment sometimes failed, and both men and women struggled to find time to work on the irrigated rice, given the demands of traditional dry-season crops. Despite these major international investments, Gambia continued to import more and more rice in subsequent years. This case highlights the social and ecological complexity of agricultural systems and, consequently, raises questions about the appropriateness of standardized, industrial production methods to improve food security.

Conclusion: why deprivation amid excess?

Conflicts, disasters, and market failures can cause acute short-term food crises, but the chronic problems of food insecurity have deeper roots, some of them intertwined with overproduction of agricultural commodities in the global North. As we illustrated in the opening case study, charitable anti-hunger efforts like food drives depend on the assumption of surplus; indeed, the entire emergency food system could not exist without the surplus foods that come through government, corporate, and household channels. Some analysts contend that food aid programs focused on the simple distribution of surplus actually contribute to long-term problems of food insecurity because they forestall more systematic and enduring solutions and the social change needed to bring them about. Examining food aid as a key dimension of the mainstream market-based food system shows how foodways are shaped by complex, manifold forces and reflect persistent inequalities.

As the paradox of deprivation amid plenty becomes even more obvious and troublesome, the scarcity myth may be losing its power. International activist groups like La Via Campesina have long argued that food is a human right, and the Food and Agriculture Organization of the United Nations concurs that "the right to adequate food has been a legally binding human right in international law for more than 35 years" (http://www.fao.org/human-right-to-food/en/). Some grassroots efforts to treat food as a human right are discussed in the next and final chapter, along with other ways in which people are looking toward food systems to solve major problems and effect meaningful social change.

Further reading

Bello, Walden. 2008. "How to Manufacture a Global Food Crisis." *Development* 51(4): 450–5. In this essay, a long-time food activist and public scholar argues that free trade policies are to blame for the current global food crisis because they undermine local production. He focuses on the experience of Mexico and the Philippines and proposes food sovereignty as an enduring solution.

Frongillo, Edward A. and Horan, Claire M. 2004. "Hunger and Aging." *Generations* 28(3): 28–33. This paper summarizes recent research on the causes and consequences of food insecurity among the elderly in the United States, for whom the lack of adequate food may stem from social isolation, mobility impairments, or lack of transportation.

Jacob, Dianne. 2003. "The Fine Art of Feeding the Hungry." *Gastronomica* 3(4): 14–20. In this essay, a long-time board member of a San Francisco-area food bank describes the struggle to consistently offer clients nutritious, culturally appropriate foods while advocating a stronger public safety net.

Poppendieck, Janet. 2014. *Breadlines Knee-Deep in Wheat: Food Assistance in the Great Depression* (updated and expanded). Berkeley, CA: University of California Press. In Poppendieck's landmark book, she explains the complex connections between abundance and scarcity in the US food system, focusing on the critical period surrounding the Great Depression. Chapter 7 tells the full story of the controversial pig slaughter, and the newly authored epilogue addresses a fascinating question: how have federal nutritional assistance programs survived amid decades of political attack on social programs?

Further exploration

1 IN CLASS: Working in groups, use the questions in Figure 8.1 to develop your own categories of household food security. What should

the categories be? How would you use responses to put households into those categories? Compare your proposal to that of other groups and the method used by the USDA (described in Coleman-Jensen et al. 2015). Which classification method would you favor if you were an anti-poverty advocate? Which would you favor if you were a budget-minded senator, interested in shrinking the SNAP program?

2 FOR DISCUSSION: What do you think would happen if, overnight, all emergency food providers in the country closed their doors? What would be the consequences for the different groups Poppendieck describes: recipients, individual donors, corporate donors, government, and service organizations?

3 ONLINE: Choose a country in the global South and see what you can learn about its food security situation from reputable online sources. Start with the UN's Food and Agriculture Organization (www.fao.org) and the World Bank's Millennium Development Goals. How many in this country are food insecure? How many food calories are produced per person in the country? Which foods are imported? Which are exported? What seem to be the direct and indirect contributors to food-security problems in that country? What would food sovereignty activists want to see changed?

9

Food and Social Change: The Value of Values

Case study

Thirty years ago, most coffee drinkers in the United States had two choices for their morning cup: regular or decaf. Sophisticated consumers might choose French roast. Nowadays, a visit to the coffee section of the supermarket reveals an expansive selection. "Half-caf" has joined the caffeine spectrum, and offerings now include beans and grounds with added flavors like hazelnut, chocolate, or caramel. The most novel development, though, is that shoppers can choose beans identified by where they were grown or roasted, as well as products identified with certain production and trade practices, such as "organically grown" and "fair trade." Most people know that "organic" implies environmental criteria; fair trade often bears more explaining.

The fair-trade label was developed within a social movement seeking non-charity solutions to poverty. The first fair-trade link was a joint effort by Mexican coffee farmers and Dutch activists, many from faith communities. Fair-trade networks have since grown to include many countries and products. The classic model works like this: an organization, such as Fair Trade USA (formerly Transfair), certifies eligible farmer cooperatives and then collects a fee from importers and roasters to cover the costs of certification. Buyers also pay a premium price to certified producer cooperatives. Some of the criteria that cooperatives must meet are environmental, such as taking measures to minimize pesticide use and enhance bird habitat; but, what makes Fair Trade unique are the criteria that address social equality and community well-being. In order to sell their coffee as fair-trade-certified, farmers have to pay a fair wage to workers, maintain democratically run cooperatives, and invest some of their revenues in projects that benefit the local community, things like schools, water systems, and other needed infrastructure. Proponents describe fair trade as a "partnership" between producers and buyers and an alternative to conventional exploitative relations (Raynolds 2009).

The potential benefits of fair trade for producers are huge. Coffee is grown in the global South and consumed in the global North, providing a crucial means for indebted countries to garner foreign currencies (Jaffee 2014). However, the basic world price of coffee has been destructively volatile in recent decades, making it impossible for producers to plan effectively. In 2000–6, the price was mostly at an unsustainable low point, far below the cost of production (Jaffee 2014). The premiums that fair-trade coffee fetches can make an enormous difference for participating farming families (Ruben and Fort 2012). And the label provides an easy way for concerned consumers to act on their humanitarian and environmental values. As of 2011, there were 991 certified producer groups in 66 countries which together included over one million growers (Jaffee 2014: 293). Beyond coffee, at least 40 different kinds of products, mostly foods grown in the South and eaten in the North, are part of fair-trade networks (Jaffee 2014: 2), and many are sold by fully mainstream retailers.

But to what extent can fair-trade food links ameliorate global poverty? Despite its success, only about 3 percent of the coffee consumed in the United States is fair trade (Raynolds 2009). The supply of fair-trade coffee far exceeds demand; many certified cooperatives sell much of their product into conventional markets for the low world price (Ruben and Fort 2012). Many other cooperatives that would like to be fair-trade-certified cannot join the limited market, and they now have to compete with fair-trade-certified plantations with hired labor as well. While coffee, and even specialty coffee, is clearly in high demand, there are limits to what consumers are willing to pay for fair-trade certification (Basu and Hicks 2008). While the fair-trade price includes a premium over the world price, it still moves up and down with conventional prices (Valkila and Nygren 2010). Overall, then, fair-trade coffee farmers do profit modestly from participating, but fair trade does not, by itself, ameliorate persistent poverty.

Some observers note a more fundamental limit to fair trade's impact. A privileged northern consumer can buy a cup of fair-trade coffee (and its feel-good effect) for US$3.50, about three times the price that fair-trade coffee farmers receive for a whole pound of beans, which makes 30–50 cups. Are consumers and producers really partners in this transaction? Is the good feeling attached to the fair-trade brand substantially different from the one associated with the smiling Juan Valdez used to market Colombian coffee in earlier decades? In the words of sociologist Daniel Jaffee (2014: 11), is fair trade "a movement or a market"?

Introduction: the decommodification of food

Many people are at least aware of the burgeoning, diverse food movements that have emerged in recent decades. From school gardens to farmers' markets to organic certification, more and more people and organizations are engaging the food system in pursuing their social and environmental missions. Some writers talk about a singular broad **food movement**, in which activists share the desire for a food system that provides healthier diets, more satisfying livelihoods, more robust agroecologies, and more opportunities to forge and renew social ties across the dinner table, market booth, garden bed, and beyond. Rather than just going with the industrial food-system flow, food activists are constructing alternative food systems and working to dismantle government and corporate policies that privilege the dominant industrial paradigm.

Why food? For one, as we have noted throughout this book, food is emotionally resonant; it is a symbol of our deepest social ties and a powerful marker of identity. Secondly, it is accessible to ordinary, concerned people. We cannot individually change the built environment to reduce our need for cars or eliminate structural poverty, for example, but we can change our diets, plant a garden, or work with one or two others to start a food pantry. Similarly, we cannot individually mitigate global inequality (chapter 8), but many of us can choose fair-trade coffee and vote with our dollars for a more just world (Johnston 2008). Another feature that makes food a salient focus is that it is, as we noted in chapter 1, "the intimate commodity" (Winson 1993); unlike other things we buy, we take it into our bodies every day. It is a meaningful and sustained arena of action, one that connects us to others on complex terms.

The food movement is a **social movement**, in that people are organizing to change society and culture. According to one useful framework, social movements are defined by five key elements: "[F]irst and foremost, they are challengers to or defenders of existing structures or systems of authority; second, they are collective rather than individual enterprises; third, they act, in varying degrees, outside existing institutional or organizational arrangements; fourth, they operate with some degree of organization; and, fifth, they typically do so with some degree of continuity" (Snow and Soule 2010: 6). The food movement clearly challenges the industrial food system and does so collectively through formal organizations and informal networks. These organizations and networks have a grassroots provenance, arising outside of major government and industrial food institutions, and their efforts have been sustained for decades. Some observers see the interest in local or sustainably produced foods as simply a fad or a niche market, and it is true that people choosing alternatively sourced foods do not necessarily consider themselves activists. However, as we explain in this chapter, the food movement goes far beyond gourmet "foodie" tastes or dietary preferences. Food is the concrete focus; but, for many participants, the true objective of the movement is a more democratic society (Hassanein 2003).

One thread that connects these diverse efforts is to say that they seek to **decommodify** food; that is, they seek to define quality in a more expansive way. As we explained in chapter 6, the quality of a commodity is defined by standardized criteria (relative to price) and confined to the physical product itself; commodification entails creating those standards and the pricing systems that use them. The food movement, in contrast, defines quality according to the broader social and environmental impact of how those foods are produced, processed, marketed and sold. Activists seek to institutionalize these more expansive notions of quality by fostering practices and relationships that are consciously embedded in their social and environmental contexts. **Embeddedness** is the notion that all economic activity both draws on and impacts the broader society and its relationships with nature (Granovetter 1985; Polanyi 2001 [1947]). Many of the criticisms, summarized in chapters 6 and 7, condemn the industrial food system for practices that are disembedded from their social and environmental contexts; that is, they are developed, promoted, and undertaken as if they didn't have any notable social or environmental impact. In response, proponents of alternative food systems seek to develop more robust and reflexive social ties among local and global neighbors to support an "ethic of care": care for the environment, for self, and for others (Kneafsey et al. 2008: 25).

As this chapter explains, and the case of fair-trade coffee illustrates, efforts to decommodify food must navigate the cultural norms and institutional imperatives of an industrialized, global food system characterized by social and geographic distance and persistent inequalities of power. Efforts to build alternatives or improve the outcomes of the industrial food system must address the complex relationships between economic values and social ones (Lang 2010b). What is gained and lost by using market forces for social good? Can the market be bypassed all together? This final chapter of the book reviews major types of alternative food projects, focusing on their expansive notions of quality and the connections they seek to forge among various participants in the food system. In the next section, we review locally based efforts to undo commodification by shortening the geographic and social distance between producers and consumers. Following that, we survey projects to decommodify food over longer geographic distances through ethical certification and labeling systems. At both scales, we see that even the most innovative and collaborative projects cannot, in themselves, fully mitigate persistent patterns of inequality, but that they can create significant positive change (Hassanein 2003). The chapter concludes with the multidimensional concept of food democracy, which can account for the gains and shortcomings of various food efforts and also help us integrate insights from throughout this volume.

Local food systems

The term **locavore** has been coined recently to describe people who eat foods produced within their local area. Alisa Smith and J. B. MacKinnon, for example, became locavore celebrities by penning a best-selling memoir (Smith and MacKinnon 2007) about eating only foods grown within one hundred miles of their British Columbia home and, subsequently, hosting a show on Food Network Canada called *The 100 Mile Challenge*. In 2007, "locavore" was declared the "word of the year" by the *New Oxford American Dictionary*, and there are now locavore organizations in most major cities in North America, Europe and elsewhere. On one hand, the rise of the locavore reveals that localized systems of food production and trade have become tremendously popular as a mode of ethical and quality eating. On the other, it raises questions about what this trend actually means (Allen 2010). Is local food necessarily more embedded or more just than food from farther away?

Perhaps the most prevalent form of local food marketing is the **farmers' market**, in which producers sell food and other agricultural products directly to shoppers. Most farmers' markets include a mix of vendors selling produce, meats and/or cheeses, jarred sauces and jams, bread, prepared foods, and non-food items like flowers, woodcrafts, or wool yarns, and some include live music or special events to add to the sociable atmosphere. Most markets require that farmers and artisans themselves staff their booths; a small-scale grocer who procures produce from several local farms, for example, would not be allowed. Farmers' markets have proven popular and have spread widely over the last four decades. In 1970, there were about 340 farmers' markets (McKibben 2008: 81); by 2014, the US Department of Agriculture counted almost 8,300 of them, continuing a steady increase for over two decades. In the United Kingdom, the number of farmers' markets grew from only one in 1997 to 550 by 2006 (Kneafsey et al. 2008: 2), where it has held steady for nearly a decade (Spiller 2012). Farmers' market associations in Canada, Australia, and New Zealand count more than 500, 150, and 50 member markets respectively. Shoppers at farmers' markets tell researchers that they are drawn by fresh, quality produce and the opportunity to support farmers and the local economy (Feagan, Morris, and Krug 2004; Smithers, Lamarche, and Joseph 2008).

Social science research indicates that farmers' markets are a boon for social ties and local economic development because they provide a regular opportunity for farmers and consumers to interact face to face. Sociologists following shoppers around the market count many more social interactions in farmers' markets than in supermarkets (McKibben 2008: 105), in part because people often go to farmers' markets in pairs or groups but to supermarkets alone (Sommer, Herrick, and Sommer 1981). Vendors also value the social interaction at the market, both with customers and with other farmer-vendors (Beckie, Kennedy, and Wittman 2012; Griffin and Frongillo 2003). Vendors share information and insights with one another in informal conversation, making these markets function as a kind of business incubator helping farmers, prepared-food vendors, and artisans expand or improve their enterprises (Hinrichs, Gillespie, and Feenstra 2004).

While festive and sociable farmers' markets can seem like the exact opposite of a chilly and manipulative supermarket, critical analyses ask to what extent the face-to-face interactions at the market can escape the forces of the conventional, industrial food system. As sociologist Clare Hinrichs (2000: 296) notes, "Social ties and personal connections in no way preclude instrumental behaviors or the relevance of price." In other words, shoppers can care deeply about farmer livelihoods, pesticides, and local economic development but also about getting a good deal for their money. Likewise, vendors may enjoy interacting with customers and take pride in providing quality food, but they must also be attuned to making a sustainable income. Hinrichs (2000: 299) explains, "Sometimes what producers are selling to consumers at farmers' markets is, in part, the aura of personal relations and social connection. Embeddedness itself then becomes some of the 'value-added' in the farmers' market experience." It is also important to note that not all farmers' markets succeed, and not everyone has equal access to these outlets (Stephenson, Lev, and

Brewer 2008). Thus, even in a highly sociable and simple form of exchange, participants and would-be participants must grapple with the inevitable tension between market values and non-market ones.

Another form of direct marketing seeks to forge even deeper ties between producers and consumers: **community supported agriculture,** or **CSA**. In CSAs, buyers purchase shares in a farm or farm collective for the growing season. In theory, the shares are priced to cover the costs of production, including a living wage for all of the producers. Then, weekly throughout the growing season, shareholders receive their portion of produce, its size and quality reflecting the farming conditions of that year. Some CSAs have only a handful of shareholders while others have hundreds. Some sell only fruits, vegetables, and herbs grown on one farm, while others offer products like eggs, maple syrup, baked goods, cheeses and other specialty products from area producers. Some CSAs invite or even require shareholders to work on the farm for a few hours to reinforce the idea that they are members of the farm, not simply customers. In one sense, CSAs are a "subscription" system, in that consumers prepay for periodic food deliveries much like one would prepay for a weekly magazine. Ideally, however, members would feel that they have a genuine stake in the farm as members. Most histories trace the roots of CSA systems to Germany and Japan in the 1960s. The first CSA in the United States was established in 1985 in Massachusetts (Hinrichs 2000: 299). In 2012, the US Census of Agriculture counted more than 12,600 farms involved in CSA-style distributions. The Ontario, Canada, CSA Directory lists about 180 for that province alone (http://csafarms.ca); CSAs can now be found around the world, from Singapore to Ghana.

As with farmers' markets, the motivations for participating in a CSA are often complex and contradictory. Amid other ethical and moral commitments, both producers and members want to get good value for their participation. As a result, CSAs rarely operate according to the ideal model. Hinrichs (2000: 300) explains, "Balanced against commitment to the CSA farmer, many CSA members remain sharply attuned to the going price for produce at farmers' markets or local grocery stores. If the share price is too high, current members will not return the following season and new ones will be difficult to recruit." Nonetheless, Hinrichs continues, the amount and quality of produce are not knowable at the time of purchasing a share, and "entering a relationship based on such indeterminacy requires some measure of trust" (2000: 301). Analyses of successful direct-marketing links highlight the value of this trust and the mutual education that takes place between producers and consumers in these forms (Ross 2006).

Another way to localize food is to encourage people to grow some of their own. As farmers' markets and CSAs flourished in recent decades, so has the movement for community gardens, school gardens, and prison gardens. **Community gardens** are spaces where groups of people grow vegetables or ornamental plants. In some gardens, everyone works together on a communal plot, but in most gardens individual participants garden their own allotted area. Sometimes water, compost, mulch, and shared tools are available to gardeners. Beginning in the 1960s and 1970s, many community gardens were founded in vacant lots in dense urban places, which provided much-needed green space and fresh vegetables while displacing drug dealing and other negative behaviors (Saldivar-Tanaka and Krasny 2004). Some community gardens host commercial urban agriculture operations, and some partner with youth development organizations to promote environmental education and entrepreneurship. No exact count of community gardens exists, but most observers agree that their numbers are growing (Clavin 2011). While exercise and fresh foods are obvious benefits of community gardens, another has been the sociability of the gardening experience. For example, Laura Saldivar-Tanaka and Marianne Krasny (2004) studied Latino community gardens in New York City and found that, in addition to the substantial produce, gardeners and visitors enjoyed spending time in the garden's *casita* (small wooden house), playing games like *pokeno* or dominoes, cooking, playing music, or simply relaxing and socializing. Similarly, a study of community gardens in Denver found that gardens strengthened community ties; as one interviewee explained, "when you get people in the garden and they're staying in the garden and coming back, you start forming those relationships and those connections and it really starts building a community and a support network for you" (quoted in Teig et al. 2009: 1117). In addition to growing food and socializing, community gardens are often sites of celebrations, voter registration drives, educational events, and picnics. In a related movement, **school gardens** serve as living classrooms that provide children and youth with opportunities to learn about nature, foods, planning, and business.

Others have sought to bring the rehabilitative and vocational benefits of gardening to people in prison or on parole. For example, the Horticultural Society of New York sponsors a training program for men and women in the Rikers Island jail complex that includes in-prison training and horticultural experience, as well as postrelease paid internships in gardening skills (Jiler 2006). At the Willard Drug Treatment Campus in upstate New York, parolees garden 25 acres of land that produce more than 200,000 pounds of produce each year. The produce goes to soup kitchens and other emergency feeding organizations, prompting one participant to tell a reporter that working the garden makes him feel he is "doing something worthwhile with his life" (Chaffie 2006). Another well-known program is the Garden Project in San Francisco, which employs people recently released from prison to produce a variety of food and flowers. The project sells vegetables to restaurants, institutions, and, more recently, to households through their own CSA. A study in the mid-1990s found that, whereas 29 percent of former prisoners reoffended within four months, only 6 percent of Garden Project participants did so ("Prison Life: The Garden's Fruit" 1997). The Garden Project website (www.gardenproject.org) boasts that people have come from around the world to learn about their successful model.

All of these efforts promote face-to-face connections through the production, distribution, and consumption of food in an effort to balance, or even replace, economic values with social ones. As we have seen, however, living in a market-based society means that relations of instrumentality and inequality cannot be easily eradicated. All participants in farmers' markets, CSAs, and community gardens have to make ends meet, and most of us are socialized to focus on the shelf price in identifying a good deal. In trying to create socially embedded food systems, activists and enthusiasts bump up against these pragmatic concerns and deep-rooted cultural patterns. Hinrichs argues that this blend of market and non-market values must be recognized and understood if these promising systems are to continue to develop (2000: 301). Moya Kneafsey and her colleagues, who use the term "reconnection" to capture the idea of embeddedness, have a similarly positive take on the challenges of forging local alternatives. They write that "'reconnection' is a *process* rather than an end-state, and it conveys a sense of 'doing and becoming'" (2008: 32; emphasis in the original). Pessimists say that consciously embedded value chains like these can never wholly replace the industrial one, while optimists emphasize that they offer millions of people a means of forging new social ties and identities and, in that way, set the stage for broader social change.

Values-based labeling

In face-to-face food systems, interested consumers can witness or ask about the social and ecological conditions under which food was produced. When growers and eaters are geographically distant, however, information like that must travel with the product. Activists have developed processes of certification and labeling to enable connections around non-market values (Taylor 2005). One social scientist calls **values-based labeling** systems "technologies of ethics": institutional means of verifying certain conditions of production and communicating those verifications to other participants in the chain from farm to eater (Du Toit 2002). These labeling systems have proliferated in this global era, from No Sweat clothing (not produced in sweatshops), to dolphin-safe tuna, to the Rainforest Alliance's Sustainable Forestry label, to corporation-specific systems like giant retailer Tesco's carbon footprint labeling or Ben & Jerry's various pledges of social and environmental responsibility (DuToit 2002). With these practices, activists hope to promote embeddedness across a distance, encouraging both producers and consumers to make consumption choices based, at least in part, on the social and environmental impacts of the production process. In this section, we profile organic certification as the most prevalent values-based labeling scheme and one emblematic of the promises and contradictions of these types of projects.

Many associate organic agriculture and food with the hippie counterculture of the late 1960s, but scholars date the origins of modern organics as a defined set of agricultural practices to the 1940s. One founding document of the organic agriculture movement, *An Agricultural Testament*, was written in 1940 by Sir Albert Howard, a botanist living in India, who was struck by the sustained productivity of traditional Indian agriculture. Another early proponent was Lady Eve Balfour, a well-to-do English farmer who experimented with organic techniques on her farm and wrote a best-selling treatise entitled *The Living Soil* in 1944. Howard and Balfour both assert that the health of agriculture and, ultimately, people depends on the health of the soil, leading them to question the long-term impact of the mineral nitrogen fertilizers and new agricultural pesticides that were becoming more prevalent during the incipient chemical revolution in agriculture (Lyson 2004; see chapter 6). Howard and Balfour argue that mimicking nutrient cycling in nature through composting, animal manures, and mixed systems would better ensure healthy soils and healthy foods. Contemporary Rudolph Steiner coined the term "biodynamic agriculture" to describe his similar approach; and J. I. Rodale played a pioneering role in bringing holistic farming ideas to the United States. When environmentalist and countercultural movements flourished in the late 1960s, activists adopted organic agriculture and natural foods as a core feature of their alternative lifestyles (Belasco 2007). In 1972, Rodale and Balfour, together with other activists, founded the International Federation of Organic Agriculture Movements (IFOAM), which is now the leading global voice of the movement (Klein and Winickoff 2011).

Since then, organic food has gone from a relatively informal countercultural practice to a highly regulated and rapidly growing global market. In the 1960s, there were no specific rules defining organic farming practices, and any producer could call his or her products "organic." By 1974, there were a dozen organic certification agencies in the United States that defined standards for organic production and created systems for certifying qualifying farmers. Typically, farmers seeking organic certification submit records on their production practices, and certification inspectors visit once or twice a year to verify them. In 1979, California passed a law prohibiting farmers and marketers from labeling products as "organic" unless they were certified by a qualified agency (Guthman 2004: 112). In the early 1990s, the Organic Foods Production Act (OFPA) in the United States and a similar EU rule sought to replace the hodge-podge of private and public certification programs with a consistent certification process and set of standards (Klein and Winickoff 2011). Japan, New Zealand, Australia, and Canada established similar regulations in the late 1990s and early 2000s (Raynolds 2004).

By relying on rule-based, auditable standards, organic certification has heightened the tension between "movement" and "market." First, the focus on auditing means that the standards tend to focus on allowable and non-allowable inputs, making them a major area of dispute (Guthman 2004). The rules cannot simply allow "natural" inputs and prohibit "unnatural" ones; some mined or botanical substances are harmful toxins, while some synthetic products are chemically indistinguishable from their naturally derived counterparts. For example, copper, a natural antifungal agent, is only allowed in organics in limited circumstances, while sulfur, another natural agent, is freely allowed. Chlorine, which does not occur in nature, is allowed for some specific uses, while unprocessed crude oil is wholly prohibited as a fertilizer, even though it is as "natural" as other mined inputs (Guthman 2004). The lists of allowable inputs have become major sites of contention. They are influenced by both corporate organic food businesses, which push for more permissiveness, and activist groups, who seek to prioritize independent producers and limit the growing influence of corporations (Jaffee and Howard 2010).

Organic standards also leave out ecological criteria that have been fundamental to the organic movement as a whole, like soil health and energy conservation. Ecologically, organic agriculture is defined by robust soil health that is achieved by mimicking processes in nature. While most organic farmers frequently use the soil-building and input-minimizing practices that originally defined the approach, some large producers can satisfy organic rules within a largely industrial model by simply replacing prohibited inputs with allowable ones (Guthman 2004). Further, farmers can follow organic rules but still have problematic outcomes. For example, organic grain growers often rely on tilling the soil to dig up weeds rather than killing them with herbicides. However, during times of high weed pressure, some organic farmers face the risk of damaging soil structure and increasing erosion through frequent tillage, a risk they may feel compelled to take if their livelihood is at stake (Shirtliffe and Johnson 2012). Similarly, many organic apples and other tree fruits are actually grown in desert conditions with underground irrigation because such systems face less pressure from insect pests and can produce blemish-free fruit as a result. Would-be organic producers in traditional apple-producing regions with much larger populations of pests find it hard to compete, even if they have a smaller ecological footprint. Alternative certification programs like Eco Apple seek to address these regional realities by minimizing, rather than eliminating, synthetic chemicals. As it stands, consumers still reject blemished fruit, even in organics (Yue, Alfnes, and Jensen 2009). Critics of organic standards often single out another example, organic bagged salad mix, as a vivid symbol of contradiction: a pound of lettuce leaves grown in California without prohibited chemicals and then washed, bagged, and shipped to the eastern United States provides only 80 food calories while using more than 4,600 calories of fossil fuel energy (Pimentel et al. 2005).

A third way that auditable standards set economic values in conflict with social ones is that they often fail to reflect social justice criteria, a key priority of the initial grassroots movement (Shreck, Getz, and Feenstra 2006). Neither operation size nor labor conditions are included in the national US standards, and IFOAM's social justice standards are notably brief: they require producers to have a "social justice policy," prohibit forced labor, affirm the right of workers to organize, require equal treatment of employees, and prohibit hired child labor or family child labor that interferes with education or well-being (IFOAM 2006: 49–50). Organic standards do not insist on non-poverty wages for farmers and farmworkers or on practices to combat gender, racial, or ethnic inequality. As with farmers' markets or CSAs, incomes are determined largely by the market and, as a result, consumers are encouraged to confine their focus to the qualities of the food product itself rather than the web of social relationships which creates that product.

Labor issues have been especially absent. "Promoting ethical consumption and demanding a shift to sustainable and just agriculture rarely include a call for justice for farmworkers," writes Margaret Gray in her aptly titled book, *Labor and the Locavore* (2013: 3). She continues, "Food advocates and their organizations display a tendency to conflate *local*, *alternative*, *sustainable* and *fair* as a compendium of virtues against the factory farm that they so vigorously demonize" (emphasis in the original). The most celebrated labor victory in US agriculture has been in the industrial tomato fields of Florida, where the Coalition of Immokalee Workers has created a certified Fair Food Program (FFP), successfully persuading large-scale buyers like fast-food chains and supermarkets to source from FFP-certified farms and pay a small premium, guaranteeing more robust worker rights and safety (ciw-online.org). A tomato worker on a giant industrial farm in Immokalee, Florida may be better off than a worker on the kind of small-scale organic farm that Margaret Gray (2013) studied in New York's Hudson Valley.

Alternative producers and activists who find nationalized organic standards unacceptable or insufficient have responded in two ways. First, many smaller farmers who market their produce directly to consumers or restaurants have declined organic certification, relying on their personal reputation and close relationships with buyers to represent the ecological and social integrity of their production practices (Guthman 2004). Second, others have developed or promoted alternatives, such as biodynamic agricultural certification or formal but noncertified pledges to use ecological practices. Some, inspired in part by the Coalition of Immokalee Workers, are exploring the feasibility of bringing fair-trade systems to domestic markets in order to account for the social dimensions of production and processing (Alvarado 2009; Howard and Allen 2010). Scholars have called these practices "beyond organic" because they seek to promote a principled authenticity with rigor that exceeds organic standards (Guthman 2004: 170–1).

A related movement seeks, somewhat paradoxically, to embed local foods at a long distance, adapting and promoting Europe's system of legally protecting place names for specialty products. Under French law, for example, only cheese produced in the Roquefort region of France that meets certain locally specified conditions can be labeled "Roquefort cheese." Called a geographic indication, this place-based labeling system is a kind of intellectual property. It is somewhat akin to a corporate brand (see chapter 5), except that it is collectively owned by qualifying producers in that defined geographic region and can never be sold. Geographic indications have become yet another bone of contention between the EU and the United States within the WTO (see chapter 7), with the EU seeking greater protections for them in the world market. The United States has resisted the move, pursuing the interests of major food corporations who prefer to see brands as property that can be bought and sold (Barham 2003). Despite this resistance, the popularity of geographic indications is growing among craft food producers and their allies in government in both the North and the South, as consumers increasingly seek out products certified to embody a unique culinary heritage (Bowen 2010).

The shortcomings of organic certification and related schemes lead some critics to claim that the current organic standards are ethically meaningless, as they fail to escape the neoliberal ideology that governs most of the food system. The structure and content of organic certification, critics contend, encourage consumers, producers, and other participants to focus on individual benefits rather than the long-term environmental and social impact of their choices (Lockie 2009). In that way, organics simply functions as a niche commodity market rather than as a mutually supportive connection among participants in an alternative food system. Some researchers have blamed these standards for a process they call **conventionalization**, when an alternative system increasingly becomes only a slightly greener version of an industrialized one (Goldberger 2011; Guptill 2009). As we discuss below, participating in alternative food systems, either face to face or at a long distance, has complicated influences on personal identity and social relationships, and thus its impacts are not immediately apparent (Guptill 2009; Lockie 2009). While local food marketing or labeling schemes may be imperfect, they are far from irrelevant.

Alternative identities

As we have seen throughout this book, food practices shape and are shaped by identity. It is unsurprising, then, that participating in alternative food systems has some influence on the identities of producers, consumers, and other participants. For producers who transition from industrial production practices to ecological ones, the concomitant shift in identity can be dramatic and emotionally challenging, as existing social ties are stressed and new ones form. For example, Neva Hassanein (1999) noted the critical importance of community in an ethnographic study of dairy farmers who feed their herds on pasture rather than keeping them confined to a barn. To most non-farmers, the idea of feeding cows on pasture seems like a natural, non-radical thing to do and it can be hard to imagine why a technical shift like that could be so personally significant. As Hassanein explains, though, these farmers were acting against dominant productivist values (see chapter 6). Hassanein (1999: 114) recounts one farmer's experience of social marginalization when he began grazing his herd: "I'd go into the feed mill down there, and everybody would shut up," explained Jim Brown. "I had several people tell me that I am crazy at the beginning. They'd say: 'You're nuts. Why are you doing that? You can't get no milk out of them cows.'" These grazing pioneers first formed networks with one another to share information and experiences. However, quite soon, Hassanein discovered, "the exchange of practical knowledge about *how* to graze was complemented by the creation and exchange of values, ideas, and beliefs, about *why* to graze" (1999: 68; emphasis in the original). For these farmers, participating in these networks not only reduces the anxiety of departing from deeply held norms, but also provides a means to collectively valorize their decisions and their new identities as grass farmers. Grazing is not just nutrient delivery; it's a symbolic departure from an industrial norm.

Identity dimensions in farming are especially apparent when looking at gender (see chapters 2 and 6). Hassanein's study included a women's network whose members benefit from mutual support as well as information sharing. These women transgressively identify as "farmers" rather than "farm wives" in a place where many of the men they interact with – on farms or in equipment dealerships, feed stores, and banks – are not inclined to take them seriously (Hassanein 1999: 160–1). Similarly, Trauger's (2004) study of a women's agricultural network in Pennsylvania finds that participants experience the social space produced by the network as comfortable and supportive, where their identities as farm operators or full partners is clearly respected. As we discussed in chapter 6, men, too, articulate their masculine identities with farming, and research shows that "the transition to sustainable agriculture . . . seems to be accompanied by changes in masculinity" (Peter et al. 2000: 231). One study finds that men in industrial farming adhere to a "monologic" masculinity, one that emphasizes mechanized control over nature and denial of pain and discomfort. Those transitioning to sustainable agriculture, in contrast, subscribe to a "dialogic" masculinity, characterized by more openness to uncertainty and sharing mistakes with peers. Similar to the pioneering grazers that Hassanein studied, these transitioning farmers value the emotional support that sustainable agriculture groups provide while forming a new identity (Peter et al. 2000).

For consumers, the relationship between alternative food practices and identity was readily apparent in the 1960s, when consuming organic or other alternative foods was largely confined to and defined by the counterculture (Belasco 2007). For them, choosing whole grain or "brown" foods over processed "white" ones was symbolic of rejecting the controlling conveniences of mass industry in favor of a lifestyle seen as more healthful and authentic (Belasco 2007: 49). Heavily criticized by mainstream society, counterculture communities played a vital role in defining and valorizing these alternative foodways (Belasco 2007). Nowadays, one can buy many of these foods from mainstream retailers, and the distinction can be muted. For example, if a consumer buys organic milk at the supermarket, is he motivated by concerns about farmer livelihoods, synthetic growth hormones in milk, or rather just a vague desire to buy "the best" for his kids to support his identity as a caring father? Studies consistently find that consumer concerns about health and taste outweigh those about environmental impact, animal welfare, or livelihood conditions for farmers and farmworkers (Hughner et al. 2007). At the same time, "green" consumption choices are often part of broader sustainability lifestyles and the values that accompany them (Gilg, Barr, and Ford 2005; Lockie 2009). For consumers as well as producers, deviating from the industrial norm involves making a new relationship with the food system.

The constantly evolving meanings associated with alternative food consumption reflect structures of inequality in broader society. The shelf prices of alternatively produced foods are generally higher; at the same time, the moral assumptions that some alternative consumers bring to their practices can work to reinforce inequality rather than undo it, particularly by race (Slocum 2007). When relatively well-off participants in the food movement seek to bring "good" food to those who do not share their race and class background, they are often surprised to find a lack of interest (Guthman 2008). Guthman (2008: 435) traces part of the disconnect to the romantic agrarian ideal that fuels the enthusiasm for alternative food, an ideal that "seems insensitive to a racialized history of agrarian land and labor relationships in the US." Because producers of color have been marginalized in American farming (see chapter 6), many do not share the dreamy notion of connecting with agriculture. It is not surprising, then, that alternative foods are sometimes derided as "yuppie chow" (Guthman 2008). Apart from the legacy of racist agricultural policy, the zeal with which white activists celebrate their own definition of "good food" reflects a tendency of members of dominant social groups to assume that their own values and perspectives are universal. Food justice advocates criticize alternative food efforts that fail to address the class and racial inequalities at the heart of food problems (Sbicca 2012). Many critical observers argue that we cannot simply shop our way to a new food system. The market cannot replace a movement.

Food democracy

Proponents of the food movement imagine a food system in which a large and diverse sector of growers make a decent living while wisely stewarding natural resources and promoting cultural integrity and social well-being; they envision more self-reliant and inclusive local economies buffered against the booms and busts of the global economy; and they frame discerning eaters as "food citizens" (rather than simply consumers) who recognize both their rights to safe, healthful food and also their responsibilities to others in the food chain (Wilkins 2005). Beyond the concrete changes in production, processing, and consumption, they promote **food democracy**: "the idea that people can and should be actively participating in shaping the food system, rather than remaining passive spectators on the sidelines" (Hassanein 2003: 79). Framing the food movement as a pro-democracy effort both simplifies and complicates the issues. It simplifies the picture by revealing an underlying continuity among the efforts, but it complicates the analysis by raising even more fundamental questions about how power is captured and wielded in the food system to create significant change in society.

These complex questions animate a recent debate about connecting local farms with educational institutions, often centered on bringing locally grown produce into the cafeterias of schools, colleges, and universities in the United States. Such projects seek to support local farmers and institute an upstream solution to childhood overweight and obesity (see chapter 4). Including local foods in cafeteria fare is a surprisingly difficult task, given government-mandated sourcing processes and cafeteria facilities that are ill-equipped for cooking from scratch. Allen and Guthman (2006) critically analyze these farm-to-school, or FTS, programs in terms of the people they serve, their operations, and how they are presented. They argue that, while FTS programs seek lasting food system change and forge important new alliances between farmers, activists, and public organizations, they nevertheless conform to conventional processes and ideas shaped by neoliberalism. Recall from chapter 7 that neoliberal ideology assumes that market forces and individual actions will solve social problems; Allen and Guthman (2006) see the stamp of neoliberalism in the ways that FTS programs depend on private resources like foundation funding and volunteer labor and, consequently, exist only in select places. Much like the charity approach to food insecurity that Poppendieck (1998) critiques (see chapter 8), this structure makes access to local foods in cafeterias a privilege that comes from private voluntaristic initiative rather than a publicly guaranteed right. They also argue that the ideas used to promote FTS programs cohere with neoliberal assumptions. Allen and Guthman (2006: 410) write, "Discourses of personal responsibility and individual success, consumerism, and choice all figure in the production of a neoliberal subjectivity." They're arguing that FTS programs may actually work against food democracy if they make it seem like only market-based approaches to food system change are feasible.

Kloppenburg and Hassanein (2006), two scholars who have been directly involved in FTS programs, offer a contrasting perspective in their direct response to Allen and Guthman's article. They note Allen and Guthman's point that FTS programs depend too heavily on voluntaristic private resources, but counter that proponents of FTS programs have been organizing statewide and national coalitions to advocate, among other things, that all schools be provided with resources for these initiatives. They also argue that Allen and Guthman (2006) focus heavily on the cafeteria connection rather than the "farmer-in-the-classroom," "classroom-to-the-farm," and other hands-on ecological learning components common to FTS programs (Kloppenburg and Hassanein 2006: 418). These other activities contradict Allen and Guthman's (2006) claim that FTS programs promote consumerism and individual choice over participatory and collaborative approaches to social change. Similarly, while Allen and Guthman (2006) see the major involvement of volunteers and private nonprofit organizations as contributing to the neoliberal push to shrink the role of government, Kloppenburg and Hassanein (2006) point to the temporary and pragmatic roles that these volunteers play. They write, "while 'volunteerism' can sometimes be used to justify cuts in state services, it is also evidence of citizen engagement" (2006: 419). Overall, they reach the opposite conclusion that

Allen and Guthman (2006) do: Kloppenburg and Hassanein (2006) argue that FTS programs, however imperfect, have positive impacts far beyond the presence of locally grown produce on cafeteria trays.

In another article, Hassanein (2003) argues that the food movement promotes food democracy pragmatically and incrementally. First, alternative food efforts draw people into an active "food citizen" role where they learn skills and values for re-embedding the food system in its social and ecological contexts. Second, however incrementally, such projects take some power and control away from major food corporations and vest it in ordinary people and their organizations. From that perspective, the tensions and contradictions between economic values and ethical ones do not signify a failed social movement, but rather the essential stuff of food democracy itself. Democracy, in this view, is messy, uncertain, and imperfect, and food democracy is no different.

This debate and others like it raise fundamental questions about how social change is defined, visualized, and achieved, as well as how power works in a food system. Many in the West, particularly the United States, are accustomed to thinking of the economy as something separate from politics, a realm of neutral technology and autonomous decision making. For social thinkers, the economy is an institution that shapes and is shaped by other social institutions, especially politics. As we have noted throughout this book, food, as both a material necessity and an intimate symbol of self, often inspires people to get involved in broader social issues, which sometimes effects a transformative shift in identity.

Conclusion

Food is, as we noted in chapter 1, an especially rich arena for exploring the dialogue between social constructionist and structuralist perspectives on society and social change. In endless ways, we can see people confronting, upholding, subverting, transforming, or restoring foodways and food systems amid larger contextual realities. The Gullah of South Carolina and Georgia renew traditional food practices to maintain a distinct ethnic identity (chapter 2) while locavores seek out foods to express their ecological and social values (this chapter). Individuals can choose how they participate in food systems, but they do so under conditions not of their making. The fine-dining practices noted in chapters 2 and 3 are socially compulsory, and the dominance of the industrial food system (chapter 6) makes it hard, though not impossible, to escape. Our first principle – that food is both material and social – is vividly illustrated by the emotional and physical experiences people have with food.

The complexity of the individual–society tension is especially apparent when it comes to the roles of food, agribusiness, and media corporations in shaping the consumption and production of food. Media corporations present seductive spectacles of food (chapter 3), as well as experiences of culinary tourism by proxy (chapter 2). Agribusiness corporations source supplies and market-farming technologies around the globe (chapters 6 and 7), and food and retail corporations carefully shape messages about healthy diets (chapter 4), quality foods (chapter 5), and, as illustrated by Coca-Cola and Vegemite, even national identity. Nevertheless, these corporations cannot dictate individual behaviors and the meanings that people attach to products and practices. Pabst Blue Ribbon (chapter 5) and the Food Sovereignty movement (chapter 8) are cases in point. In this way, we see the second principle at work: food is both profoundly individual and fundamentally social.

On both global and national scales, food systems produce abundance for some and deprivation for others (chapters 7 and 8). On a smaller scale, practices of production, processing, preparation, and consumption reflect, and often reinforce, inequality by gender, as we see in notes about Gambian farmers (chapter 8), gendered eating norms (chapter 2), and the burdens and privileges of restaurant work (chapter 3). Similarly, many foodways depend on the persistence of sharp economic inequalities. Privileged consumers enjoy the results of low-paid restaurant work (chapter 3), the resource-intensive global food value chains that deliver raw fish for sushi and baby vegetables from Africa (chapter 7), and the good feelings that come from choosing ethnic foods (chapter 2) or fair-trade coffee (this chapter). Foodways and food systems can be used to reinforce or dismantle structures of inequality (our third principle) in sometimes surprising and subtle ways.

Our three principles point to a broader insight: because foodways are, at once, material and symbolic, individual and social, liberating and oppressive, they constantly change. McDonald's changed from exotic to mundane (chapter 7), and Thanksgiving from a religious ritual to a national one (chapter 2). Even practices that persist can take on new meanings. Cocoa production in Ghana originated with colonial incursion but then became a tenuous hope for independent economic viability (chapter 7), and feeding dairy cows on pasture, once standard and sensible, became a heretical practice under productivism (this chapter).

People seeking food democracy must grapple with these formidable and shifting challenges to forge more equal relationships in the food system, as well as to pursue more participatory modes of engagement. The impacts of food democracy can be tremendous because food systems play a major role in several of the global crises we face: human-induced climate change, declining oil reserves, freshwater scarcity, and the disruptions of financial speculation (Sage 2011). As we have noted throughout the book, food is an especially meaningful realm for engaging with these larger forces and forging new connections to one another. In many ways, you are what you eat, but you are also what you grow, process, prepare, serve, and choose. Frances Moore Lappé (2005), a public intellectual who was among the first to insist that food system problems are far from inevitable, writes, "Democracy isn't something we have, it is something we do." Under normal circumstances, food is something we do every day, and, as we have seen, it provides much more than a bundle of nutrients. We hope this introduction to the overt and hidden worlds of food helps you more deliberately navigate this fascinating landscape. To close, we return to the oft-quoted Marx and Engels (1969 [1945]: para. 11): "the philosophers have only interpreted the world in various ways; the point is to change it."

Further reading

Alkon, Alison Hope and Agyeman, Julian (eds). 2011. *Cultivating Food Justice: Race, Class, and Sustainability*. Boston, MA: MIT Press. This edited collection tackles food justice issues, with chapters focusing on farm labor, food insecurity on household and national levels, and tensions within food-related social movements.

Feagan, Robert B. and Morris, David. 2009. "Consumer Quest for Embeddedness: A Case Study of the Brantford Farmers' Market." *International Journal of Consumer Studies* 33(3): 235–43. This paper uses the concept of embeddedness to understand and compare the different motivations that consumers report for shopping at a farmers' market. They add new insights to the research on embeddedness by Hinrichs (2000) that we discussed in this chapter.

Freidberg, Susanne and Goldstein, Lissa. 2011. "Alternative Food in the Global South: Reflections on a Direct Marketing Initiative in Kenya." *Journal of Rural Studies* 27(1): 24–34. This is one of few studies of localized agricultural marketing projects in the global South. This analysis reveals the importance of historical and geographic context in understanding the operation and significance of alternative agriculture efforts and, indirectly, the extent to which projects in the global North depend on relatively affluent consumers.

Jarosz, Lucy. 2011. "Nourishing Women: Toward a Feminist Political Ecology of Community Supported Agriculture in the United States." *Gender, Place and Culture* 18(3): 307–26. Jarosz provides a thorough review of research on gender in alternative agriculture as well as findings from interviews with women CSA farmers. She frames this work within political ecology, a field of research and analysis about how inequalities of power and environmental problems are interrelated.

Further exploration

1 FOR DISCUSSION: This chapter ends with the concept of food democracy. What does it mean to live in a democratic society, that is, not just under a democratic government? How would you define "democratization"? What other realms of social life, besides food, seem like important arenas of democratization?

2 FOR DISCUSSION: To what extent can the fair-trade model be applied to addressing labor issues within national-scale food systems? Could it be used to support rights for hired workers on both large and small farms? Or to support the livelihoods of independent producers? A three-minute video about the Coalition of Immokalee Workers' Fair Food Program provides one example; it can be found at http://www.fairfoodprogram. org/.

3 IN CLASS: Watch *The Garden* (a film by Scott Hamilton Kennedy, Black Valley Films), a feature-length documentary film about a community garden in South-Central Los Angeles, and chart out the positions within the debate. What outcome does each side want? How does each side define property rights? How might things have come out differently?

4 ONLINE: Break into groups and do some online research on a particular dietary practice to answer these questions: (1) Which individuals or organizations are prominent proponents of this practice? (2) What are the key principles motivating these dietary choices? (3) To what extent do the practitioners see it as a social movement? (4) To what extent does it promote food democracy and why? Each group should research one of the following dietary practices: Bible diet, gluten-free, keeping kosher, low-carbohydrate diets (including Atkins), macrobiotic, raw food, slow food, and vegetarianism or veganism.

References

Abu-Lughod, Janet L. 1989. *Before European Hegemony: The World System AD 1250–1350*. New York: Oxford University Press.

Achenbach, Joel. 2008. "A 'Dead Zone' in the Gulf of Mexico: Scientists Say Area that Cannot Support Some Marine life is Near Record Size." *The Washington Post*, July 31. Retrieved from LexisNexis on January 1, 2009.

Adams, Carol. 1990. *The Sexual Politics of Meat: A Feminist-Vegetarian Critical Theory*. New York: Continuum.

Adams, Jane and Gorton, D. 2009. "This Land Ain't My Land: The Eviction of Sharecroppers by the Farm Security Administration." *Agricultural History* 83(3): 323–51.

Adams, Jean and White, M. 2015. "Prevalence and Socio-Demographic Correlates of Time Spent Cooking by Adults in the 2005 UK Time Use Survey: Cross-Sectional Analysis." *Appetite* 92(1): 185–91.

Adams, Julia. 1996. "Principals and Agents, Colonialists and Company Men: The Decay of Colonial Control in the Dutch East Indies." *American Sociological Review* 61(1): 12–28.

Aga, Myleeta and Soholt, Rennik (producers). 2007. "Namibia." *No Reservations*. The Travel Channel, January 22.

Agunos, Agnes, Léger, D. F., Avery, B. P., et al. 2014. "Ciprofloxacin-Resistant Campylobacter in Broiler Chicken in Canada." *Canada Communicable Disease Report* 40(S2): 36.

Ahmadi, Brahm. 2009. RE: Re: Re: food apartheid COMFOOD thread. COMFOOD listserve, June 29, 2009.

Alkon, Alison Hope and Agyeman, Julian (eds). 2011. *Cultivating Food Justice: Race, Class, and Sustainability*. Boston, MA: MIT Press.

Allahyari, Rebecca. 2000. *Visions of Charity: Volunteer Workers and Moral Community*. Berkeley, CA: University of California Press.

Allen, Patricia. 1999. "Reweaving the Food Security Safety Net: Mediating Entitlement and Entrepreneurship." *Agriculture and Human Values* 16(2): 117–29.

Allen, Patricia. 2010. "Realizing Justice in Local Food Systems." *Cambridge Journal of Regions, Economy and Society* 3(2): 295–308.

Allen, Patricia and Guthman, Julie. 2006. "From 'Old School' to 'Farm-to-School': Neoliberalization from the Ground Up." *Agriculture and Human Values* 23(4): 401–15.

Allen, Patricia and Wilson, Alice Brooke. 2008. "Agrifood Inequalities: Globalization and Localization." *Development* 51(4): 534–40.

Allison, Anne. 1991. "Japanese Mothers and Obentōs: The Lunch-Box as Ideological State Apparatus." *Anthropological Quarterly* 64(4): 195–208.

Alter, Karen J. and Meunier, Sophie. 2006. "Nested and Overlapping Regimes in the Transatlantic Banana Trade Dispute." *Journal of European Public Policy* 13(3): 362–82.

Alvarado, Jesus. 2009. "Fair Trade in Mexico and Abroad: An Alternative to the Walmartopia?" *Journal of Business Ethics* 88: 301–17.

American Academy of Pediatrics. 2006. Policy Statement: Children, Adolescents, and Advertising. Retrieved October 5, 2009 (http://aap policy.aappublications.org/cgi/content/short/pediatrics;118/6/2563).

American Farm Bureau Federation. 2009. "Food and Farm Facts." Retrieved October 20, 2009 (http://fb.org/index.php?fuseaction=yourag. facts).

American Farm Bureau Federation. 2015. "Preserving Antibiotic Access." Retrieved September 15, 2015 (http://www.fb.org/issues/docs/antibiot ics15.pdf).

American Psychological Association. 2004. Report of the APA Task Force on Advertising and Children; Section: Psychological Issues in the Increasing Commercialization of Childhood. Retrieved October 5, 2009 (www.apa.org/releases/childrenads.pdf).

Amiraian, Dana and Sobol, Jeffery. 2009. "Dating and Eating. Beliefs about Dating Foods among University Students." *Appetite* 53: 226–32.

Anderson, Benedict. 1991. *Imagined Communities*. New York: Verso.

Andrieu, E., Darmon, Nicole, and Drewnowski, Adam. 2006. "Low Cost Diets: More Energy, Fewer Nutrients." *European Journal of Clinical Nutrition* 60: 434–6.

Arnould, Eric J. and Thompson, Craig J. 2005. "Consumer Culture Theory (CCT): Twenty Years of Research." *Journal of Consumer Research* 31(4): 868–82.

Atkins, Peter. 2010. *Liquid Materialities: A History of Milk, Science and the Law*. Farnham, UK: Ashgate.

"Australian Athletes Get Vegemite in Welcome Pack." 2008. *The Daily Telegraph*, July 31. Retrieved February 21, 2012 (www.dailytelegraph. com.au/news/australian-athletes-get-vegemite-in-welcome-pack/story-e6 freyp0- 1111117071758).

Baker, James W. 2009. *Thanksgiving: The Biography of an American Holiday*. Durham, NH: University of New Hampshire Press.

Balfour, Evelyn Barbara. 1944. *The Living Soil: Evidence of the Importance to Human Health of Soil Vitality*. London: Faber and Faber.

Barham, Elizabeth. 2003. "Translating Terroir: The Global Challenge of French AOC Labeling." *Journal of Rural Studies* 19(1): 127–38.

Basow, Susan and Kobrynowicz, Diane. 1993. "What is She Eating? The Effects of Meal Size on Impressions of a Female Eater." *Sex Roles* 28(5/6): 335–44.

Basu, Arnab K. and Hicks, Robert L. 2008. "Label Performance and the Willingness to Pay for Fair Trade Coffee: A Cross-national Perspective." *International Journal of Consumer Studies* 32(5): 470–8.

Bauman, Zygmunt. 1992. *Intimations of Postmodernity*. London: Routledge.

Beagan, Brenda, Chapman, Gwen E., D'Sylva, Andrea, and Bassett, B. Raewyn. 2008. "'It's Just Easier for Me to Do It': Rationalizing the Family Division of Foodwork." *Sociology* 42(4): 653–71.

Becker, Howard. 1998. *Tricks of the Trade: How to Think about Your Research While You're Doing It*. Chicago, IL: University of Chicago Press.

Beckie, Mary A., Kennedy, Emily Huddart, and Wittman, Hannah. 2012. "Scaling Up Alternative Food Networks: Farmers' Markets and the Role of Clustering in Western Canada." *Agriculture and Human Values* 29: 333–45.

Belasco, Warren. 1987. "Ethnic Fast Foods: The Corporate Melting Pot." *Food and Foodways* 2: 1–30.

Belasco, Warren. 2002. "Food Matters: Perspectives on an Emerging Field," in W. Belasco and P. Scranton (eds), *Food Nations*. New York: Routledge, pp. 2–23.

Belasco, Warren. 2007. *Appetite for Change: How the Counterculture Took on the Food Industry*. Ithaca, NY: Cornell University Press.

Belasco, Warren. 2008. *Food: The Key Concepts*. Oxford and New York: Berg.

Bello, Walden. 2008. "How to Manufacture a Global Food Crisis." *Development* 51(4): 450–5.

Bentley, Amy. 2004. "The Other Atkins Revolution: Atkins and the Shifting Culture of Dieting." *Gastronomica* 4(3): 34–45.

Beoku-Betts, Josephine. 1995. "'We Got Our Way of Cooking Things': Women, Food and the Preservation of Ethnic Identity Among the Gullah." *Gender & Society* 9(5): 535–56.

Bernstein, Adam M., Bloom, David E., Rosner, Bernard A., Franz, Mary, and Willet, Walter C. 2010. "Relation of Food Cost to Healthfulness of Diet among US Women." *The American Journal of Clinical Nutrition* 92(5): 1197–1203.

Berry, Sara. 1993. *No Condition is Permanent: The Social Dynamics of Agrarian Change in Sub-Saharan Africa*. Madison, WI: University of Wisconsin Press.

Bezner Kerr, Rachel. 2010. "The Land is Changing: Contested Agricultural Narratives in Northern Malawi," in P. McMichael (ed.), *Contesting*

Development: Critical Struggles for Social Change. New York: Routledge, pp. 98–115.

Blanchard, Troy C. and Matthews, Todd L. 2007. "Retail Concentration, Food Deserts, and Food-Disadvantaged Communities in Rural America," in C. C. Hinrichs and T. A. Lyson (eds), *Remaking the North American Food System: Strategies for Sustainability.* Lincoln, NE: University of Nebraska Press, pp. 201–15.

Block, Daniel. 2005. "Saving Milk through Masculinity: Public Health Officers and Pure Milk, 1880–1930." *Food and Foodways* 13(1–2): 115–34.

Block, Daniel and Kouba, Joanne. 2006. "A Comparison of the Availability and Affordability of a Market Basket in Two Communities in the Chicago Area." *Public Health Nutrition* 9(7): 837–45.

Block, Donna. 2010. "Report: Pabst Sold to Metropolous." Daily Deal, May 26. Retrieved from LexisNexis on July 26, 2010.

Blum, Janet E. Whatley, Davee, Anne-Marie, Beaudoin, Christina M., Jenkins, Paul L., Kaley, Lori A., and Wigand, Debra A. 2008. "Reduced Availability of Sugar-Sweetened Beverages and Diet Soda has a Limited Impact on Beverage Consumption Patterns in Maine High School Youth." *Journal of Nutrition Education and Behavior* 40(6): 341–7.

Bock, Beth and Kanarek, Robin. 1995. "Women and Men Are What They Eat: The Effects of Gender and Reported Meal Size on Perceived Characteristics." *Sex Roles* 33(1/2): 109–19.

Boero, Natalie. 2012. *Killer Fat: Media, Medicine, and Morals in the American "Obesity Epidemic."* New Brunswick, NJ: Rutgers University Press.

Bordo, Susan. 1993. *Unbearable Weight: Feminism, Western Culture, and the Body.* Berkeley, CA: University of California Press.

Bosch, Torie. 2006. "Is Vegemite Banned in the United States?" *Slate,* October 25. Retrieved January 15, 2012 (www.slate.com/id/2152218/).

Boulud, Daniel. 2003. *Letters to a Young Chef: The Art of Mentoring.* London and New York: Basic Books.

Bourdieu, Pierre. 1984. *Distinction: A Social Critique of the Judgement of Taste.* Cambridge, MA: Harvard University Press.

Bowen, Sarah. 2010. "Embedding Local Places in Global Spaces: Geographical Indications as a Territorial Development Strategy." *Rural Sociology* 75(2): 209–43.

Breen, T. H. 1988. "'Baubles of Britain': The American and Consumer Revolutions of the Eighteenth Century." *Past and Present* 119: 73–104.

Brembeck, Helene. 2005. "Home to McDonald's: Upholding the Family Dinner with the Help of McDonald's." *Food, Culture and Society* 8(2): 215–26.

Brenner, Leslie. 2003. *The Fourth Star: Dispatches from Inside Daniel Boulud's Celebrated New York Restaurant.* New York: Three Rivers Press.

Brett, John A. 2010. "The Political-Economics of Developing Markets versus Satisfying Food Needs." *Food and Foodways* 18(1/2): 28–42.

Brewster, Zachary W. and Lynn, Michael. 2014. "Black–White Earnings Gap among Restaurant Servers: A Replication, Extension, and Exploration of Consumer Racial Discrimination in Tipping." *Sociological Inquiry* 84(4): 545–69.

Broadway, Michael J. and Stull, Donald D. 2010. "The Wages of Food Factories." *Food and Foodways* 18(1–2): 43–65.

Brown, Doug. 2004. "Haute Cuisine." *American Journalism Review* 26(1): 50–5.

Brown, Patricia Leigh. 2006. "A Rare Kind of Food Bank, and Just Maybe the Hippest, Flourishes." *The New York Times*, September 26. Retrieved from LexisNexis on March 10, 2010.

Brown, Rachael and Ogden, Jane. 2004. "Children's Eating Attitudes and Behavior: A Study of the Modeling and Control Theories of Parental Influence." *Health Education Research* 19(3): 261–71.

Brown, Vincent. 2008. "Eating the Dead: Consumption and Regeneration in the History of Sugar." *Food and Foodways* 16(2): 117–26.

Bruni, Frank. 2006. "A Critic at Every Table," in H. Hughes (ed.), *Best Food Writing* 2008. Cambridge, MA: De Capo Press, pp. 318–25.

Buford, Bill. 2006. "TV Dinners." *The New Yorker*, October 2, 41–7.

Buzby, Jean C., Wells, Hodan F., and Hyman, Jeffrey. 2014. *The Estimated Amount, Value, and Calories of Postharvest Food Losses at the Retail and Consumer Levels in the United States*, EIB-121, US Department of Agriculture, Economic Research Service.

Cade, Janet, Upmeier, Hendrike, Calver, Claire, and Greenwood, Darren. 1999. "Cost of a Healthy Diet: Analysis from the UK Women's Cohort Study." *Public Health Nutrition* 2(4): 505–12.

Camilleri, Michael. 2006. "Probiotics and Irritable Bowel Syndrome: Rationale, Putative Mechanisms, and Evidence of Clinical Efficacy." *Journal of Clinical Gastroenterology* 40(3): 264–9.

Campos, Paul. 2004. *The Obesity Myth: Why America's Obsession with Weight is Hazardous to Your Health*. New York: Gotham.

Caplan, Patricia. 1997. "Approaches to the Study of Food, Health, and Identity," in P. Caplan (ed.), *Food, Health, and Identity*. London: Routledge, pp. 1–31.

Carney, Judith. 2008. "Reconsidering Sweetness and Power through a Gendered Lens." *Food and Foodways* 16(2): 127–34.

Carrington, Christopher. 1999. *No Place Like Home: Relationships and Family Life among Lesbians and Gay Men*. Chicago, IL: University of Chicago Press.

Carroll, Rory. 2009. "World: Now Coca-Cola Feels Force of Chavez's Colourful Revolution." *The Observer*, March 15, p. 38. Retrieved from LexisNexis on July 16, 2009.

Carson, Rachel. 1962. *Silent Spring*. Greenwich, CT: Fawcett.

"Cattle Farmers and Ranchers Fighting Hunger: Fact Sheet." 2010.

Retrieved January 13, 2012 (www.explorebeef.org/CMDocs/ExploreBeef/FactSheet_FarmersFightingHunger.pdf).

Centers for Disease Control and Prevention (CDC). 2013. *Antibiotic Resistance Threats in the United States, 2013*. Retrieved August 28, 2015 (http://www.cdc.gov/drugresistance/pdf/ar-threats-2013-508.pdf).

Chaffie, Neil. 2006. "Parolees' Garden Grows in Record Numbers." *Ithaca Journal*, October 16.

Chan, Andrew. 2003. "'La Grande Bouffe': Cooking Shows as Pornography." *Gastronomica* 3(4): 46–53.

Chang, Wen-Ruey, Courtney, Theodore K., Huang, Yueng-Hsiang, Li, Kai Way, Filiaggi, Alfred J., and Vermaa, Santosh K. 2011. "Safety in Fast-Food Restaurants." *Professional Safety* 56(5): 62–9.

Charles, Nikki and Kerr, Marion. 1988. *Women, Food and Families*. New York: St Martin's Press.

Cheng, Hsiang-tai. 2005. "Competitive Relationships among Potato Production Areas in Northeastern America." *Journal of Food Distribution Research* 36(1): 27–32.

Child, Julia. 1961. *Mastering the Art of French Cooking*. New York: Knopf.

Chin, Elizabeth. 2001. *Purchasing Power: Black Kids and American Consumer Culture*. Minneapolis, MN: University of Minnesota Press.

Cidell, Julie L. and Alberts, Heike C. 2006. "Constructing Quality: The Multinational Histories of Chocolate." *Geoforum* 37(6): 999–1007.

Clapp, Jennifer and Helleiner, Eric. 2012. "Troubled Futures? The Global Food Crisis and the Politics of Agricultural Derivatives Regulation." *Review of International Political Economy* 19(2): 181–207.

Clavin, Alma Anne. 2011. "Realising Ecological Sustainability in Community Gardens: A Capability Approach." *Local Environment* 16(10): 945–62.

Cochrane, Willard W. 1958. *Farm Prices: Myth and Reality*. Minneapolis, MN: University of Minnesota Press.

Cogan, Jeanine C. 1999. "Re-evaluating the Weight-Centered Approach Toward Health," in J. Sobal and D. Maurer (eds), *Interpreting Weight: The Social Management of Fatness and Thinness*. Hawthorne, NY: Aldine de Gruyter, pp. 229–53.

Cohen, Kate. 2003. "Fen Phen Nation." Retrieved February 18, 2012 (www.pbs.org/wgbh/pages/frontline/shows/prescription/hazard/fenphen.html).

Cohen, Lizabeth. 2003. *A Consumer's Republic*. New York: Vintage.

Cohen, Patricia. 2010. "'Culture of Poverty' Makes a Comeback." *New York Times*, October 17. Retrieved from LexisNexis on February 8, 2011.

Coleman-Jensen, Alisha, Rabbitt, Michael, Gregory, Christian, and Singh, Anita. 2015. *Household Food Security in the United States in 2014*. Economic Research Service, United States Department of Agriculture. Retrieved September 20, 2015 (http://www.ers.usda.gov/publications/err-economic-research-report/err194.aspx)

Collins, Kathleen. 2009. *Watching What We Eat: The Evolution of Television Cooking Shows.* New York: Continuum.

Coltrane, Scott. 2000. "Research on Household Labor: Modeling and Measuring the Social Embeddedness of Routine Family Work." *Journal of Marriage and Family* 62(4): 1208–33.

Connors, M., Bisogni, C. A., Sobal, J., and Devine, C. M. 2001. "Managing Values in Personal Food Systems." *Appetite* 36(3): 189–200.

Conway, Gordon. 1997. *The Doubly Green Revolution: Food for All in the Twenty-First Century.* Ithaca, NY: Cornell University Press.

Coontz, Stephanie. 1998. *The Way We Really Are: Coming to Terms with America's Changing Families.* New York: Basic Books.

"Corporation." *Encyclopedia Britannica.* Retrieved February 2, 2010 (www. search.eb.com/eb/article-9026395).

Cotula, Lorenzo. 2013. *The Great African Land Grab? Agricultural Investments and the Global Food System.* London: Zed Books.

Counihan, Carole. 1992. "Food Rules in the United States: Individualism, Control and Hierarchy." *Anthropological Quarterly* 65: 55–66.

Counihan, Carole and Kaplan, Steven (eds). 1998. *Food and Gender: Identity and Power.* Amsterdam: Harwood Academic Publishers.

Cronon, William. 1992. *Nature's Metropolis: Chicago and the Great West.* New York: W. W. Norton.

Crossman, Ashley, Sullivan, Deborah Anne, and Benin, Mary. 2006. "The Family Environment and American Adolescents' Risk of Obesity as Young Adults." *Social Science and Medicine* 63: 2255–67.

Cunningham, Solveig A. and Zavodny, Madeline. 2011. "Does the Sale of Sweetened Beverages at School Affect Children's Weight?" *Social Science and Medicine* 73: 1332–9.

Damrosch, Phoebe. 2007. *Service Included: Four-Star Secrets of an Eavesdropping Waiter.* New York: Harper.

Dannon, Inc. n.d. "Activia." Retrieved January 10, 2012 (www.activia. us.com/).

Davey, Stephen S. and Richards, Carol. 2013. "Supermarkets and Private Standards: Unintended Consequences of the Audit Ritual." *Agriculture & Human Values* 30: 271–81.

de la Peña, Carolyn. 2010. *Empty Pleasures: The Story of Artificial Sweeteners from Saccharin to Splenda.* Chapel Hill, NC: University of North Carolina Press.

del Ninno, Carlo, Dorosh, Paul A., and Subbarao, Kalanidhi. 2007. "Food Aid, Domestic Policy and Food Security: Contrasting Experiences from South Asia and Sub-Saharan Africa." *Food Policy* 32(4): 413–35.

DeLind, Laura B. 1994. "Celebrating Hunger in Michigan: A Critique of an Emergency Food Program and an Alternative for the Future." *Agriculture and Human Values* 11(4): 58–68.

De Paula, Nilson and Pessali, Huáscar. 2014. "Agricultural Trade

Negotiations and the Challenges of Food Security." *Agrarian South: Journal of Political Economy* 3(3): 313–35.

Deutsch, Jonathan. 2005. "'Please Pass the Chicken Tits': Rethinking Men and Cooking at an Urban Firehouse." *Food and Foodways* 13(1/2): 91–114.

DeVault, Marjorie. 1991. *Feeding the Family: The Social Organization of Caring as Gendered Work.* Chicago, IL: University of Chicago Press.

DeVault, Marjorie L. and Pitts, James P. 1984. "Surplus and Scarcity: Hunger and the Origins of the Food Stamp Program." *Social Problems* 31(5): 545–57.

Dey, Jennie. 1981. "Gambian Women: Unequal Partners in Rice Development Projects?" *Journal of Development Studies* 17(3): 109–22.

Díaz-Sánchez, Sandra, Moscoso, S., Solís de los Santos, Fauso, Andino, Ana, Hanning, Irene. 2015. "Antibiotic Use in Poultry: A Driving Force for Organic Poultry Production." *Food Protection Trends* 35(6): 440–7.

Dinour, Lauren M., Bergen, Dara, and Yeh, Ming-Chen. 2007. "The Food Insecurity–Obesity Paradox: A Review of the Literature and the Role Food Stamps May Play." *Journal of the American Dietetic Association* 107(11): 1952–61.

Dixon, Jane. 2007. "Supermarkets as New Food Authorities," in D. Burch and G. Lawrence (eds), *Supermarkets and Agri-Food Supply Chains: Transformations in the Production and Consumption of Foods.* Cheltenham: Edward Elgar, pp. 29–50.

Dixon, Jane, Banwell, Cathy, Hinde, Sarah, and McIntyre, Heather. 2007. "Car-centered Diets, Social Stratification and Cultural Mobility: Food Systems Research Directions." *Food, Culture and Society* 10(1): 131–47.

Dobkin, Leah. 2008. "Quinoa Comeback." *Americas* 65(5): 28037.

Dole Food Company. 2009. "Dole Banana Diet." Pamphlet.

Douglas, Mary. 1972. "Deciphering a Meal." *Daedalus* 101(1): 61–81.

Douglas, Mary and Nicod, Michael. 1974. "Taking the Biscuit: The Structure of British Meals." *New Society* 19: 744–7.

Du Toit, Andres. 2002. "Globalizing Ethics: Social Technologies of Private Regulation and the South African Wine Industry." *Journal of Agrarian Change* 2(3): 356–80.

Dublanica, Steve. 2008. *Waiter Rant: Behind the Scenes of Eating Out.* New York: Harper.

Dulsrud, Arne and Jacobsen, Eivind. 2009. "In-Store Marketing as a Mode of Discipline." *Journal of Consumer Policy* 32(3): 203–18.

DuPuis, E. Melanie. 2002. *Nature's Perfect Food: How Milk Became America's Drink.* New York: New York University Press.

Durkheim, Emile. 1965. *Elementary Forms of the Religious Life.* New York: Free Press.

Dzanku, Fred M. and Sarpong, Daniel. 2010. "Agricultural Diversification, Food Self-Sufficiency and Food Security in Ghana – The Role of Infrastructure and Institutions," in Goran Djurfeldt, Ernest Aryeetey, and

Aida Isinika (eds), *African Smallholders: Food Crops, Markets, and Policy.* Wallingford, UK: CABI Publishing, pp. 189–213.

Edge, John T. (ed.). 2007. *The New Encyclopedia of Southern Culture, Vol. 7: Foodways.* Chapel Hill, NC: University of North Carolina Press.

Edin, Kathryn and Kefalas, Maria. 2005. *Promises I Can Keep: Why Poor Women Put Motherhood Before Marriage.* Berkeley, CA: University of California Press.

Ehrenreich, Barbara. 2001. *Nickel and Dimed: On (Not) Getting By in America.* New York: Metropolitan.

Ehrmann, Thomas, Meiseberg, Brinja, and Ritz, Christian. 2009. "Superstar Effects in Deluxe Gastronomy – An Empirical Analysis of Value Creation in German Quality Restaurants." *Kyklos* 62(4): 526–41.

Elliott, Charlene. 2011. 'It's Junk Food and Chicken Nuggets": Children's Perspectives on 'Kids' Food' and the Question of Food Classification. *Journal of Consumer Behaviour* 10: 133–40.

Ellis, Lee and Engh, Tim. 2000. "Handedness and Age of Death: New Evidence on a Puzzling Relationship." *Journal of Health Psychology* 5(4): 561–5.

Ellis, Luke (producer). 2006. "The Supermarket." Modern Marvels. The History Channel, November 16.

English, Ben. 2008. "Beijing Bans our Athletes' Vegemite." *Adelaide Now*, April 29. Retrieved January 15, 2012 (www.adelaidenow.com.au/news/beijing-bans-our-athletes-vegemite/story-e6freo8c-1111116202433).

Erickson, Karla. 2004. "Bodies at Work: Performing Service in American Restaurants." *Space and Culture* 7(1): 76–89.

Eurostat. 2011. "HICP – Household Consumption Patterns." Retrieved December 14, 2011 (http://epp.eurostat.ec.europa.eu/statistics_explained/index.php/HICP_-_Household_consumption_patterns).

Evenson, Robert E. and Gollin, Douglas. 2003. "Assessing the Impact of the Green Revolution, 1960 to 2000." *Science* 300(5620): 758–62.

Feagan, Robert B. and Morris, David. 2009. "Consumer Quest for Embeddedness: A Case Study of the Brantford Farmers' Market." *International Journal of Consumer Studies* 33(3): 235–43.

Feagan, Robert, Morris, David, and Krug, Karen. 2004. "Niagara Region Farmers' Markets: Local Food Systems and Sustainability Considerations." *Local Environment* 9: 235–54.

Fears, Daryl. 2008. "USDA is Called Lax on Bias: GAO Accuses Agency of Inaction on Racial Discrimination." *The Washington Post*, May 13. Retrieved from LexisNexis on December 30, 2009.

Federal Trade Commission. 2011a. Decision and Order, Dannon Company. Retrieved August 11, 2015 (https://www.ftc.gov/sites/default/files/documents/cases/2011/02/110204dannondo.pdf).

Federal Trade Commission. 2011b. Complaint Exhibit F, Dannon Company, Exhibits A-G. Retrieved August 11, 2015 (https://www.ftc.gov/sites/default/files/documents/cases/2011/02/101215dannonexhibits.pdf).

Ferguson, Priscilla P. and Zukin, Sharon. 1995. "What's Cooking?" *Theory and Society* 24(2): 193–9.

Fernando, Jeewani. 2013. "Consumer Corner: Changing Food Retail Landscape in Canada and Alberta." Alberta Agriculture and Rural Development. Retrieved July 15, 2015 (http://www1.agric.gov.ab.ca/$department/deptdocs.nsf/all/sis14494)

Field, Sean, Masakure, Oliver, and Henson, Spencer. 2010. "Rethinking Localization – A Low-Income Country Perspective: The Case of Asian Vegetables in Ghana." *Cambridge Journal of Regions, Economy and Society* 3(2): 261–77.

Fields, Scott. 2004. "The Fat of the Land: Do Agricultural Subsidies Foster Poor Health?" *Environmental Health Perspectives* 112(14): A820–A823.

Fine, Gary Alan. 1996. *Kitchens: The Culture of Restaurant Work.* Berkeley, CA: University of California Press.

Fitchen, Janet M. 1991. *Endangered Spaces, Enduring Places: Change, Identity and Survival in Rural America.* Boulder, CO: Westview Press.

Flegal, Katherine M., Carroll, Margaret D., Kit, Brian K., and Ogden, Cynthia L. 2012. "Prevalence of Obesity and Trends in the Distribution of Body Mass Index among US Adults, 1999–2010." *Journal of the American Medical Association* 307(5): 491–7.

Flegal, Katherine M., Graubard, Barry I., Williamson, David F., and Gail, Mitchell H. 2007. "Excess Deaths Associated with Underweight, Overweight, and Obesity." *Journal of the American Medical Association* 293(15): 1861–7.

Fold, Niels. 2001. "Restructuring of the European Chocolate Industry and its Impact on Cocoa Production in West Africa." *Journal of Economic Geography* 1(4): 405–20.

Food and Agriculture Organization of the United Nations. 2011. "Food Security Data and Definitions." Retrieved December 14, 2011 (http://www.fao.org/economic/ess/ess-fs/fs-data/ess-fadata/en/).

Food and Drug Administration (FDA). 2013. *2013 Summary Report on Antimicrobials Sold or Distributed for Use in Food-Producing Animals.* Retrieved August 20, 2015 (http://www.fda.gov/AnimalVeterinary/NewsEvents/CVMUpdates/ucm440585.htm).

Food & Water Watch. 2012. Why Walmart Can't Fix The Food System. February. Retrieved July 15, 2015 (http://www.foodandwaterwatch.org/reports/why-walmart-cant-fix-the-food-system/).

Forero, Juan. 2007. "Colombia May Seek Chiquita Extraditions." *The Washington Post*, March 21. Retrieved from LexisNexis on February 14, 2010 (www.washingtonpost.com/wp-dyn/content/article/2007/03/20/AR2007032001698.html).

Forsberg, Kevin J., Reyes, Alejandro, Wang, Bin, Selleck, Elizabeth M., Sommer, Morten O. A., and Dantas, Gautam. 2012. "The Shared Antibiotic Resistome of Soil Bacteria and Human Pathogens." *Science* 337(6098): 1107–11.

Frazão, Elizabeth, Meade, Birgit, and Regmi, Anita. 2008. "Converging Patterns in Global Food Consumption and Food Delivery Systems." *Amber Waves* 6(1): 22–9.

Freidberg, Susanne. 2009. *Fresh: A Perishable History.* Cambridge, MA: Harvard University Press.

Freidberg, Susanne and Goldstein, Lissa. 2011. "Alternative Food in the Global South: Reflections on a Direct Marketing Initiative in Kenya." *Journal of Rural Studies* 27(1): 24–34.

Fridell, Gavin. 2011. "The Case against Cheap Bananas: Lessons from the EU–Caribbean Banana Agreement." *Critical Sociology* 37(3): 285–307.

Fried, Ellen and Simon, Michele. 2007. "The Competitive Food Conundrum: Can Government Regulations Improve School Food?" *Duke Law Journal* 56: 1491–1539.

Friedman-Rudovsky, Jean. 2012. "Quinoa: The Dark Side of an Andean Superfood." *Time*, April 3. Retrieved September 17, 2015 (http://content.time.com/time/world/article/0,8599,2110890-2,00.html).

Friedmann, Harriet. 1982. "The Political Economy of Food: The Rise and Fall of the Postwar International Food Order." *American Journal of Sociology* 88 (Supplement): 248–86.

Frongillo, Edward A. and Horan, Claire M. 2004. "Hunger and Aging." *Generations* 28(3): 28–33.

Fyksen, Jane. 2006. "Skinny Cows Aren't So Sexy: The 'Dairyness' Debacle." *Agriview*, November 9. Retrieved December 12, 2007 (www.agriview.com/articles/2006/11/09/dairy_news/feature_stories/producer02.txt).

Gabaccia, Donna R. 1998. *We Are What We Eat: Ethnic Food and the Making of Americans.* Cambridge, MA: Harvard University Press.

Gal, David and Wilkie, James. 2010. "Real Men Don't Eat Quiche: Regulation of Gender-Expressive Choices by Men." *Social Psychological and Personality Science* 1(4): 291–301.

General Mills. n.d. "Grow Up Strong with Big G Kid Cereals." Retrieved January 10, 2012 (http://growupstrong.com/).

Genoways, Ted. 2015. "Corn Wars." *The New Republic*, August 16. Retrieved August 27, 2015 (http://www.newrepublic.com/article/122441/corn-wars).

Germann Molz, Jennie. 2004. "Tasting an Imagined Thailand: Authenticity and Culinary Tourism in Thai Restaurants," in L. M. Long (ed.), *Culinary Tourism.* Lexington, KY: University of Kentucky Press, pp. 53–75.

Germov, John and Williams, Lauren. 2004. "Introducing the Social Appetite: Towards a Sociology of Food and Nutrition," in J. Germov and L. Williams (eds), *A Sociology of Food and Nutrition: The Social Appetite.* Oxford: Oxford University Press, pp. 3–26.

"Ghana Cocoa Crisis." 2000. *Africa News*, August 7. Retrieved from LexisNexis on January 28, 2010.

Gilbert, Christopher L. 2009. "Cocoa Market Liberalization in Retrospect." *Review of Business and Economics* 54(3): 294–312.

Gilg, Andrew, Barr, Stewart, and Ford, Nicholas. 2005. "Green Consumption or Sustainable Lifestyles? Identifying the Sustainable Consumer." *Futures* 37(6): 481–504.

Glassner, Barry. 2006. *The Gospel of Food: Everything You Think You Know About Food is Wrong*. New York: Ecco.

Glazer, Nona Y. 1993. *Women's Paid and Unpaid Labor: The Work Transfer in Health Care and Retailing*. Philadelphia, PA: Temple University Press.

Glenn, LaShanda M., Lindsey, Rebecca L., Folster, Jason P., et al. 2013. "Antimicrobial Resistance Genes in Multidrug-Resistant *Salmonella enterica* Isolated from Animals, Retail Meats, and Humans in the United States and Canada." *Microbial Drug Resistance* 19(3): 175–84. doi:10.1089/mdr.2012.0177.

Goffman, Erving. 1959. *The Presentation of Self in Everyday Life*. New York: Anchor.

Goldberger, Jessica R. 2011. "Conventionalization, Civic Engagement, and the Sustainability of Organic Agriculture." *Journal of Rural Studies* 27(3): 288–96.

Gonzalez, Wendy, Jones, Sonya J., and Frongillo, Edward A. 2009. "Restricting Snacks in US Elementary Schools is Associated with Higher Frequency of Fruit and Vegetable Consumption." *Journal of Nutrition* 139: 142–4.

Goodman, David, Sorj, Bernardo, and Wilkinson, John. 1987. *From Farming to Biotechnology: A Theory of Agro-Industrial Development*. New York: Blackwell.

Gragg, Maryanne. 2013. "17 Superfoods That Fight Disease – ABC News." Retrieved August 10, 2015 (http://abcnews.go.com/Health/Wellness/17-superfoods-fight-disease/story?id=19348767).

Granovetter, Mark. 1985. "Economic Action and Social Structure: The Problem of Embeddedness." *American Journal of Sociology* 91(3): 481–510.

Gray, Margaret. 2013. *Labor and the Locavore: The Making of a Comprehensive Food Ethic*. Berkeley, CA: University of California Press.

Grazian, David. 2003. *Blue Chicago: The Search for Authenticity in Urban Blues Clubs*. Chicago, IL: University of Chicago Press.

Grier, Beverly. 1992. "Pawns, Porters, and Petty Traders: Women in the Transition to Cash Crop Agriculture in Colonial Ghana." *Signs* 17(2): 304–28.

Griffin, Matthew R. and Frongillo, Edward A. 2003. "Experiences and Perspectives of Farmers from Upstate New York Farmers' Markets." *Agriculture and Human Values* 20(2): 189–203.

Guptill, Amy. 2009. "Exploring the Conventionalization of Organic Dairy: Trends and Counter-Trends in Upstate New York." *Agriculture and Human Values* 26: 29–42.

Guptill, Amy and Welsh, Rick. 2014. "The Declining Middle of American

Agriculture: A Spatial Phenomenon" in C. Bailey, L. Jensen, and E. Ransom (eds), *Rural America in a Globalizing World: Problems and Prospects for the 2010s*. Morgantown, WV: West Virginia University Press, pp. 36–50.

Gustavsson, Jenny, Cederberg, Christel, and Sonesson, Ulf. 2011. *Food Losses and Food Waste: Extent, Causes and Prevention*. FAO, Rome.

Guthman, Julie. 2004. *Agrarian Dreams: The Paradox of Organic Farming in California*. Berkeley, CA: University of California Press.

Guthman, Julie. 2008. "Bringing Good Food to Others: Investigating the Subjects of Alternative Food Practice." *Cultural Geographies* 15(4): 431–47.

Guthman, Julie. 2011. *Weighing In: Obesity, Food Justice, and the Limits of Capitalism*. Berkeley, CA: University of California Press.

Hall, Kevin D., Guo, Juen, Dore, Michael, and Chow, Carson C. 2009. "The Progressive Increase of Food Waste in America and Its Environmental Impact." *PLoS ONE* 4(11): e7940. doi:10.1371/journal.pone.0007940.

Halloran, Vivian. 2004. "Biting Reality: Extreme Eating and the Fascination with the Gustatory Subject." *Iowa Journal of Cultural Studies* 4: 24–42.

Hansen, Signe. 2008. "Society of the Appetite: Celebrity Chefs Deliver Consumers." *Food, Culture and Society* 11(1): 49–67.

Harnack, Lisa, Story, Mary, Martinson, Brian, Neumark-Sztainer, Dianne, and Stang, Jamie. 1998. "Guess Who's Cooking? The Role of Men in Meal Planning, Shopping, and Preparation in US Families." *Journal of the American Dietetic Association* 98(9): 995–1000.

Harris, B. L. and Kolver, E. S. 2001. "Review of Holsteinization on Intensive Pastoral Dairy Farming in New Zealand." *Journal of Dairy Science* 84: E56–E61.

Harris, Deborah A. and Giuffre, Patti. 2015. *Taking the Heat: Women Chefs and Gender Inequality in the Professional Kitchen*. New Brunswick, NJ: Rutgers University Press.

Harris, Jessica B. 2011. *High on the Hog: A Culinary Journey from Africa to America*. New York: Bloomsbury.

Harris, Marvin. 1985. *Good to Eat: Riddles of Food and Culture*. Longgrove, IL: Waveland Press.

Hassanein, Neva. 1999. *Changing the Way America Farms: Knowledge and Community in the Sustainable Agriculture Movement*. Lincoln, NE: University of Nebraska Press.

Hassanein, Neva. 2003. "Practicing Food Democracy: A Pragmatic Politics of Transformation." *Journal of Rural Studies* 19(1): 77–86.

Healey, Kelvin. 2006. "Ultimate Insult as US Bans Vegemite." *The Sunday Mail*, October 22, p. 35.

Hesterman, Oran. 2011. *Fair Food: Growing a Healthy, Sustainable Food System for All*. New York: PublicAffairs.

Higgins, Janine A., Higbee, Dana R., Donahoo, William T., Brown, Ian L., Bell, Melanie L., and Bessesen, Daniel H. 2004. "Resistant Starch

Consumption Promotes Lipid Oxidation." *Nutrition and Metabolism* 1: 8–18.

Higman, B. W. 1995. *Slave Population of the British Caribbean, 1807–1834*. Kingston, Jamaica: University Press of the West Indies.

Himes, Christine and Reynolds, Sandra. 2005. "The Changing Relationship between Obesity and Educational Status." *Gender Issues* 22(2): 45–57.

Hinrichs, C. Clare. 2000. "Embeddedness and Local Food Systems: Notes on Two Types of Direct Agricultural Market." *Journal of Rural Studies* 16(3): 295–303.

Hinrichs, C. Clare, Gillespie Jr, Gilbert W., and Feenstra, Gail W. 2004. "Social Learning and Innovation at Retail Farmers' Markets." *Rural Sociology* 69(1): 31–58.

Hitt, Jack. 1996. "The Science of Supermarkets." *The New York Times*, March 10, p. 56. Retrieved from LexisNexis on July 15, 2010.

Hobsbawm, Eric. 1983. "Introduction: Inventing Traditions," in E. Hobsbawm and T. Ranger (eds), *The Invention of Tradition*. Cambridge, UK: Cambridge University Press, pp. 1–14.

Hochschild, Arlie R. 1983. *The Managed Heart: Commercialization of Human Feeling*. Berkeley. CA: University of California.

Holt, Douglas B. 2006. "Toward a Sociology of Branding." *Journal of Consumer Culture* 6: 299–302.

Howard, Albert. 1940. *An Agricultural Testament*. Oxford: Oxford University Press.

Howard, Judith. 2000. "The Social Psychology of Identities." *Annual Review of Sociology* 26: 367–93.

Howard, Philip H. and Allen, Patricia. 2010. "Beyond Organic and Fair Trade? An Analysis of Ecolabel Preferences in the United States." *Rural Sociology* 75(2): 244–69.

Hughes, Alex. 2006. "Geographies of Exchange and Circulation: Transnational Trade and Governance." *Progress in Human Geography* 30(5): 635–43.

Hughner, Renée Shaw, McDonagh, Pierre, Prothero, Andrea, Shultz, Clifford J., and Stanton, Julie. 2007. "Who are Organic Food Consumers? A Compilation and Review of Why People Purchase Organic Food." *Journal of Consumer Behaviour* 6: 94–110.

IFOAM. 2006. *The IFOAM Basic Standards for Organic Production and Processing: Version 2005*.

Inness, Sherrie. 2005. *Secret Ingredients: Race, Gender, and Class at the Dinner Table*. New York: Palgrave Macmillan.

Issenberg, Sasha. 2007. *The Sushi Economy: Globalization and the Making of a Modern Delicacy*. New York: Gotham.

Jacob, Dianne. 2003. "The Fine Art of Feeding the Hungry." *Gastronomica* 3(4): 14–20.

Jaffee, Daniel. 2004. *Brewing Justice: Fair Trade Coffee, Sustainability, and Survival* (updated edition). Berkeley, CA: University of California Press.

Jaffee, Daniel and Howard, Philip H. 2010. "Corporate Cooptation of Organic and Fair Trade Standards." *Agriculture and Human Values* 27(4): 387–99.

Jarosz, Lucy. 2011. "Nourishing Women: Toward a Feminist Political Ecology of Community Supported Agriculture in the United States." *Gender, Place and Culture* 18(3): 307–26.

Jaslow, Ryan. 2012. "Obesity Pill Qsymia Gains FDA Approval." Retrieved August 12, 2015 (http://www.cbsnews.com/news/obesity-pill-qsymia-gains-fda-approval/).

Jiler, James. 2006. *Doing Time in the Garden: Life Lessons through Prison Horticulture*. Oakland, CA: New Village Press.

John, Deborah Roedder. 1999. "Consumer Socialization of Children: A Retrospective Look at Twenty-Five Years of Research." *Journal of Consumer Research* 26(3): 183–213.

Johnston, Josée. 2008. "The Citizen-Consumer Hybrid: Ideological Tensions and the Case of Whole Foods Market." *Theory and Society* 37(3): 229–70.

Johnston, Josée and Baker, Lauren. 2005. "Eating Outside the Box: FoodShare's Good Food Box and the Challenge of Scale." *Agriculture and Human Values* 22(3): 313–25.

Johnston, Josée and Baumann, Shyon. 2015. *Foodies: Democracy and Distinction in the Gourmet Foodscape, Second Edition*. New York: Taylor & Francis.

Jordan, Jennifer A. 2007. "The Heirloom Tomato as Cultural Object: Investigating Taste and Space." *Sociologia Ruralis* 47(1): 20–41.

Kahn, Barbara E. and McAllister, Leigh M. 1997. *Grocery Revolution: The New Focus on the Consumer*. Reading, MA: Addison-Wesley.

Kamp, David. 2006. *The United States of Arugula: How We Became a Gourmet Nation*. New York: Broadway Books.

Kantor, Linda Scott, Lipton, Kathryn, Manchester, Alden, and Oliveira, Victoria. 1997. "Estimating and Addressing America's Food Losses." *Food Review* 20(1): 2–12.

Kasson, John F. 1991. *Rudeness & Civility: Manners in Nineteenth-Century Urban America*. New York: Macmillan.

Kastner, J. J. and Pawsey, R. K. 2002. "Harmonising Sanitary Measures and Resolving Trade Disputes through the WTO–SPS Framework. Part I: A Case Study of the US–EU Hormone-treated Beef Dispute." *Food Control* 13(1): 49–55.

Kaufman, Frederick. 2009. *A Short History of the American Stomach*. New York: Houghton Mifflin Harcourt.

Kawecka Nenga, Sandi. 2011. "Volunteering to Give up Privilege? How Affluent Youth Volunteers Respond to Class Privilege." *Journal of Contemporary Ethnography* 40(3): 263–89.

Kenner, Robert. 2008. *Food, Inc.* Magnolia Home Entertainment.

Ketchum, Cheri. 2005. "The Essence of Cooking Shows: How the Food

Network Constructs Consumer Fantasies." *Journal of Communication Inquiry* 29(3): 217–34.

Khanna, Vikramaditya S. 2005. "The Economic History of the Corporate Form in Ancient India." Unpublished manuscript. Retrieved January 29, 2010 (www/law.yale.edu/documents/pdf/cbl/Khanna_Ancient_India_informal.pdf).

Kilman, Scott. 2000. "Monsanto's Biotech Spud is Being Pulled from the Fryer at Fast-Food Chain" (press release). Retrieved January 4, 2010 (www.organicconsumers.org/ge/gepotatoban.cfm).

Kirkman, Michael A. 2007. "Global Markets for Processed Potato Products," in D. Vreugdenhil, J. Bradshaw, C. Gephardt, F. Govers, M. A. Taylor, D. K. L. MacKerron, and H. A. Ross (eds), *Potato Biology and Biotechnology: Advances and Perspectives*. New York: Elsevier, pp. 27–44.

Klein, Kendra and Winickoff, David E. 2011. "Organic Regulation across the Atlantic: Emergence, Divergence, Convergence." *Environmental Politics* 20(2): 153–72.

Klinenberg, Eric. 2002. *Heat Wave: A Social Autopsy of Disaster in Chicago.* Chicago, IL: University of Chicago Press.

Kloppenburg, Jack and Hassanein, Neva. 2006. "From Old School to Reform School?" *Agriculture and Human Values* 23(4): 417–21.

Knai, Cécile, Pomerleau, Joceline, Lock, Karen, and McKee, Martin. 2006. "Getting Children to Eat More Fruit and Vegetables: A Systematic Review." *Preventive Medicine* 42(2): 85–95.

Kneafsey, Moya, Cox, Rosie, Holloway, Lewis, Dowler, Elizabeth, Venn, Laura, and Tuomainen, Helena. 2008. *Reconnecting Consumers, Producers and Food: Exploring Alternatives.* Oxford and New York: Berg.

Kolata, Gina. 2012. "Studies Question the Pairing of Food Deserts and Obesity." *The New York Times*, April 17. Retrieved from Lexis-Nexis March 1, 2016.

Konefal, Jason, Bain, Carmen, Mascarenhas, Michael, and Busch, Lawrence. 2007. "Supermarkets and Supply Chains in North America," in D. Burch and G. Lawrence (eds), *Supermarkets and Agri-food Supply Chains: Transformations in the Production and Consumption of Foods.* Cheltenham: Edward Elgar, pp. 268–88.

Konefal, Jason, Mascarenhas, Michael, and Hatanaka, Maki. 2005. "Governance in the Global Agro-food System: Backlighting the Role of Transnational Supermarket Chains." *Agriculture and Human Values* 22(3): 291–302.

Korczynski, Marek and Ott, Ursula. 2004. "When Production and Consumption Meet: Cultural Contradictions and the Enchanting Myth of Customer Sovereignty." *Journal of Management Studies* 41: 575–99.

Kroshus, Emily. 2008. "Gender, Marital Status, and Commercially Prepared Food Expenditure." *Journal of Nutrition Education and Behavior* 40(6): 355–60.

Kuh, Patric. 2001. *The Last Days of Haute Cuisine*. New York: Penguin.

Kurdek, Lawrence A. 2007. "The Allocation of Household Labor by Partners in Gay and Lesbian Couples." *Journal of Family Issues* 28: 132–48.

Kwan, Samantha and Graves, Jennifer. 2013. *Framing Fat: Competing Constructions in Contemporary Culture*. New Brunswick, NJ: Rutgers University Press.

Lam, Francis. 2006. "Life on the Line," in H. Hughes (ed.), *Best Food Writing 2006*. Cambridge, MA: De Capo Press, pp. 263–8.

Lang, Tim. 2010a. "Crisis? What Crisis? The Normality of the Current Food Crisis." *Journal of Agrarian Change* 10(1): 87–97.

Lang, Tim. 2010b. "From 'Value-For-Money' to 'Values-For-Money'? Ethical Food and Policy in Europe." *Environment and Planning A* 42: 1814–32.

Lang, Tim and Heasman, Michael. 2004. *Food Wars: The Global Battle for Mouths, Minds and Markets*. London: Earthscan.

Lanz, Rainer and Miroudot, Sebastien. 2011. "Intra-Firm Trade." OECD Trade Policy Working Papers No. 114.

Lappé, Frances Moore. 2005. *Democracy's Edge: Choosing to Save Our Country by Bringing Democracy to Life*. New York: Jossey-Bass.

Laudan, Rachel. 2001. "A Plea for Culinary Modernism: Why We Should Love New, Fast, Processed Food." *Gastronomica* 1(1): 36-44.

La Via Campesina. 2008. *Food Sovereignty for Africa: A Challenge at Fingertips*. Retrieved February 24 2010 (http://viacampesina.net/downloads/PDF/Brochura_em_INGLES.pdf).

Lawrence, Geoffrey and Burch, David. 2007. "Understanding Supermarkets and Agri-food Supply Chains," in D. Burch and G. Lawrence (eds), *Supermarkets and Agri-food Supply Chains: Transformations in the Production and Consumption of Foods*. Cheltenham: Edward Elgar, pp. 1–25.

LeBesco, Karen and Naccarato, Peter. 2008. "Julia Child, Martha Stewart, and the Rise of Culinary Capital," in K. LeBesco and P. Naccarato (eds), *Edible Ideologies: Representing Food and Meaning*. Albany, NY: State University of New York Press, pp. 223–38.

Le Billon, Karen. 2012. *French Kids Eat Everything*. New York: HarperCollins/Morrow.

Lechner, Frank J. 2009. *Globalization: The Making of World Society*. Chichester, UK and Malden, MA: Wiley-Blackwell.

Lee, Jennifer 8. 2008. *The Fortune Cookie Chronicles: Adventures in the World of Chinese Food*. New York: Twelve.

Lee, Wan-chen Jenny, Shimizu, Mitsuru, Kniffin, Kevin M., and Wansink, Brian. 2013. "You Taste What You See: Do Organic Labels Bias Taste Perceptions?" *Food Quality and Preference* 29(1): 33–9.

Leidner, Robin. 1993. *Fast Food, Fast Talk: Service Work and the Routinization of Everyday Life*. Berkeley, CA: University of California.

Leschziner, Vanina. 2007. "Kitchen Stories: Patterns of Recognition in Contemporary High Cuisine," in *Sociological Forum* 22(1): 77–101.

Levine, Susan. 2010. *School Lunch Politics: The Surprising History of America's Favorite Welfare Program*. Princeton, NJ: Princeton University Press.

Lévi-Strauss, Claude. 1983. *Structural Anthropology*. Chicago, IL: University of Chicago Press.

Lind, David and Barham, Elizabeth. 2004. "The Social Life of the Tortilla: Food, Cultural Politics, and Contested Commodification." *Agriculture and Human Values* 21(1): 47–60.

Locher, Julie L., Yoels, William C., Maurer, Donna, and Van Ells, Jillian. 2005. "Comfort Foods: An Exploratory Journey into the Social and Emotional Significance of Food." *Food and Foodways* 13(4): 273–97.

Lockie, Stewart. 2009. "Responsibility and Agency within Alternative Food Networks: Assembling the 'Citizen Consumer.'" *Agriculture and Human Values* 26(3): 193–201.

Loewen, James W. 2008. *Lies My Teacher Told Me: Everything Your American History Textbook Got Wrong*. New York: The New Press.

Logsdon, Gene. 2004. *All Flesh is Grass: The Pleasures and Promises of Pasture Farming*. Athens, OH: Ohio University Press.

"LSSU Continues its New Year Tradition with 40th List of Banished Words." 2015. Lake Superior State University, January 1. Retrieved August 15, 2015 (http://www.lssu.edu/whats_new/articles.php?articleid=3033).

Lu, Shun and Fine, Gary Alan. 1995. "The Presentation of Ethnic Authenticity: Chinese Food as a Social Accomplishment." *Sociological Quarterly* 36(3): 535–53.

Lupton, Deborah. 1996. *Food, the Body and the Self*. Thousand Oaks, CA: Sage.

Lydersen, Kari. 2009. "Herbicide Found in Water May Pose Greater Danger." *The Washington Post*, August 25. Retrieved from LexisNexis on January 2, 2010.

Lyon, Alexandra, Bell, Michael M., Gratton, Claudio, and Jackson, Randall. 2011. "Farming Without a Recipe: Wisconsin Graziers and New Directions for Agricultural Science." *Journal of Rural Studies* 27(4): 384–93.

Lyson, Thomas A. 2004. *Civic Agriculture: Reconnecting Farm, Food, and Community*. Medford, MA: Tufts University Press.

Lyson, Thomas A., Stevenson, G. W., and Welsh, Rick. 2008. *Food and the Mid-level Farm: Renewing an Agriculture of the Middle*. Cambridge, MA: MIT Press.

Marks, Robert. 2007. *The Origins of the Modern World: A Global and Ecological Narrative from the Fifteenth to the Twenty-first Century*. Lanham, MD: Rowman & Littlefield.

Martens, Bobby J. 2008. "The Effect of Entry by Wal-Mart Supercenters on Retail Grocery Concentration." *Journal of Food Distribution Research* 39(3): 13–28.

Marx, Karl. 2001 (1852). *The Eighteenth Brumaire of Louis Bonaparte*. London: Electric Book Company.

Marx, Karl and Engels, Friedrich. 1969 (1845). *Theses on Feuerbach.* Moscow, USSR: Progress Publishers. Retrieved January 13, 2012 (www.marxists.org/archive/marx/works/1845/theses/theses.htm).

Matejowsky, Ty. 2007. "SPAM and Fast-food 'Glocalization' in the Philippines." *Food, Culture and Society* 10(1): 23–41.

Mattes, Richard. 2002. "Ready-to-Eat Cereal Used as a Meal Replacement Promotes Weight Loss in Humans." *Journal of the American College of Nutrition* 21(6): 570–7.

Maurer, Donna. 2002. *Vegetarianism: Movement or Moment?* Philadelphia, PA: Temple University Press.

McBride, Anne E. 2010. "Food Porn." *Gastronomica* 10(1): 38–46.

McCullum, Christine, Desjardins, Ellen, Kraak, Vivica I., Ladipo, Patricia, and Costello, Helen. 2005. "Evidence-based Strategies to Build Community Food Security." *Journal of the American Dietetic Association* 105(2): 278–83.

McKibben, Bill. 2008. *Deep Economy: The Wealth of Communities and the Durable Future.* New York: Macmillan.

McKinlay, John B. 2005. "A Case for Refocusing Upstream: The Political Economy of Illness," in P. Conrad (ed.), *The Sociology of Health and Illness*, 7th edn. New York: Worth.

McLaughlin, Katy. 2009. "Rock-Star Chefs." *The Wall Street Journal*, October 2. Retrieved from LexisNexis on January 4, 2012.

McMichael, Philip. 2009. "A Food Regime Analysis of the 'World Food Crisis.'" *Agriculture and Human Values* 26(4): 281–95.

McMichael, Philip. 2011. *Development and Social Change: A Global Perspective*, 5th edn. Thousand Oaks, CA: Pine Forge.

McMillan, Tracie. 2012. *The American Way of Eating: Undercover at Walmart, Applebee's, Farm Fields and the Dinner Table.* New York: Scribner.

Mihesuah, Devon A. 1996. *American Indians: Stereotypes and Realities.* Atlanta, GA: Clarity Press.

Mikell, Gwendolyn. 1989. *Cocoa and Chaos in Ghana.* New York: Paragon House.

Milburn, Josephine. 1970. "The 1938 Gold Coast Cocoa Crisis: British Business and the Colonial Office." *African Historical Studies* 3(1): 57–74.

Miller, Daniel. 1998a. *A Theory of Shopping.* Ithaca, NY: Cornell University Press.

Miller, Daniel (ed.). 1998b. *Material Cultures: Why Some Things Matter.* Chicago, IL: University of Chicago Press.

Miller, John. 2009. "McDonald's Fries the Holy Grail for Potato Farmers." *Salon*, October 23. Retrieved January 3, 2010 (www.salon.com/wires/ap/us/2009/09/23/ D9ASV9F80_us_spud_stud/index.html).

Mills, C. Wright. 1958. *The Sociological Imagination.* New York: Oxford University Press.

Mintz, Sidney W. 1985. *Sweetness and Power: The Place of Sugar in Modern History.* New York and London: Sifton.

Monsivais, Pablo, Aggarwal, Anju, and Drewnowski, Adam. 2010. "Are Socio-Economic Disparities in Diet Quality Explained by Diet Cost?" *Journal of Epidemiology and Community Health* 66(6): 530–5.

Morales, A. (2011). "Growing Food *and* Justice: Dismantling Racism through Sustainable Food Systems," in A. H. Alkon and J. Agyeman (eds), *Cultivating Food Justice: Race, Class, and Sustainability*. Cambridge, MA: MIT Press, pp. 149–76.

Morton, Lois W., Bitto, Ella Annette, Oakland, Mary Jane, and Sand, Mary. 2008. "Accessing Food Resources: Rural and Urban Patterns of Giving and Getting Food." *Agriculture and Human Values* 25(1): 107–19.

Moss, Michael. 2013. *Salt Sugar Fat: How the Food Giants Hooked Us*. NY: Random House.

National Agricultural Statistics Service. 2009. "QuickStats." Retrieved November 18, 2009 (www.nass.usda.gov/QuickStats).

National Center for Farmworker Health. 2010. "About America's Farmworkers." Retrieved January 1, 2010 (www.ncfh.org/?pid=4).

Nestle, Marion. 2006. *What to Eat: An Aisle-by-Aisle Guide to Savvy Food Choices and Good Eating*. New York: North Point Press.

Nestle, Marion. 2007. *Food Politics: How the Food Industry Influences Nutrition and Health*. Berkeley, CA: University of California Press.

Nestle, Marion. 2011. "Deconstructing the USDA's New Food Plate." Retrieved January 28, 2012 (www.foodpolitics.com/2011/06/deconstructing-the-usdas-new-food-plate/).

Neumark-Sztainer, Dianne, French, Simone A., Hannan, Peter J., Story, Mary, and Fulkerson, Jayne A. 2005. "School Lunch and Snacking Patterns among High School Students: Associations with School Food Environment and Policies." *International Journal of Behavioral Nutrition and Physical Activity* 2: 14–20.

Nichols, Michelle. 2006. "Vegemite Outrage Spreads." Herald Sun, October 24. Retrieved December 2, 2009 (www.heraldsun.com.au/news/world/vegemite-outrage-spreads/story-e6frf7lf-1111112408593).

O'Brien, Ashley M., Hanson, Blake M., Farina, Sarah S., et al. 2012. "MRSA in Conventional and Alternative Retail Pork Products." *PLoS ONE* 7(1): e30092. doi: 10.1371/journal.pone.0030092.

O'Connor, Kaori. 2008. "The Hawaiian Luau: Food as Tradition, Transgression, Transformation, and Travel." *Food, Culture and Society* 11(2): 149–72.

Ogden, Cynthia L., Carroll, Margaret D., Kit, Brian K. and Flegal, Katherine M. 2012. "Prevalence of Obesity and Trends in Body Mass Index among US Children and Adolescents, 1999–2010." *Journal of the American Medical Association* 307(5): 483–90.

Ogden, Cynthia L., Carroll, Margaret D., Kit, Brian K. and Flegal, Katherine M. 2014. "Prevalence of Childhood and Adult Obesity in the United States, 2011–2012." *Journal of the American Medical Association* 311(8): 806–14.

Oldenburg, Ray. 1989. *The Great Good Place: Cafes, Coffee Shops, Bookstores, Bars, Hair Salons and Other Hangouts at the Heart of a Community*. New York: Marlowe.

Oliver, J. Eric. 2006. *Fat Politics: The Real Story Behind America's Obesity Epidemic*. Oxford: Oxford University Press.

Olivera, S. A., Ellison, R. C., Moore, L. L., Gillman, M. W., Garrahie, E. J., and Singer, M. R. 1992. "Parent–Child Relationships in Nutrient Intake: The Framingham Children's Study." *American Journal of Clinical Nutrition* 56(3): 593–8.

O'Neill, Molly. 2003. "Food Porn." *Columbia Journalism Review* 42(3): 38–45.

Opie, Frederick Douglass. 2008. *Hog and Hominy: Soul Food from Africa to America*. New York: Columbia University Press.

Owings, Alison. 2002. *Hey, Waitress! The USA from the Other Side of the Tray*. Berkeley, CA: University of California Press.

Paige, Jeffery M. 1997. *Coffee and Power: Revolution and the Rise of Democracy in Central America*. Cambridge, MA: Harvard University Press.

Painter, Kim. 2014. "FDA Approves a Third New Weight-Loss Pill." *USA TODAY*. Retrieved August 12, 2015 (http://www.usatoday.com/story/news/nation/2014/09/10/fda-approves-weight-loss-pill/15426453/).

Parker, Suzi. 2000. "The Vanishing Black Farmer." *Christian Science Monitor*, July 13. Retrieved from LexisNexis on December 31, 2009.

Parker-Pope, Tara. 2009. "Probiotics: Looking Underneath the Yogurt Label." *The New York Times*, September 28. Retrieved January 11, 2012 (www.nytimes. com/2009/09/29/health/29well.html?_r=1&scp=2&sq=activia%20 lawsuit&st=cse).

Patel, Raj. 2007. *Stuffed and Starved: The Hidden Battle for the World Food System*. Brooklyn, NY: Melville House.

Patterson, Eliza. 2001. "The US–EU Banana Dispute." ASIL Insights. Retrieved October 4, 2011 (www.asil.org/insigh63.cfm).

Paules, Greta Foff. 1991. *Dishing It Out: Power and Resistance Among Waitresses in a New Jersey Restaurant*. Philadelphia, PA: Temple University Press.

Pearlman, Alison. 2013. *Smart Casual: The Transformation of Gourmet Restaurant Style in America*. Chicago, IL: University of Chicago Press.

Pendergrast, Mark. 2000. *For God, Country, and Coca-Cola: The Definitive History of the Great American Soft Drink and the Company That Makes It*. New York: Basic Books.

Penfold, Steve. 2008. *The Donut: A Canadian History*. Toronto: University of Toronto Press.

Peter, Gregory, Bell, Michael M., Jarnagin, Susan, and Bauer, Donna. 2000. "Coming Back Across the Fence: Masculinity and the Transition to Sustainable Agriculture." *Rural Sociology* 65(2): 215–33.

Phillips, Peter W. B. 2007. *Governing Transformative Technological Innovation: Who's in Charge?* Cheltenham: Edward Elgar.

Pimentel, David, Hepperly, Paul, Hanson, James, Douds, David, and Seidel, Rita. 2005. "Environmental, Energetic, and Economic Comparisons of Organic and Conventional Farming Systems." *BioScience* 55(7): 573–82.

Pirog, Rich and Benjamin, Andrew. 2003. "Checking the Food Odometer: Comparing Food Miles for Local versus Conventional Produce Sales to Iowa Institutions." Leopold Center for Sustainable Agriculture. Retrieved February 14, 2010 (www.leopold.iastate.edu/pubs/staff/files/food_travel072103.pdf).

Pittman, David. 2013. "AMA House Votes Against Council, Calls Obesity a Disease." Retrieved August 12, 2015 (http://www.medpagetoday.com/MeetingCoverage/AMA/39952).

Pleck, Elizabeth. 1999. "The Making of the Domestic Occasion: The History of Thanksgiving in the United States." *Journal of Social History* 32(4): 773–89.

Poe, Tracey N. 2002. "The Origins of Soul Food in Black Urban Identity: Chicago, 1915–1947," in C. Counihan (ed.), *Food in the USA*. New York: Routledge, pp. 91–108.

Polanyi, Karl. 2001 (1947). *The Great Transformation: The Political and Economic Origins of Our Time*. Boston, MA: Beacon Press.

Pollack, Andrew. 2009. "Rules on Modified Corn Skirted, Study Says." *The New York Times*, November 6. Retrieved from LexisNexis on January 2, 2010.

Pollack, Andrew. 2010. "Abbott Labs Withdraws Meridia from the Market." *The New York Times*, October 8. Retrieved August 14, 2015 (http://www.nytimes.com/2010/10/09/health/09drug.html).

Pollack, Andrew. 2013. "A.M.A. Recognizes Obesity as a Disease." *The New York Times*, June 18. Retrieved August 11, 2015 (http://www.nytimes.com/2013/06/19/business/ama-recognizes-obesity-as-a-disease.html).

Pollan, Michael. 2006. *The Omnivore's Dilemma: A Natural History of Four Meals*. New York: Penguin Press.

Pollan, Michael. 2009. *In Defense of Food: An Eater's Manifesto*. New York: Penguin Press.

Poppendieck, Janet. 1998. *Sweet Charity? Emergency Food and the End of Entitlement*. New York: Penguin.

Poppendieck, Janet. 2010. *Free for All: Fixing School Food in America*. Berkeley, CA: University of California Press.

Poppendieck, Janet. 2014. *Breadlines Knee-Deep in Wheat: Food Assistance in the Great Depression (Updated and Expanded)*. Berkeley, CA: University of California Press.

Pretty, Jules N. 2002. *Agri-culture: Reconnecting People, Land and Nature*. London: Earthscan.

"Prison Life: The Garden's Fruit." 1997. *The Economist* 342(8005): 29–30.

Pritchard, Bill and Tonts, Matthew. 2011. "Market Efficiency, Agriculture and Prosperity in Rural Australia," in M. Tonts and M. A. B. Siddique (eds), *Globalisation, Agriculture and Development: Perspectives from the Asia-Pacific*. Northampton, MA: Edward Elgar, pp. 29–53.

Puhl, Rebecca and Brownell, Kelly D. 2001. "Bias, Discrimination, and Obesity." *Obesity* 9(12): 788–805.

Rao, Mayuree, Afshin, Ashkan, Singh, Gitanjali, and Mozaffarian, Dariush. 2013. "Do Healthier Foods and Diet Patterns Cost More than Less Healthy Options? A Systematic Review and Meta-analysis." *BMJ Open* 3(12): e004277.

Raynolds, Laura T. 2003. "The Global Banana Trade," in S. Striffler and M. Moberg (eds), *Banana Wars: Power, Production, and History in the Americas*. Durham, NC: Duke University Press, pp. 23–47.

Raynolds, Laura T. 2004. "The Globalization of Organic Agro-Food Networks." *World Development* 32(5): 725–43.

Raynolds, Laura T. 2009. "Mainstreaming Fair Trade Coffee: From Partnership to Traceability." *World Development* 37(6): 1083–93.

Relyea, Rick A. 2005. "The Lethal Impact of Roundup on Aquatic and Terrestrial Amphibians." *Ecological Applications* 15(4): 1118–24.

Richard, Sophie, Moslemi, Safa, Sipahutar, Herbert, Benachour, Nora, and Seralini, Gilles-Eric. 2005. "Differential Effects of Glyphosate and Roundup on Human Placental Cells and Aromatase." *Environmental Health Perspectives* 113(6): 716–20.

Richardson, Kay. 2003. "Vegemite, Soldiers, and Rosy Cheeks." *Gastronomica* 3(4): 60–2.

Rist, Gilbert. 2002. *The History of Development: From Western Origins to Global Faith*. London and New York: Zed Books.

Rochman, Bonnie. 2009. "The Sugary Brands Doing the Most Kid-Chasing." *Time*, October 23. Retrieved January 25, 2012 (www.time.com/time/specials/packages/article/0,28804,1931891_1931889_1931865,00.html).

Rose, Mike. 2004. *The Mind at Work: Valuing the Intelligence of the American Worker*. New York: Viking.

Roseberry, William. 1996. "The Rise of Yuppie Coffees and the Reimagination of Class in the United States." *American Anthropologist* 98(4): 762–75.

Ross, Bruce. 2005. "Fat or Fiction? Weighing the 'Obesity Epidemic,'" in M. Gard and J. Wright (eds), *The Obesity Epidemic: Science, Morality and Ideology*. New York: Routledge, pp. 86–106.

Ross, Nancy J. 2006. "How Civic Is It? Success Stories in Locally Focused Agriculture in Maine." *Renewable Agriculture and Food Systems* 21(2): 114–23.

Rosset, Peter. 2008. "Food Sovereignty and the Contemporary Food Crisis." *Development* 51(4): 460–3.

Rozin, Paul and Siegal, Michael. 2003. "Vegemite as a Marker of National Identity." *Gastronomica* 3(4): 63–7.

Ruben, Ruerd, and Fort, Ricardo. 2012. "The Impact of Fair Trade

Certification for Coffee Farmers in Peru." *World Development* 40(3): 570–82.

Ruhlman, Michael. 2006. *The Reach of a Chef: Professional Cooks in the Age of Celebrity.* New York: Penguin.

Rusche, Sarah E. and Brewster, Zachary W. 2008. "'Because They Tip for Shit!': The Social Psychology of Everyday Racism in Restaurants." *Sociology Compass* 2(6): 2008–29.

Sachs, Carolyn, Allen, Patricia, Terman, A. Rachel, Hayden, Jennifer, and Hatcher, Christina. 2013. "Front and Back of the House: Sociospatial Inequalities in Food Work." *Agriculture and Human Values* 31: 3–17.

Sack, Daniel. 2000. *Whitebread Protestants: Food and Religion in American Culture.* New York: Palgrave.

Sage, Colin. 2011. *Environment and Food.* London and New York: Routledge.

Saguy, Abigail C. 2013. *What's Wrong with Fat?* New York: Oxford University Press.

Saguy, Abigail and Riley, Kevin W. 2005. "Weighing Both Sides: Morality, Mortality, and Framing Contests over Obesity." *Journal of Health Politics, Policy and Law* 30(5): 869–921.

Saldivar-Tanaka, Laura and Krasny, Marianne E. 2004. "Culturing Community Development, Neighborhood Open Space, and Civic Agriculture: The Case of Latino Community Gardens in New York City." *Agriculture and Human Values* 21(4): 399–412.

Sanderson, Steven E. 1986. "The Emergence of the 'World Steer': International and Foreign Domination in Latin American Cattle Production," in F. L. Tullis and W. L. Hollist (eds), *Food, the State, and International Political Economy: Dilemmas of Developing Countries.* Lincoln, NE: University of Nebraska Press, pp. 123–48.

Sandler, Lauren. 2008. "Gut Instinct: What Health Benefits, Exactly, is Activia Yogurt Supposed to Offer?" *Slate*, July 3. Retrieved January 25, 2012 (www.slate.com/articles/news_and_politics/hey_wait_a_ minute/ 2008/07/gut_instinct.html).

Sbicca, Joshua. 2012. "Growing Food Justice by Planting an Anti-Oppression Foundation: Opportunities and Obstacles for a Budding Social Movement." *Agriculture and Human Values* 29: 455–66.

Scanlan, Stephen J., Jenkins, J. Craig, and Peterson, Lindsey. 2010. "The Scarcity Fallacy." *Contexts* 9(1): 34–9.

Schardt, David. 2006. "Soyonara? Tough Times for the Miracle Bean." *Nutrition Action Health Letter* 33(8): 1, 3–6.

Schardt, David. 2010. "Probiotics." *Nutrition Action Health Letter* 37(3): 9–11.

Schlosser, Eric. 2002. *Fast Food Nation: The Dark Side of the All-American Meal.* Boston, MA: Houghton Mifflin.

Schor, Juliet. 2004. *Born to Buy: The Commercialized Child and the New Consumer Culture.* New York: Simon and Schuster.

Schor, Juliet and Holt, Douglas B. 2000. *The Consumer Society Reader*. New York: New Press.

Schultz, E. J. 2011. "Dannon Goes Greek, Takes on (Former) Little Guy." *Advertising Age* 82(34): 22.

Segan, Francine. 2010. "Behind the Scenes." *The Chicago Tribune*, January 6, p. 5.

Shaw, Gareth, Curth, Louise, and Alexander, Andrew. 2004. "Selling Self-Service and the Supermarket: The Americanisation of Food Retailing in Britain, 1945–60." *Business History* 46: 568–82.

Shelton, Allen. 1990. "A Theater for Eating, Looking, and Thinking: The Restaurant as Symbolic Space." *Sociological Spectrum* 10(4): 507–26.

Shirtliffe, Steven J. and Johnson, Eric N. 2012. "Progress Towards No-Till Organic Weed Control in Western Canada." *Renewable Agriculture and Food Systems* 27(1): 60–7.

Shortridge, Barbara and Shortridge, James (eds). 1998. *The Taste of American Place: A Reader on Regional and Ethnic Foods*. New York: Rowman & Littlefield.

Shreck, Aimee, Getz, Christy, and Feenstra, Gail. 2006. "Social Sustainability, Farm Labor, and Organic Agriculture: Findings from an Exploratory Analysis." *Agriculture and Human Values* 23(4): 439–49.

Singh, Sukhpal. 2008. "Marketing Channels and their Implications for Smallholder Farmers in India," in E. B. McCullough, P. L. Pingali, and K. G. Stamoulis (eds), *The Transformation of Agri-Food Systems: Globalization, Supply Chains and Smallholder Farmers*. London: Earthscan, pp. 279–310.

Siró, István, Kápolna, Emese, Kápolna, Beáta and Lugasi, Andrea. 2008. "Functional Food. Product Development, Marketing and Consumer Acceptance – a Review." *Appetite* 51(3): 456–67.

Siskind, Janet. 2002. "The Invention of Thanksgiving: A Ritual of American Nationality," in C. Counihan (ed.), *Food in the USA*. New York: Routledge, pp. 41–58.

Skerrett, P. J. 2011a. "New Dietary Guidelines Offer Little New Guidance." *Harvard Health Blog*. Retrieved June 9, 2011 (www.health.harvard.edu/blog/new-dietary-guidelines-offer-little-new-guidance-201102011292).

Skerrett, P. J. 2011b. "Crumbling, Confusing Food Pyramid Replaced by a Plate." *Harvard Health Blog*. Retrieved June 9, 2011 (www.health.harvard.edu/blog/crumbling-confusing-food-pyramid-replaced-by-a-plate-201106032767?utm_source=hhp&utm_medium=pressrelease&utm_campaign=myplate0511).

Slater, Don. 1999. *Consumer Culture and Modernity*. Cambridge, UK: Polity.

Slocum, Rachel. 2007. "Whiteness, Space and Alternative Food Practice." *Geoforum* 38(3): 520–33.

Smith, Alisa Dawn and MacKinnon, J. B. 2007. *The 100-Mile Diet: A Year of Local Eating*. Toronto, ON: Random House of Canada.

Smith, Kylie J., McNaughton, Sarah A., Gall, Seana L., Blizzard, Leigh,

Dwyer, Terence, and Venn, Alison J. 2010. "Involvement of Young Australian Adults in Meal Preparation: Cross-Sectional Associations with Sociodemographic Factors and Diet Quality." *Journal of the American Dietetic Association* 110(9): 1363–7.

Smith, Tara C., Male, Michael J., Harper, Abby L., et al. 2009. "Methicillin-Resistant Staphylococcus aureus (MRSA) Strain ST398 is Present in Midwestern US Swine and Swine Workers." *PLoS ONE* 4(1): e4258. doi:10.1371/journal.pone.0004258.

Smithers, John, Lamarche, Jeremy, and Joseph, Alun E. 2008. "Unpacking the Terms of Engagement with Local Food at the Farmers' Market: Insights from Ontario." *Journal of Rural Studies* 24(3): 337–50.

Snow, David A. and Soule, Sarah A. 2010. *A Primer on Social Movements.* New York: W. W. Norton.

Sobal, Jeffery. 2005. "Men, Meat and Marriage: Models of Masculinity." *Food and Foodways* 13: 135–58.

Sommer, Robert, Herrick, John, and Sommer, Ted R. 1981. "The Behavioral Ecology of Supermarkets and Farmers' Markets." *Journal of Environmental Psychology* 1(1):13–19.

South, Scott and Spitze, Glenna. 1994. "Housework in Marital and Non-marital Households." *American Sociological Review* 59: 327–47.

Spang, Rebecca L. 2000. *The Invention of the Restaurant: Paris and Modern Gastronomic Culture.* Cambridge, MA: Harvard University Press.

Spector, Malcolm and Kitsuse, John I. 1977. *Constructing Social Problems.* Menlo Park, CA: Cummings.

Spiller, Keith. 2012. "It Tastes Better Because . . . Consumer Understandings of UK Farmers' Market Food." *Appetite* 59(1): 100–7.

Stephenson, Garry, Lev, Larry, and Brewer, Linda. 2008. "'I'm Getting Desperate': What We Know about Farmers' Markets That Fail." *Renewable Agriculture and Food Systems* 23(3): 188–99.

Stern, Lisë. 2004. *How to Keep Kosher: A Comprehensive Guide to Understanding Jewish Dietary Laws.* New York: HarperCollins.

Striffler, Steve. 2005. *Chicken: The Dangerous Transformation of America's Favorite Food.* New Haven, CT: Yale University Press.

Szajewska, Hania, Setty, Mala, Mrukowicz, Jacek, and Guandalini, Stefano. 2006. "Probiotics in Gastrointestinal Diseases in Children: Hard and Not-So-Hard Evidence of Efficacy." *Journal of Pediatric Gastroenterology and Nutrition* 42(5): 454–75.

Tarasuk, Valerie and Eakin, Joan M. 2003. "Charitable Food Assistance as Symbolic Gesture: An Ethnographic Study of Food Banks in Ontario." *Social Science and Medicine* 56(7): 1505–15.

Taxel, Laura F. 2008. "Welcome to Dante's Inferno," in H. Hughes (ed.), *Best Food Writing 2008*. Cambridge, MA: De Capo Press, pp. 196–204.

Taylor, Peter Leigh. 2005. "In the Market But Not of It: Fair Trade Coffee and Forest Stewardship Council Certification as Market-Based Social Change." *World Development* 33(1): 129–47.

Tedlow, Richard. 1990. *New and Improved: The Story of Mass Marketing in America*. New York: Basic Books.

Teig, Ellen, Amulya, Joy, Bardwell, Lisa, Buchenau, Michael, Marshall, Julie A., and Litt, Jill S. 2009. "Collective Efficacy in Denver, Colorado: Strengthening Neighborhoods and Health through Community Gardens." *Health and Place* 15(4): 1115–22.

Thomas, Carol. 2002. "Disability Theory: Key Ideas, Issues, and Thinkers," in C. Barnes, M. Oliver, and L. Barton (eds), *Disability Studies Today*. Malden, MA: Blackwell.

Trauger, Amy. 2004. "'Because They Can Do the Work': Women Farmers in Sustainable Agriculture in Pennsylvania, USA." *Gender, Place and Culture* 11: 289–307.

United Nations Development Program. 2015. *About Ghana*. Retrieved July 15, 2015 (http://www.gh.undp.org/content/ghana/en/home/countryinfo/).

US Department of Agriculture. "Mission Statement." Retrieved February 19, 2012 (www.usda.gov/wps/portal/usda/usdahome?navid= MISSION_STATEMENT).

US Department of Agriculture Economic Research Service. 2010. "Adoption of Genetically Engineered Crops in the US." Retrieved October 12, 2010 (www.ers.usda.gov/Data/BiotechCrops).

US Department of Agriculture Economic Research Service. 2011a. "ERS/ USDA Briefing Room – Food CPI and Expenditures." Retrieved December 14, 2011 (www.ers.usda.gov/Briefing/CPIFoodAndExpenditures/).

US Department of Agriculture Economic Research Service. 2011b. "ERS/ USDA Data – Food Availability (Per Capita) Data System: Nutrient Availability." Retrieved December 14, 2011 (www.ers.usda.gov/Data/ FoodConsumption/NutrientAvailIndex.htm).

US District Court. 2010. "Amended Stipulation of Settlement." Retrieved August 11, 2015 (http://www.casewatch.org/civil/dannon/settlement.pdf).

"US Government Denies It's Banned Vegemite." 2006. *NineMSN*. Retrieved April 1, 2012. (http://news.ninemsn.com.au/article.aspx?id=155019).

Valenze, Deborah. 2011. *Milk: A Local and Global History*. New Haven, CT: Yale University Press.

Valkila, Joni and Nygren, Anja. 2010. "Impacts of Fair Trade Certification on Coffee Farmers, Cooperatives, and Laborers in Nicaragua." *Agriculture and Human Values* 27(3): 321–33.

van der Geest, Kees. 2011. "North–South Migration in Ghana: What Role for the Environment?" *International Migration* 49: e69–e94.

van der Lippe, Tanja, Tijdens, Kea, and de Ruijter, Esther. 2004. "Outsourcing of Domestic Tasks and Time-Saving Effects." *Journal of Family Issues* 25(2): 216–40.

van Hook, Jennifer and Altman, Claire E. 2012. "Competitive Food Sales in Schools and Childhood Obesity: A Longitudinal Study." *Sociology of Education* 85: 23–39.

van Puyvelde, Eric. 2011. "EU/Canada: Provisional Solution Found to

Hormone-Treated Beef Dispute." *Europolitics,* March 21. Retrieved from LexisNexis on November 26, 2011.

van Trijp, H. C. M. and van der Lans, I. A. 2007. "Consumer Perceptions of Nutrition and Health Claims." *Appetite* 48: 305–24.

Vardi, Itai. 2010. "Feeding Race: Eating Contests, the Black Body, and the Social Production of Group Boundaries through Amusement in Turn of the Twentieth Century America." *Food, Culture and Society* 13(3): 371–96.

"The Vegemite Story." 2012. Retrieved January 15, 2012 (www.kraft brands.com/kraftvegemite/Pages/the-vegemite-story.aspx).

Voight, Joan. 2007. "The New Brand Ambassadors." *AdWeek.com,* December 31. Retrieved from LexisNexis on October 5, 2009.

Vorley, Bill. 2007. "Supermarkets and Agri-food Supply Chains in Europe: Partnership and Protest," in D. Burch and G. Lawrence (eds), *Supermarkets and Agri-food Supply Chains: Transformations in the Production and Consumption of Foods.* Cheltenham: Edward Elgar, pp. 243–67.

Wald, Sarah D. 2011. "Visible Farmers/Invisible Workers: Locating Immigrant Labor in Food Studies." *Food, Culture and Society* 14(4): 567–86.

Waldman, Amy. 2002. "Poor in India Starve as Surplus Wheat Rots." *The New York Times,* December 2. Retrieved from LexisNexis on March 22, 2010.

Walker, Rob. 2008. *Buying In: The Secret Dialogue Between What We Buy and Who We Are.* New York: Random House.

Wansink, Brian. 2003. "Overcoming the Taste Stigma of Soy." *Journal of Food Science* 68(8): 2604–6.

Wansink, Brian. 2007. *Mindless Eating: Why We Eat More Than We Think.* New York: Bantam Books.

Wansink, Brian, Cheney, Matthew M., and Chan, Nina. 2003. "Exploring Comfort Food Preferences across Age and Gender." *Physiology and Behavior* 79: 739–47.

Wansink, Brian and Park, Se-Bum. 2002. "Sensory Suggestiveness and Labeling: Do Soy Labels Bias Taste?" *Journal of Sensory Studies* 17: 483–91.

Warde, Alan and Martens, Lydia. 2000. *Eating Out: Social Differentiation, Consumption, and Pleasure.* Cambridge, UK and New York: Cambridge University Press.

Warde, Alan, Martens, Lydia, and Olsen, Wendy. 1999. "Consumption and the Problem of Variety: Cultural Omnivorousness, Social Distinction and Dining Out." *Sociology* 33(1): 105–27.

Wardle, Jane. 1995. "Parental Influences on Children's Diets." *Proceedings of the Nutrition Society* 54(3): 747–58.

Wardyn, Shylo E., Forshey, Brett M., Farina, Sarah A., et al. 2015. "Swine Farming is a Risk Factor of Infection with and High Prevalence of Carriage of Multidrug Resistant *Stapholococcus aureus*." *Clinical Infectious Disease* 61(1): 59–66.

Warnes, Andrew. 2004. *Hunger Overcome? Food and Resistance in Twentieth-Century African American Literature*. Athens, GA: University of Georgia Press.

Watson, James L. 2005. "China's Big Mac Attack," in J. L. Watson and M. L. Caldwell (eds), *The Cultural Politics of Food and Eating*. Malden, MA: Blackwell, pp. 80–102.

Webber, Caroline B., Sobal, Jeffery, and Dollahite, Jamie S. 2007. "Physical Disabilities and Food Access among Limited Resource Households." *Disability Studies Quarterly* 27(3). http://dsq-sds.org/article/view/20/20.

Weiner, Mark. 1996. "Consumer Culture and Participatory Democracy: The Story of Coca-Cola during World War II." *Food and Foodways* 6(2): 109–29.

Wendakoon, Chitra N., Thomson, Alan B. R., and Ozimek, Lech. 2002. "Lack of Therapeutic Effect of a Specially Designed Yogurt for the Eradication of *Helicobacter pylori* Infection." *Digestion: International Journal of Gastroenterology* 65: 16–20.

Wiley, Andrea S. 2011. "Milk for 'Growth': Global and Local Meanings of Milk Consumption in China, India, and the United States." *Food and Foodways* 19(1–2): 11–33.

Wilk, Richard. 2006. "Bottled Water: The Pure Commodity in the Age of Branding." *Journal of Consumer Culture* 6: 303–25.

Wilkins, Jennifer L. 2005. "Eating Right Here: Moving from Consumer to Food Citizen." *Agriculture and Human Values* 22(3): 269–73.

Williams, Timothy. 2010. "Dannon Settles with F.T.C. over Some Health Claims." *The New York Times*, December 16. Retrieved April 1, 2012 (www. nytimes.com/2010/12/16/business/16yogurt.html).

Winson, Anthony. 1993. *The Intimate Commodity: Food and the Development of the Agro-Industrial Complex in Canada*. Toronto, ON: Garamond Press.

Witt, Doris. 1999. *Black Hunger: Food and the Politics of US Identity*. Oxford: Oxford University Press.

World Health Organization (WHO). 2006. "Online Q&A: What are the Health Consequences of Being Overweight?" Retrieved February 20, 2012 (www.who.int/features/qa/49/en/index.html).

World Health Organization (WHO). 2011. "Obesity and Overweight." Fact Sheet No. 311. Retrieved February 20, 2012 (www.who.int/mediacentre/factsheets/fs311/en/index.html).

World Health Organization (WHO). 2014. "Antimicrobial Resistance: Global Report on Surveillance." April. Retrieved August 28, 2015 (http://www.who.int/drugresistance/documents/surveillancereport/en/).

Yan, Yunxiang. 2005. "Of Hamburger and Social Space: Consuming McDonald's in Beijing," in J. L. Watson and M. L. Caldwell (eds), *The Cultural Politics of Food and Eating*. Malden, MA: Blackwell, pp. 80–102.

Young, Meredith E., Mizzau, Madison, Mai, Nga T., Sirisegaram, Abby, and Wilson, Margo. 2009. "Food for Thought: What You Eat Depends on Your Sex and Eating Companions." *Appetite* 53: 268–71.

Yue, Chengyan, Alfnes, Frode, and Jensen, Helen H. 2009. "Discounting Spotted Apples: Investigating Consumers' Willingness to Accept Cosmetic Damage in an Organic Product." *Journal of Agricultural and Applied Economics* 41(1): 29–46.

Zenk, Shannon N., Schulz, Amy, Israel, Barbara A., James, Sherman A., Bao, Shuming, and Wilson, Mark L. 2005. "Neighborhood Racial Composition, Neighborhood Poverty, and the Spatial Accessibility of Supermarkets in Metropolitan Detroit." *American Journal of Public Health* 95(4): 660–7.

Zoomers, Annalies. 2010. "Globalisation and the Foreignisation of Space: Seven Processes Driving the Current Global Land Grab. *The Journal of Peasant Studies* 37(2): 429–47.

Zukin, Sharon, and Maguire, Jennifer Smith. 2004. "Consumers and Consumption." *Annual Review of Sociology* 30(1): 173–97.

Zwick, Detlev, Bonsu, Samuel K., and Darmody, Aron. 2008. "Putting Consumers to Work: 'Co-creation' and New Marketing Governmentality." *Journal of Consumer Culture* 8(2): 163–96.

Glossary

absolute poverty – when a person or household lacks the basic needs for survival and well-being, including food, shelter, health care, and freedom from violence or threat

appropriationism – the corporate practice of selling inputs (such as seeds) to farmers that were previously produced on the farm itself; enables corporations to avoid the risks of farming

authenticity – a social accomplishment; when the expectations of consumers (e.g., diners) and the behaviors of producers (e.g., restaurants) interact to give the consumer a sense of having truly experienced a foreign culture

Body Mass Index (BMI) – a simple measure of overweight and obesity calculated as a person's weight in kilograms divided by height in meters squared

brand – a commercially developed symbol

brand ambassador – a person who promotes a branded item among his or her friends and family and then communicates their activities to the brand's company, usually unpaid

branding – the creation and promotion of meaning-laden symbols that represent particular products with compelling values and ideas

category management – a retail system in which retailers and manufacturers collaborate to determine the array of goods within a given category, such as pasta sauce, with hopes of maximizing the profit of each unit of shelf space

claims maker – a term from social constructionism to refer to an interest group within a broad social debate

comfort foods – dishes and products consumed specifically for an emotional boost

commodification – the process of shaping products to be inter-changeable mass-produced goods that take their value from the prices they fetch on the market

community food security – "a condition in which all community residents obtain a safe, culturally acceptable, nutritionally adequate diet through a sustainable food system that maximizes community self-reliance and social justice" (www.foodsecurity.org/views_cfs_faq.html)

community gardens – spaces where groups of people grow fruits, vegetables or ornamental plants on either a communal or an individual plot

community supported agriculture (CSA) – a form of direct marketing in which buyers purchase seasonal shares in a farm or farm collective that cover the costs of production and, in return, receive a weekly portion of produce and other products throughout the growing season

competitive foods – foods in US schools that compete with those available through the National School Lunch Program (NSLP) and the School Breakfast Program

consumer culture – a system of symbols in which identity is shaped and communicated through brands and other consumption choices

consumer sovereignty – the revered idea in capitalist culture that consumers should (and do) make their own free consumption choices based on their own unique tastes and wants, favoring the best and cheapest among competing selections

conventionalization – the process through which an alternative food system increasingly becomes only a slightly different version of an industrialized one

corporation – a chartered organization with limited liability, transferability of shares, legal personhood, and indefinite duration

corporatization – a process in which products and practices that existed outside the mainstream increasingly become produced and promoted by large corporations

cuisine – a distinctive set of ingredients, flavor principles, and cooking techniques, usually associated with a particular geographic region

culinary capital – the components of cultural capital that relate to food and eating

culinary tourism – a food-based encounter with an unfamiliar culture that reinforces the tourist's identity as an adventuresome and sophisticated person

cultural capital – the relatively rare and highly valued knowledge, skills, attitudes, and tastes that define an elite status

culture of poverty thesis – the claim that families and communities become trapped in poverty because they have developed cultural traits that perpetuate poverty, including an inability to delay gratification or plan for the future; an approach to poverty that "blames the victim"

decommodification – the process of redefining a product's quality to take into account its cultural, environmental, or social impacts, not simply its price on the market

development project – the global effort to modernize the societies and economies of the South

domestic outsourcing – purchasing products or services in order to shift work done in the home to people and businesses outside

"eat more" – a general category of nutritional advice, favored by the food industry, that encourages consumers to eat various foods without restriction

embeddedness – the notion that all economic activity both draws on and impacts the broader society and its relationship with nature

emergency food system – the network of food banks, food pantries, soup kitchens, and other organizations that provide food to the needy on a volunteer, charitable basis

emotion management – producing and maintaining a desired state of mind in others

emotional labor – the work to "induce or suppress feelings in order to sustain the outward countenance" needed for emotion management (Hochschild 1983: 7)

entitlement programs – government assistance programs such as SNAP or WIC that are theoretically available to anyone who meets eligibility requirements

epidemic – "the rapid and episodic onset of infectious diseases . . . historically associated with fear and sudden widespread death" (Saguy and Riley 2005: 892)

ethnic revival – a period in the 1970s when many Americans sought to reclaim a distinct ethnic heritage as a response to the hegemonic process

eutrophication – the reduction of dissolved oxygen in water due to nutrient pollution that creates aquatic and marine dead zones

excess death – a method of assessing the impact of a disease or condition such as obesity by calculating the number of deaths over and above what would normally be expected in a population

farmers' market – a form of local food marketing in which producers sell food and other agricultural products directly to shoppers

fat acceptance – a movement to contest the medical model of overweight and obesity and the social stigma against larger body sizes that such a model may promote

feeding work – the sum of mental, emotional, and physical effort that goes into planning, provisioning, preparing, and serving meals, as well as cleaning after them; includes knowing others' tastes and monitoring home food stores

financialization of food – the growing power of financial institutions and transactions in shaping the global food system

food apartheid – a term coined by food justice advocates to describe the stark inequalities in food environments by race that arise from public and corporate policies

food banks – part of the emergency food system; organizations that act as wholesale agents by collecting food donations from food drives and corporate sources and distributing them to member organizations such as food pantries and soup kitchens

food democracy – "the idea that people can and should be actively participating in shaping the food system, rather than remaining passive spectators on the sidelines" (Hassanein 2003: 79)

food deserts – communities that lack full-line supermarkets, forcing typically low-income residents to make do with fast-food restaurants and convenience stores or travel long distances to access a supermarket; *see also* food apartheid

food icon – a brand or food item that constitutes an especially powerful symbol of group identity

food insecurity – limited access or lack of access to a nutritionally sound and culturally appropriate diet from reliable mainstream sources

(the) food justice movement – a network of activists focused on "dismantling racism as part of [achieving] food security" (Morales 2011: 158)

(the) food movement – a multidimensional social movement aimed at bringing about a food system that will provide healthier diets, more satisfying livelihoods, more robust agroecologies, and more opportunities to forge and renew social ties

food pantries – part of the emergency food system; organizations that distribute unprepared foods to food-insecure persons for use at home

food porn – food spectacles that are similar to pornography in that they are designed to induce desire and are based on fantasy rather than reality

food rescue programs – part of the emergency food system; organizations that collect and transport leftover prepared foods from catered events and food services to soup kitchens

food sovereignty – "the right of peoples to healthy and culturally appropriate food produced through ecologically sound and sustainable methods, and their right to define their own food and agriculture systems" (La Via Campesina 2008)

(the) food system – the set of vast, interlinked institutions and processes that transform sunlight, water, and soil into meaning-laden foods

foodways – the patterns that establish "what we eat, as well as how and why and under what circumstances we eat" (Edge 2007: 8)

frames – definitions of reality advanced by claims makers to influence public perception

functional food – one that purports to provide health benefits beyond food's normal nutritional properties, typically because of added nutrients or other beneficial ingredients

genetic pollution – when unwanted genetic material contaminates crops through uncontrollable pollination

gleaning – the practice of harvesting crops that would otherwise rot in fields or orchards for distribution through the emergency food system

(the) global land grab – the rapidly increasingly purchase or lease of prime agricultural lands in poor countries by global investors since the economic downturn of 2007–8

(the) global North – the set of high-income countries in North America, Europe, Asia, and Oceania; the term has largely replaced "first world"

(the) global South – the set of low-income countries in Africa, the Americas, and Asia; most were formerly European colonies; the term has largely replaced "third world"

globalization project – the effort to expand the global economy by promoting production and marketing networks that transcend national boundaries

(the) Green Revolution – poverty-reduction efforts in the 1960s and 1970s that sought to increase agricultural production in the global South through the use of industrial agriculture techniques and technologies

health halo – when the focus on healthy ingredients influences consumers to regard an entire product containing those ingredients as healthy

hegemonic process – the way dominant cultural forms incorporate and thereby erase cultural distinctions

household food security – the ability of a household to access culturally acceptable and sufficient food supplies in a socially acceptable manner without relying on food assistance programs or illegitimate means

hunger – the pervasive lack of food that causes immediate physiological discomfort

identity work – activity through which we define for ourselves and others who we are, socially and culturally

imagined communities – political theorist Benedict Anderson's description of nations, based on the fact that members are not all acquainted with one another, "yet in the minds of each lives the image of their communion" (Anderson 1991: 6)

(the) international division of labor – the pattern, established under colonialism, in which countries of the global South produce primary products and countries of the global North produce manufactured goods

invented tradition – a set of practices based largely on an idealized and fictionalized past; important for promoting social solidarity, establishing new social institutions and legitimizing existing ones, and socializing individuals into a culture

line extension – the industry practice of creating new products and marketing them with an already successful brand

locavore – a person who seeks to eat foods produced only within a specified local or regional area

mass marketing – a food industry practice of encouraging broad consumer desire for branded goods and then making those goods widely available for purchase

meal replacement diets – weight-loss eating regimens based on regularly substituting a particular food for one or more daily meals

meal solutions – foods that are mostly prepared by manufacturing or retail companies, requiring little attention at home to be ready to eat

medical model of obesity – the dominant view that defines overweight and obesity as medical issues and high rates of overweight and obesity in a population as a health crisis; this model promotes individual weight loss as the appropriate solution

medicalization – the process of redefining human problems or issues as medical problems or issues

micro-marketing – a food industry practice of promoting specific products to narrowly defined consumer groups based on age, gender, ethnicity, and other social statuses; contrasts with mass marketing

national food security – a measure of the number of food-insecure households coupled with an assessment of threats to food security affecting a nation or a distinct population within a nation

neo-ethnicity – a consciously reinvigorated cultural heritage that had been previously lost

neoliberalism – an ideology that views any barriers to trade as illegitimate barriers to growth, progress, and peace

nutrient pollution – when excessive nitrogen and phosphorus enter bodies of water, prompting the overgrowth of algae and aquatic plants

obesity – "abnormal or excessive fat accumulation that may impair health" (World Health Organization 2011: para 1); people with a Body Mass Index (BMI) of more than 30 are assumed to be obese

obesogenic environments – settings such as families, neighborhoods, and schools that encourage overconsumption of foods believed to contribute to overweight and obesity

pesticide resistance – when a growing proportion of individuals within a pest population are unaffected by a pesticide; occurs when immune individuals within a population outcompete vulnerable ones and successfully pass on their immunity to offspring

private label – store-specific brands produced in supply chains managed by the retailing company itself; also called "own brands"

productivism – the relentless effort to increase output with the assumption that greater output is inherently positive

relative poverty – when people and households are deprived of the comforts and privileges that most people in their society enjoy

ritual – a scripted and repeated set of acts performed primarily for their symbolic significance rather than for practical ends

role loss – the disappearance of an important social role, leading to a painful readjustment of one's identity

satiety – a feeling of fullness after eating

(the) scarcity fallacy – the false assumption that hunger is caused by insufficient food production

school gardens – gardens that serve as living classrooms, providing children and youth with opportunities to learn about nature, foods, planning, and entrepreneurship

social constructionism – a tradition within social inquiry that focuses on how social patterns are produced and reproduced via the actions and interactions of individuals and groups

social exclusion – when a person or group is barred from or left out of many of the key social institutions in mainstream society

social inequality – persistent patterns in which some people enjoy more material and cultural privileges than others

social institution – a stable pattern of roles and relationships in society; sometimes as a formal organization, such as a government agency or corporation, and sometimes as a widely recognized pattern, such as the family or the supermarket

social movement – an organized collection of people working to change key features of society and culture by challenging or defending existing social structures

social problem – a pattern in society that is widely regarded as both undesirable and changeable, making it an appropriate target for policy or other social interventions

social solidarity – the feelings of "we-ness" within groups, often created and renewed through ritual

social unifier – a symbol that helps promote unity within a divided society

soup kitchens – part of the emergency food system; organizations that prepare and serve meals to food-insecure persons

status symbol – an object that represents one's social status, most often used to refer to social class status

structuralism – a tradition within social inquiry that focuses on how enduring social patterns shape human behavior

substitutionism – the corporate practice of designing food value chains that enable flexibility in sourcing primary products; for example, being easily able to substitute beet sugar for cane sugar, or cocoa from Ghana for cocoa from Brazil

super foods – a marketing term used to refer to foods that are high in a single nutrient or have a dense nutritional profile overall

symbol – anything that carries a shared meaning in a culture

technology treadmill – a process in which falling unit prices force farmers to adopt costly new technologies to garner higher yields to replace lost income; however, the technology also creates an oversupply of products that pushes prices down further

third places – sites of social interaction, separate from home and work, that are important for forging ties across social difference

values-based labeling – a certification and labeling practice that carries information about the social and environmental conditions under which a product was produced; examples include dolphin-safe tuna and fair trade

yo-yo dieting – the repeating pattern of losing weight through dieting, regaining it, followed by more dieting, and so on

Index

CPSIA information can be obtained
at www.ICGtesting.com
Printed in the USA
BVHW050338051121
620516BV00002B/12